american popular music

Recent Titles in
American Popular Culture

Series Editor: *M. Thomas Inge*

Film: A Reference Guide
Robert A. Armour

Women's Gothic and Romantic Fiction: A Reference Guide
Kay Mussell

Animation: A Reference Guide
Thomas W. Hoffer

Variety Entertainment and Outdoor Amusements: A Reference Guide
Don B. Wilmeth

Women in Popular Culture: A Reference Guide
Katherine Fishburn

Sports: A Reference Guide
Robert J. Higgs

Play and Playthings: A Reference Guide
Bernard Mergen

american popular music
A REFERENCE GUIDE

Mark W. Booth

American Popular Culture

GREENWOOD PRESS
WESTPORT, CONNECTICUT • LONDON, ENGLAND

Library of Congress Cataloging in Publication Data

Booth, Mark W., 1943-
  American popular music.

  (American popular culture, ISSN 0193-6859)
  Bibliography: p.
  Includes index.
  1. Music, Popular (Songs, etc.)—United States—
Dictionaries.   2. Music, Popular (Songs, etc.)—United
States—Bio-bibliography.   3. Music, Popular (Songs,
etc.)—United States—History and criticism.   I. Title.
II. Series.
ML102.P66B65   1983   016.78'042'0973   82-21062
ISBN 0-313-21305-4

Library of Congress Catalog Card Number: 82-21062
ISBN: 0-313-21305-4
ISSN: 0193-6859

First published in 1983

Greenwood Press
A division of Congressional Information Service, Inc.
88 Post Road West
Westport, Connecticut 06881

Printed in the United States of America

10 9 8 7 6 5 4 3 2 1

Contents

Preface

This book is an inventory of resources for studying American popular music. It offers brief descriptions of books, periodicals, and special library collections where the user can seek out the many kinds of popular music, past and present, and information about that music and its makers.

I have written about books I have been able to examine, over eleven hundred of them, most found in libraries in Richmond, Washington, New York, and Boston, or brought to me through the patient help of the Interlibrary Loan office of the James Branch Cabell Library of Virginia Commonwealth University. I have examined most of the journals listed at the Library of Congress. Some journals, the books listed in a separate category in chapter 1 (manuals for songwriters), and most of the library reference collections around the country are described at second hand from published sources. Elsewhere, I have chosen not to list all reported books but only those that I can attest to and describe directly.

The intent of the book is to give the user quick but thorough and reliable command of resources in any corner of the large subject of American popular music, including in that subject Tin Pan Alley, bands, Broadway, Hollywood, blues, black pop, ragtime, jazz, country, commercial folk, and rock, along with a few predecessors and loose ends. Chapters follow, with small variations, a consistent plan: bibliography and discography of the particular subject; general reference; collective and individual biography; history and criticism; and a bibliography of books and magazines mentioned in the chapter. Within each section of a chapter, related materials are grouped in paragraphs to be described and compared, and sometimes they are given brief critical evaluation.

Quick access to the information is offered not only by consistent and labelled chapter divisions but by writing intended to be easily scanned. Perhaps at some cost in stylistic elegance, paragraphs almost always begin with the subject of the paragraph, in a word or a phrase. In the biographical sections, the paragraphs are arranged in alphabetical order by the names of the subjects. Mention of a book gives the full main title and sometimes a subtitle if the subtitle gives information or flavor; in all cases full subtitles are given in the lists at the ends of chapters. The publication data given there may be useful particularly to readers served by the spreading modern computer network for interlibrary borrowing.

The idea for this book and for others in this series belongs to Tom Inge, and I want to thank him. Staff members of several libraries have been graciously helpful to me; I must thank particularly Elizabeth Brewer Coughman, formerly of VCU, and Myra Kight of the Art and Music collection of the Richmond Public Library. Thanks to Rob Goldblum for jazz expertise; what is inexpert on that and other subjects in this book is only mine.

Introduction: A Sketch of the History of American Popular Music

Some of the music that European colonists brought to the New World was formal and sophisticated music for genteel recreation; some of their music was what we now call *folk music,* belonging freely to the traditional communities from which they had come. Some, however, was *popular music.* It often had the form of penny broadsides sold in the city streets or of commercial entertainment performed to paying audiences. In the colonial period of our history, America had colonial popular music; our broadsides and ballad operas were simply imported from England. Even when American residents began writing songs and shows or writing and printing broadsides, what they first wrote was colonial in its close imitation of music from England.

During the years of the Revolution, the sentiments of Americans were expressed in anti-British songs that could hardly have had British writers but were still firmly in the vein known there, learned there, and brought here. Many were specific parodies of particular British songs. The new nation began with a largely British popular culture.

When did we acquire an American popular music? To determine when the new nation could really claim such music of its own, signs of a clear American stamp upon the music must be found that will show that it was not only written, printed, sold, performed, and enjoyed in America, but that it gave some distinct expression of the life of the new society, not just of its imported heritage.

English and other European music remained in the American marketplace as well as the American concert hall throughout the nineteenth century, gradually mixing more and more with what was distinctly native to the new nation. When this genuine American popular music really began cannot be said for certain. A sign of the beginning can be identified in 1827. Among the scattered relics of the music sold or professionally performed a century and a half ago, two songs of 1827 suggest in hindsight the turning point. In Julius Mattfeld's chronicle, *Variety Music Cavalcade, 1620-1969,* four songs are listed as hits of the year 1827, and two of them, "My Long-Tail Blue" and "The Coal-Black Rose," were popularized by the minstrel singer George Washington Dixon. Dixon, whom Mattfeld calls "a Negro minstrel," was a white man performing in blackface. He was not the first or the most successful performer in that masquerade tradition that was still alive more than a century later, but his two hit songs are a portent. The native American note we are looking for was struck in the meeting of Afro-American and Euro-American styles of music.

Most popular songs in the years after 1827 continued to be the work of English writers or were indistinguishable from English work. Tunes continued to be borrowed, as the tunes of "Yankee Doodle" and "The Star-Spangled Banner" had been borrowed, from English songs. Still, a new way had been opened. The music that slaves brought with them from west Africa evolved into an Afro-American folk music and then evolved into a variety of black styles of performance for black audiences that were in themselves an American popular music. Throughout their history, in all their forms, they have also had the broadest influence on all the rest of what is distinctively American popular music.

Alec Wilder argues that the first truly native American popular songs are those a generation after George Washington Dixon, at the next stage of interaction between black and white music: the songs of Stephen Foster. Foster was influenced not only by the minstrel mimicry of slave music but also by Negro church music. After Foster's death in 1864, Wilder contends, the disruption of the Civil War and Reconstruction in the lives of black Americans kept black music away from the ears of white Americans, and popular music entered a recession that ended in the 1890s when the sounds of ragtime played by young black pianists began to be heard by a white public. The distinctly American feeling that derived from ragtime rhythm entered the mainstream of those major songwriters of the twentieth century whose work Wilder traces. Often very remote from ragtime itself or from the blues and jazz styles that most directly expressed black experience and culture in America, American music continued to be inspired by black tradition in its rhythm, melody, and performance, whether in Tin Pan Alley, in swing bands, in country, or in rock.

Popular music is a marketplace art. American popular music was the commercial extension of the eighteenth-century publishing and theater businesses as they had evolved in London and had been imitated in New York, Philadelphia, and other colonial cities. In nineteenth-century American cities and towns, those businesses met with an American buying public and gradually learned to offer them music with American flavor. The evolution came slowly, and when something clearly American predominated at the end of the nineteenth century, it was the product of American musicians and of the American genius for commercial promotion. A massive market was built up by promoters and salesmen for shows, for sheet music, and for pianos to play the music. Even then some of the commercial entertainment purveyed by such business had the prestige of claiming European origin, but the booming music business was coming to be brassily American.

Thomas Edison built the first phonograph in 1877, but for half a century phonograph records would be only a minority of the trade carried on by the music business. The first million-selling record came in 1902 and two dozen more followed by the 1920s for home phonographs and juke boxes. In a scramble for sales, record companies diversified their productions. They discovered jazz as it arrived in Chicago and New York, and they ventured into the south to find saleable rural black and white music. Ralph Peer of Okeh Records opened one door by recording black blues singer Mamie Smith in 1920 and another when he recorded pioneer, though not actually the first, "hillbilly" white country musicians. On two successive days in 1927 he discovered and claimed for the commercial empire the Carter Family and Jimmie Rodgers.

At the opening of the twentieth century, the decisive influence of the ragtime pianists was taking effect. At the same time the American band was being heard everywhere, promoted by the most successful musician of his time, John Philip Sousa. The two influences met in a craze for dance bands that played vigorous dance music. Burgeoning displays of sheet music in neighborhood stores, often called *rag,* attracted a large public, many of whom never heard the concerts of the creators of ragtime. Even modest homes across the country could boast a parlor piano or the less expensive reed organ: the industry built 107,000 harmoniums a year in 1900, and 177,000 pianos. By 1909 the figure was 364,000 pianos. A household did not need to have an accomplished pianist in order to enjoy the benefits of piano music and to enter the circle of buyers of sheet music: by 1925 more than half the pianos produced were automatics and could use player rolls to reproduce the popular songs of the day (see Cyril Ehrlich, *The Piano: A History*). These home instruments made better music than the early record players or the first radio receivers, but in the 1920s those artificial voices were already competing for the ears of many families.

A boom in social dancing began during the second decade of the twentieth century along with the first national awareness of a new music called jass or *jazz.* Nat Shapiro quotes *Variety's* estimate that in the middle 1920s there were sixty thousand dance bands playing on the dance floors of jazz-age America. Both live and on record Americans were hearing the infectious ensemble jazz sound that coalesced in New Orleans around the turn of the century, spread up the river to Chicago, was joined by the sounds of Harlem pianists and large bands in Kansas City and New York, and diversified into swinging and sweeter orchestra sounds in the 1930s. It diversified more with the radical bop soloists of the 1940s. Perhaps the broadest public jazz ever had, though not when it was most purely jazz, was in the age of swing in the later 1930s and the 1940s when big-band arranged jazz or at least jazz-influenced bands and vocalists were the mainstream of urban popular music, live and on records and radio.

Records were where the money was in popular music in the 1920s, replacing the sheet music market. But two challenges were waiting before record sales could assert their lasting dominance over other music markets. Beginning in 1920, radio brought live and recorded music into homes—for free if you had a receiver. Radio set sales boomed. When the Depression struck in 1929 the expense of records suddenly seemed too great and sales of records were decimated; they struggled slowly back toward the end of the 1930s. A second challenge came when Al Jolson sang on screen in the first sound movie in 1927. At first only a curiosity, sound films soon drove theater organists out of work, and the films not only made their own dialogue but their own music. A fad for movies featuring numerous songs took hold and became an institution, the movie musical, one of the standards of escapist movie fare in the tight-money 1930s when going out to films became the nation's leading entertainment expenditure. Hollywood had become one of the influential sources of popular songs.

As the record industry regained a large market with big bands and their vocalists, the city ballroom, city stage, and Hollywood glamour streams of popular music came to a significant crisis. The American Society of Composers, Authors, and Publishers (ASCAP) had been formed in 1914 to collect performance royalties for the owners of song copyrights. By 1939 it represented a music establishment, and it held a monopoly power over popular music. A dispute arose between ASCAP and the radio broadcasters over terms for a new royalty contract, and a ten-month interval followed in 1941 during which no ASCAP music could be played on the air. Stations and networks scrambled to find classical fare, folk music, anything in the public domain to fill the void. An alternative guild called Broadcast Music Incorporated, BMI, was formed to compete with ASCAP. When a contract was finally signed the new BMI remained and grew. It came to represent popular music from outside the sophisticated New York-Hollywood circles, with more interest in local markets and regional music as opposed to the network emphasis of ASCAP. Eventually the two organizations would have a great overlap of interests, but the birth of BMI reflected new importance for the regional (especially southern), rural, and minority interests that would gain still more in importance after the war.

When the war ended, the entertainment industry responded to the ready money of a new public, more urbanized (but much of it with fresh country roots), less in touch with high-hat sophistication, and with expanding young families that would grow up to adopt rock 'n' roll. Carl Belz describes the recording industry in the years after the war as dividing its market in the interest of stability and consequently producing dull, or at least highly controlled and predictable, music for a general market. Small, independent record companies sold to the country and western and to the rhythm and blues or "race" record markets, while the major companies guided the music of the largest popular market down a narrow channel with a slow succession of new songs and much repetitive recording of them by competing established stars.

Into this hit parade world, in 1954, came *rock 'n' roll*. Old divisions broke down. Some listeners couldn't tell whether Elvis Presley was white or black; to the white market he brought another infusion of the black music influence that has always participated in the evolution of vital new eras of American pop. Some of Elvis' records and those of other artists who were called *rockabilly* performers also sold well to the country-and-western fans. For a time, the new pop music of young white Americans fell in with the vocal styles already established for singing piano players and vocal groups from New Orleans and Harlem that had been targeted to black audiences under the general denomination of *rhythm and blues*. Some of these black performers acquired large new white audiences; many more saw their work profitably imitated by white stars.

Rock 'n' roll, which the industry learned to ride to a staggering new sales volume, also jarred that industry into new patterns: new companies, new small-group recording economics, new audience definitions, and new relationships to radio broadcasting. Some of the story can be told in terms of technological innovations. Television, the surging new home entertainment medium, turned radio stations toward the disc-jockey format of record programming. New sizes, speeds, and materials for the records themselves may have had broad implications. Belz makes an interesting analysis of the cultural meaning of the shift from 78 to 45 rpm records that streamlined the experience of recorded music in the direction of casualness, especially for the young audience: their parents bought the more substantial 33 rpm long-playing records that emerged at the same time in the early 1950s. When later rock artists began to tailor their music toward 33 LP record albums, it would be a sign both of their dominance of the industry and all the marketing resources it could command and of their increasing musical confidence, sophistication, and ambition.

A new phase of music, based on rock 'n' roll but with several new accents, arrived in 1962—music called *rock*. One of its accents was British. The Beatles led a British invasion, but that invasion only brought back across the Atlantic basic American pop sounds. Charlie Gillett analyzes their novelty for British and then American listeners as a new combination of hard rock 'n' roll and of soft gospel-style black pop. Whatever the elements, their fresh musical energy gave them at one point all five top records on the American charts. But the new rock had many other voices too, including the harsher London sound of the Rolling Stones, the soft southern California surf music of the Beach Boys, and soon the psychedelic evocations of San Francisco groups. If rock 'n' roll had been associated with the disaffected rebel without a cause, rock in the 1960s sounded at the heart of a culture against a culture, a counterculture with powerful causes, especially their opposition to the Vietnam War. Popular music became expressive of deep splits and changes in American values. The challenging of established values and habits of American culture was especially clear in the *folk* and *folk-rock* styles popular with collegiate audiences of the decade.

No single style emerged in the 1970s of comparable novelty and power. As the confrontational politics of the Vietnam era waned and as economic pressures seemed to foster conservatism in both younger and older Americans, popular music styles included several waves of cosmetic flashiness and mechanical regularity—glitter rock, high-technology loud sound, disco, and punk. Rock also accommodated the challenge of the new popularity of new kinds of *country music*. The Grand Ole Opry had made Nashville the center of southern white rural music since the 1920s, and for a half a century the music had stood for music of old times and old values for its fans in the country and, increasingly, in the cities. By the 1970s, Nashville was a major recording center and a major popular music business center, and new slick country music was taking over radio stations in the biggest nonsouthern urban markets. Generally it still stood for old values: Merle Haggard's "Okie from Muskogee" denounced "the hippies out in San Francisco" to middle America. But if, in Haggard, country music defied rock, it edged toward rock style and the rock audience in the music of other stars, including those who called themselves the Outlaws (not a performing group but a circle of nonconformist separate singers). A rock and country alliance was heralded by Willie Nelson and friends in performances and festivals around Austin, Texas.

A generation after the rock 'n' roll explosion, the electric guitar dominates American popular music as the big band once did. Rock is the establishment, and the rock generation, the postwar baby boom, moves toward middle age: such stars as the Rolling Stones, playing what has always been a youth music, are in their forties. Whatever coming of age means for the music itself, it means increasingly that rock and its culture are firmly established as something to be reckoned with in society, in politics (Jimmy Carter quoted Bob Dylan as he campaigned for the presidency), in history, and among the arts. The great cultural and economic importance of rock has meant much publicity and a growing amount of serious attention from journalists, critics, and scholars. The study of popular culture and of all the popular arts has been fostered by the prominence of rock and by commentary on it, by its detractors and by its articulate loyalists. The spectacular rise of rock has helped bring about new interest in the meaning of American popular music, including the story of where it came from and how it grew.

american popular music

CHAPTER I

American Popular Music in General

This chapter surveys resources for the study of American popular music that are relevant to all its modern diversity or to long stretches of its history. Books and other resources that deal specifically with the early history, however broadly, will be taken up in chapter 2. Materials concerned with limited areas of the music, however long their history, come up in succeeding chapters.

A. BIBLIOGRAPHICAL RESOURCES

GUIDES TO BOOKS

David Horn's *The Literature of American Music in Books and Folk Music Collections: A Fully Annotated Bibliography* gives detailed descriptions of a large number of books published through mid-1975. The scope of Horn's book includes cultivated as well as folk and popular music, but half of its listings are within the fields of "Black Music," "Jazz," and "Popular Currents," with about 250 books in each of those categories. Horn's annotations are often long review paragraphs that summarize and sometimes evaluate; there is a helpful full index. Richard Jackson's *United States Music: Sources of Bibliography and Collective Biography* is a much briefer but also very illuminating annotated survey with brisk, authoritative descriptions and judgments on a hundred books, two-thirds of them relevant to popular music. Vincent Duckles' *Music Reference and Research Materials: An Annotated Bibliography* is a comprehensive scholarly guide to reference works in musicology, and the second and third editions include several categories that touch on popular and jazz materials. Duckles' notes on the books include mention of published reviews. The *Chicorel Bibliography to Books on Music and Musicians,* volume 10 of a series of conspicuous bright yellow reference-room books, is much less useful. It gives trade information only for books that were in print in 1974.

Each issue of *Notes: The Quarterly Journal of the Music Library Association* has an extensive section of reviews of new books in musicology, with listings of new books not reviewed. Reflecting the increasing seriousness and scholarly acceptance of popular music studies, *Notes* has begun to devote some of its reviews to such books in the past decade. Books on black music are listed and reviewed in *Black Perspective in Music* (see section C, below).

GUIDES TO SCHOLARSHIP AND JOURNALISM

In 1974, Rita H. Mead published *Doctoral Dissertations in American Music: A Classified Bibliography* which includes a scattering of work on popular music, especially under the headings "Opera and Other Musical Theater," "Jazz and Country Music," "Socio-Cultural Studies," "Racial and Ethnic Groups," "Special Topics," and "Communications Media." Dissertations on popular subjects are still not numerous, but for succeeding years they can be located in the annual *American Doctoral Dissertations;* listings are by school under such topics as "Music" (very few are popular) and "Folklore," where studies of country music are filed. There is no subject index beyond these general topics. *Dissertation Abstracts International: A—The Humanities and Social Sciences* provides summaries of some but not all such dissertations (Harvard University, for example, does not participate).

Published writing on popular music other than books can be tracked down through a variety of reference tools. About sixty magazines concerned mostly with popular music are indexed by subject and author in the *Popular Music Periodicals Index,* compiled by Dean Tudor and others, so far covering the years 1973-1976. The other most specific index is provided by *Abstracts of Popular Culture,* which selects and summarizes articles from over three hundred periodicals. Entries are by author, with a subject index; many of the works represented are on music.

Other indexes and guides cast broader nets over different groups of publications and also have some popular music materials. *RILM Abstracts of Music Literature,* a musicological library service, attempts to list and describe "all significant" current music articles and books worldwide, noting published reviews of books. Its "Ethnomusicology" section has a heading for "Jazz, Pop, and Rock." *The Music Index* is a subject and author index of music periodicals including many popular and jazz magazines. General readers' magazines are indexed in the *Readers' Guide to Periodical Literature.* In 1973 a *Popular Periodical Index* was begun to cover a variety of generally more nonestablishment magazines, but its two specifically musical magazines, *Down Beat* and *Rolling Stone* (see chapters 5 and 7), have now been picked up by *Readers' Guide.*

Essays and articles collected in books are covered by the *Essay and General Literature Index.* Coverage goes back to 1900 in cumulative volumes published in 1934 and continues monthly. This index has always had the Library of Congress catalog heading "Music, Popular (Songs, etc.)" and some other relevant categories such as "Jazz music" and "Musical comedies."

Scholarly articles in several disciplines may bear on popular music. The *MLA International Bibliography* of the Modern Language Association of

America publishes three volumes each year of literary and linguistics studies. In volume 1 there is a category "Folklore," subcategory "Songs," that lists books and articles on folk songs and also popular songs. Ballad and folksong coverage is long standing, but in the 1970s considerable popular material has been appearing: see the sub-subsections "Bibliography" and "North America." There are separate *Social Sciences Index* and *Humanities Index* as of 1975 succeeding the *Social Sciences and Humanities Index* that began in 1916, with coverage back to 1907, as a more scholarly supplement to the *Readers' Guide.* Academic sociology has *Sociological Abstracts* in which there is a "mass culture" category: some studies of popular music have appeared, for example, in the *American Journal of Sociology.*

A specialized magazine index relevant to current popular music is the *Annual Index to Popular Music Record Reviews*, by Andrew Armitage and others, published so far for the years 1972-1977, which locates such reviews in about fifty-five periodicals.

Newspapers, of course, often carry reviews, features, and entertainment and business coverage that bears on popular music. Files of the *New York Times* and its annual index are available in many libraries throughout the country, and, according to region, libraries also may have files and the indexes that are published for such papers as the *Wall Street Journal,* the *Christian Science Monitor,* the *Washington Post,* the New Orleans *Times-Picayune,* the Chicago *Tribune,* or the *Los Angeles Times.* There is an *Alternative Press Index* for a hundred "underground" newspapers, beginning in 1969; these papers may have more coverage than, and a different slant from, writing in the established papers. Files and index are also available for the *Times* of London (it will be noticed in this survey that American popular music is often also English). Local newspaper writing in 190 U.S. newspapers can be located and read through *NewsBank,* a monthly microfiche collection of clipped and cataloged articles since 1975. There is a monthly subcollection of "Performing Arts" articles that locates interviews and reviews from around the country.

Women in American Music: A Bibliography, compiled by JoAnn Skowronski, lists books, periodicals, and articles on women's participation in popular and other American music since the American Revolution, with brief annotations. A larger volume, *Women in American Music: A Bibliography of Music and Literature* by Adrienne Fried Block and Carol Neuls-Bates, is devoted almost entirely to art music; it has brief sections listing musical works by and literature about women in "vernacular music" prior to 1920.

LIBRARIES

There is now available an extremely useful guide to collections of all sizes and kinds in the United States relevant to popular as well as other American music history: *Resources of American Music History: A Directory of Source Materials from Colonial Times to World War II,* by D. W. Krummel and others. Sponsored by the Music Library Association, the American Musicological Society, and the National Endowment for the Humanities, *Resources* surveys music history holdings in public libraries and other institutions and also many in private hands throughout the country. Inventories give the size of collections in categories such as popular songbooks, popular sheet music, and local archival materials; the more specialized holdings, especially, are described in considerable detail. There is a large index.

Many public and university libraries hold extensive collections of printed music, of books about music, and of sound recordings. Such libraries, beyond those to be mentioned here, may be identified in *Resources* or by consulting the *Directory of Special Libraries and Information Centers* edited by Margaret L. Young and Harold C. Young (6th edition) or by Lois Lenroot-Ernt (7th). It has an index category "Music, popular American," but libraries listed there are oddly selected, and many of the larger collections, as described elsewhere in the same volume, are not mentioned there. Lee Ash's *Subject Collections* similarly lists library collections under various headings such as "Music—American," "Music, Country," "Music, Pop," and "Blues." The two works vary considerably in institutions they list under these topics. Useful information can be found by going beyond the subject groupings to check the holdings of particular libraries accessible to the user.

Libraries with special collections of sound recordings may be identified in *A Preliminary Directory of Sound Recordings Collections in the United States and Canada,* which lists both public libraries and substantial private collections, with brief characterizations of their holdings.

The greatest collection of music and music literature is in the Library of Congress in Washington, D.C., in its Music and Recorded Sound Divisions, the latter housing over a million records, though not all of music. The next largest is in the New York Public Library's Lincoln Center branch, with its great Rodgers and Hammerstein Archive of Recorded Sound, and an Americana Collection in its music division. A very large collection specifically of popular recordings is housed at the Bowling Green State University Library in Bowling Green, Ohio. Some other large collections (excluding jazz collections, cited in chapter 5) include the following, alphabetically by state: the UCLA Music Library Archive of Popular American Music (350,000 popular song sheets); the University of Florida Belknap Collection for the Performing Arts in Gainesville (sheet music); the University of Rochester Eastman Music School Sibley Music Library (sheet music); the Barnard A. and Morris N. Young Library of Early American Popular Music in Manhattan (mostly 1790-1910); the University of Oregon in

Eugene; the Free Library of Philadelphia; and the Brown University Library in Providence, Rhode Island.

Holdings of books and recordings in major libraries can often be checked without a visit to the library in question, since printed catalogs of many libraries are now available in other libraries. Most prominently, of course, Library of Congress cards are widely deployed as sets of reference volumes in library reference rooms, and in particular there is a separate publication called *Music: Books on Music, and Sound Recordings,* or variations of that title, a continuing and cumulative bibliography, now of works in the Library of Congress and seven other libraries. Sets of volumes of catalog cards for many other major and special libraries are published by G. K. Hall and Company; some in which music is prominent are those for the Boston Public Library Music Collection, the Sibley Library of the Eastman School of Music, the New York Public Library Music Collection, and separately, the New York Public Library Rodgers and Hammerstein Archives.

In a separate corner of the Library of Congress in the American Folklife Center is housed the Archive of Folk Song. Its materials are generally outside the scope of the present survey, but there is overlap. Among the bibliographies provided by the archive on request are those on "Charles Edward 'Chuck' Berry"; "Blues"; "Country and Western Music"; "Bob Dylan"; "Folksong Revival"; and "She Is More to Be Pitied than Censured."

B. GENERAL REFERENCE

No guide or encyclopedia attempts to control information on songs and people throughout the whole span of history of American popular music, although several histories, to be described in section C, below, outline the whole story. The greatest range of a general reference work belongs to Roger D. Kinkle's *The Complete Encyclopedia of Popular Music and Jazz, 1900-1950,* in four volumes: the first surveys shows, songs, and recordings year by year throughout the half century; two more are devoted to short biographies that include inventories of the works of writers and performers; the fourth contains indexes and various supplementary lists. Irwin Stambler's *Encyclopedia of Popular Music* has 380 entries, most falling between 1925 and 1964, on performers, selected songs, shows, and topics like "Lyric" and "Mambo"; appendixes list various award winners and give discography and bibliography. When Stambler's *Encyclopedia of Pop, Rock, and Soul* came out a decade later (see chapter 7) the first encyclopedia was retrospectively labeled volume 1; with Grelun Landon, Stambler also has produced an *Encyclopedia of Folk, Country, and Western Music* (see chapter 6), so that his works make a fairly comprehensive set, although they are seldom found together. Peter Gammond and Peter Clayton, two British writers, compiled *A Guide to Popular Music* in 1960, a small handy-reference encyclopedia with many American biographical and subject entries, especially on jazz and Broadway, but with no country or rock. Several more specialized "encyclopedias" will be described in the following chapters.

SONGS

Song indexes are books that index the contents of song books, so that the user can track down the words and music of a song more easily than by searching a sheet music archive for the separately published song or by casual search through books where it might be collected. The first such index was by Minnie E. Sears, *Song Index: An Index to More than 12,000 Songs in 177 Song Collections,* in 1926; there followed a *Supplement: An Index to More than 7,000 Songs in 104 Song Collections* in 1934, and the two have now been reprinted in one volume. Entries are by title, first line, author, and composer. One successor was Robert Leigh's *Index to Song Books: A Title Index to Over 11,000 Copies of Almost 6,800 Songs in 111 Song Books Published between 1933 and 1962;* note in this self-description that access is only by title. A fuller continuation is *Songs in Collections: An Index* by Desiree De Charms and Paul F. Breed: 9,493 songs in 411 collections, 1940-1957. As compared to the other indexes this one leans toward art songs and arias, although many folk and popular collections are included. Songs are listed by title, first line, and author. The *Popular Song Index* by Patricia Havlice covers three hundred books from 1940 to 1972, by title, composer, and author; there is a *First Supplement* with seventy-two more books, 1972-1975. All of these indexes are best considered as a set and used with the awareness that their reference lists are different—what is not in one may be in another. They give no information about a song except where to find it, and when it is found in the song book referred to, the user must judge whether the words and music printed there are likely to be accurate enough for the purposes of the search.

Information about songs can be found in Nat Shapiro's *Popular Music: An Annotated Index of American Popular Songs:* volume 1, covering 1950-1959; 2, 1940-1949; 3, 1960-1964; 4, 1930-1939; 5, 1920-1929; 6, 1965-1969 (note that this sequence of volumes is not chronological). Shapiro's work is an alphabetical catalog year by year, giving author, composer, copyright owner, and who introduced the song. For each volume there is a cumulative title list and publishers' directory, and all but the first volume have brief historical introductions that together make a good brief history of the half century of popular music. Shapiro's list and all other lists are, of course, selective; his is the largest available. Another large list is Julius Mattfeld's *Variety Music Cavalcade, 1620-1969: A Chronology of Vocal and Instrumental Music Popular in the United States* ("Variety" because at an earlier stage it was serialized in *Variety* magazine). Although Mattfeld's title indicates sweeping historical coverage, the years before 1800 pass in less than nine pages. Still, his coverage is extensive for the century before Shapiro's listings begin. Mattfeld concludes each yearly list in the nineteenth and twentieth centuries with a compilation of historical and human interest notes on that year, giving the music some social context. John H. Chipman's *Index to Top-Hit Tunes (1900-1950)* selects some three thousand songs by sales success. About the same size is Chappell and Company's *80 Years of American Song Hits 1892-1972,* another yearly title-and-author listing of varying numbers of songs, two for the first year, more than sixty for the last. Richard Lewine and Alfred Simon's *Songs of the American Theater: A Comprehensive Listing of More Than 12,000 Songs, Including Selected Titles from Film and Television Productions* will be noticed again in chapter 3, as will *The Index of American Popular Music* by Jack Burton.

A different perspective on songs is offered by David Ewen's *American Popular Songs from the Revolutionary War to the Present.* Ewen's index is an alphabetical catalog of songs and writers, so that songs can be looked up for anecdotal commentary or browsed over, rather than seen in yearly groupings. Ewen also offers an "All-Time Hit Parade" chronology, an "All-Time Best-Selling Popular Recordings" list, and a performers list. Some thirty-six hundred songs are presented, excluding jazz. Another view again comes from the *Stecheson Classified Song Directory* (1961) and its *Supplement* (1978). They order an enormous number of songs, 100,000 titles, according to the subjects of the songs. The intended purpose is to enable program directors "to compile a program of songs about the skies" or about virtually anything else. Other users may find it illuminating to see what subjects have been represented and when and to what relative extent they have been represented in popular songs. (Compare the work by Macken, Fornatale, and Ayres on rock music, chapter 7.) Some further information is also presented by Stecheson. Under "Motion Pictures," "Musicals," and "Operas," show titles are followed by song inventories, and under "Composers-Authors" (a large section between "Comical" and "Conga"), writers are listed with their principal works. Publishers and distributors are listed at the back.

A scholarly look into the histories of individual songs makes up two books by James J. Fuld. Its first form was *American Popular Music (Reference Book) 1875-1950* in 1955 and a *Supplement* in 1956, which gave bibliographic descriptions of sheet music and some historical notes on about 250 songs, illustrated with sheet music covers. It was greatly expanded in 1966 and again enlarged in 1971 as *The Book of World-Famous Music: Classical, Popular and Folk.* Here Fuld traces the bibliographical and historical trail back to the first printed appearance of each of about a thousand well-known melodies. Various tabulated and other data are given in a general introduction.

The lyrics of the most popular current songs have been published for forty years in magazines of the Charlton Press: *Hit Parader* and *Song Hits* magazines since 1942, joined by *Country Song Roundup* in 1947 and *Rock and Soul Songs* in 1956. Back files of these magazines are rare.

RECORDS

The sales history of records is another profile of the history of popular music. The weekly sales charts in *Billboard* magazine (similar charts also appear in its rival, *Cashbox*) make a base of data about popular music that is gathered into various forms in several books. Joel Whitburn is the most prominent collector of the data. His *Top Pop Records, 1955-1970: Facts about 9,800 Recordings Listed in Billboard's "Hot 100" Charts, Grouped under the Names of the 2,500 Recording Artists* assembles the numbers cumulatively to give for each record the dates and the length and the highest standing of chart appearance. His next work, *Joel Whitburn's Top Pop Records, 1940-1955*, extends the tabulation back to the beginning of the *Billboard* charts. In these years the magazine listed top forties, and Whitburn indexes seventeen hundred records by four hundred artists, adding lists of first-place records and other information. He extended the coverage laterally in *Joel Whitburn's Top Rhythm and Blues Records 1949-1971* from the separate charts in the same source, and he made similar compilations on country and western, long-playing records, and "easy listening" music. A rearrangement of the data produced *Joel Whitburn's Pop Annual, 1955-1977* where they are given by year, including fuller listing for the first three years than were previously tabulated, revising some rankings in his earlier books. Elston Brooks' *I've Heard Those Songs Before: The Weekly Top Ten Tunes for the Past Fifty Years* tabulates for the years 1930-1980 with notes on events of each year, and includes a title index. Other catalogs of hit data belong specifically to the history of Tin Pan Alley or of rock 'n' roll and will be discussed in later chapters. One may be mentioned here: *The Miles Chart Display* is a mammoth compilation of graphs of sales of individual records.

A more elite set of hits is chronicled in *The Book of Golden Discs* compiled by Joseph Murrells, which gives annotated entries for all the artists recording million-selling records by year from 1903 to 1969. Biographical data appear with the first listing of any given artist, and short notes on the records make up subsequent entries.

"Discography" often means a list of records. It also names a science, the disciplined cataloging of records (the two uses parallel the two meanings of "bibliography"). Systematic discographic surveys of various segments of the vast territory of phonograph record production will be mentioned throughout this book. A preface to all of them is *Brian Rust's Guide to Discography,* an explanation of the art by its most eminent practitioner, including a bibliography of book-length discographies, a glossary, and directories of organizations and magazines concerned with the subject.

Current record production in all fields can be surveyed to some extent in the Schwann and Phono-Log commercial catalogs. *The Schwann-1 Record and Tape Guide,* founded in 1949, is a selective list, revised each month, of facts supplied by the record companies about their current offerings. The sections on "Musicals," "Current Popular," and "Jazz" are sketchy compared to the classical section, making up together less than a quarter of the book. For most artists represented in the "Current Popular" list only one record will be entered. The *Schwann-2* book is a semiannual supplement of miscellaneous records, including "Non-Current Popular," but this listing also is very incomplete, and the two catalogs together do not cover nearly all records that are actually available in stores and from record companies. *Phono-Log Reporter* is the large looseleaf yellow reference book displayed on the counters of record stores, continuously updated, but still less than a full catalog of records actually offered for sale, especially those of smaller companies. The same publisher issues *List-o-Tapes,* a similar looseleaf book for the various tape configurations, with weekly replacement sheets.

An evaluative rather than quantitive or availability survey of recordings is provided in a series edited by Dean Tudor and Nancy Tudor called collectively American Popular Music on Elpee. There are four volumes with similar layout: *Contemporary Popular Music, Black Music, Jazz,* and *Grass Roots Music.* These companion volumes are extensively annotated buying guides to a total of about five thousand long-playing records. The Tudors are librarians, writing partly for other librarians developing public record collections; their annotations attempt to report a consensus of published reviews (they have also produced the *Index* of such reviews—see above) on all significant records produced at any time if still available for purchase. The four books share a bibliography that is referred to in separate bibliographic and historical introductions to sections of each book, for example, "Bop, Cool, Modern" in *Jazz.*

A bigger body of recordings, with more contemporary emphasis and briefer commentary, is *The Rolling Stone Record Guide: Reviews and Ratings of Almost 10,000 Currently Available Rock, Pop, Soul, Country, Blues, Jazz, and Gospel Albums,* edited by Dave Marsh and John Swenson. In the Tudors' *Contemporary* volume, only about 250 albums are listed in the "Rock" section; the ten thousand records in Marsh and Swenson are all either rock or somehow associated with rock, mostly in the 1970s. The notes and value judgments are curt, lively, and opinionated, aimed at the individual record customer rather than the sober institutional buyer. More general advice for the consumer is given in *The New York Times Guide to Listening Pleasure* edited by Howard Taubman (1968), a collection of chapters of advice by various critics on how to understand and enjoy diverse forms of "good music." The last third includes pieces by Alfred Simon on the musical theater, John S. Wilson on jazz, Robert Sherman on folk music, and Pru Devon on music from Latin America. Discographies for the various chapters are at the end.

SHEET MUSIC AND RECORD COLLECTING

Some information about the history of popular music is in forms directed at collectors of old or rare song sheets and records.

Sheet music collecting was given an extensive introduction in 1941 in Harry Dichter and Elliott Shapiro's *Early American Sheet Music, Its Lure and Lore,* reprinted in 1977 as *Handbook of Early American Sheet Music, 1768-1889,* giving a bibliographic catalog by periods and by types within periods, with directories of publishers and of lithographers and artists. Marian Klamkin's *Old Sheet Music: A Pictorial History* presents briefly introduced photographs of covers, four to a page, some in color, about equally from the nineteenth and twentieth centuries.

Prices for some old sheet music are suggested in several hobbyist's guides which also make casual histories and hit-or-miss bibliographies. *Collectors Guide to Sheet Music,* perhaps itself collectible as an anonymous publication from Gas City, Indiana, is a slim paperback price guide by various categories and in general, illustrated with many small black-and-white reproductions; items range from the mid-nineteenth to the mid-twentieth century. Helen Westin's *Introducing the Song Sheet: A Collector's Guide with Current Price List* is similar, graced with 148 color reproductions. Daniel B. Priest's *American Sheet Music: A Guide to Collecting Sheet Music from 1775 to 1975* has minichapters on various aspects of the history, business, and art of sheet music and a forty-page price list with small reproductions. Relevant here although aimed at a broader reading audience are the works of Lester Levy and the book by David Tatham described in chapter 2.

Collectors of old records have similar guides. Peter A. Soderbergh has published two. In *78 RPM Records and Prices,* the last quarter is a price guide, the rest miscellaneous data: a chronology, a chapter of advice for beginning collectors, a table of 550 classic recording dates (mainly for big bands), a list of band theme songs, a label catalog, and a million-sellers list. *Olde Records Price Guide, 1900-1947: Popular and Classical 78 RPM's* is principally a price guide discography organized by recording artist—the classical section is brief—focusing on jazz bands, with "Intermissions" of historical and bibliographic notes. The *1915-1965 American Premium Record Guide: Identification and Values, 78's, 45's and LP's* by L. R. Docks is a large 737-page listing, with a section illustrating several hundred labels and a performers' index. Gary S. Felton has compiled *The Record Collector's International Directory* to locate American, English, and some other dealers in rare or collector's records.

C. BIOGRAPHY AND HISTORY

BIOGRAPHY

Access to facts about some ten thousand men and women of American music up to the 1930s is possible through the *Bio-Bibliographical Index of Musicians in the United States of America Since Colonial Times* that was prepared under the Work Projects Administration and completed in 1941. The index gives dates, an identifying word or phrase, and reference to a book in which information can be found; a small minority of those listed are popular music figures.

Fuller biographical information for many men and women in a single volume can be found in the *Biographical Dictionary of American Music* by Charles Eugene Claghorn. Again, both classical and popular careers are covered from colonial times to the 1970s in fifty-two hundred entries on musicians, composers, lyricists, and singers. *Baker's Biographical Dictionary of Musicians* (sixth edition, 1978), edited by Nicolas Slonimsky, is the latest form of a book that has been a standard reference work on classical music since 1900. It began to include popular musicians in its 1958 edition, and coverage is extended a bit in the newest version, though still with some diffidence. Entries include bibliographic references. An *ASCAP Biographical Dictionary* has eight thousand life and career summaries (but not every member has found his way in) for both living and deceased members since 1914. After 1940, a share of popular music figures have belonged to the rival BMI guild and so will not appear in this directory. Warren Craig's *Sweet and Lowdown: America's Popular Song Writers* registers the most successful songwriting careers (no country or rock 'n' roll) with short narratives and surveys of hits written, sternly excluding some recognized figures if sales data do not place them in the successful elite.

Article-length entries compose *The Best of the Music Makers: From Acuff to Ellington to Presley to Sinatra to Zappa and 279 More of the Most Popular Perfomers of the Last Fifty Years* by George T. Simon "and friends," venturing beyond Simon's interest in jazz and swing performers to assemble with them some rock and country performers, up to about a third of the total. Entries have about a page and a half each with photographs but without record lists or references. David Ewen produced *Popular American Composers from Revolutionary Times to the Present* in 1962, with a *Supplement* in 1972. The first version had 130 biographies of both classical and popular composers; the supplement added new figures, including more pop and a few country and rock 'n' roll writers. Also in 1972, Ewen enlarged his *Great Men of American Popular Song* which gives chatty biographies of twenty-eight composers and thirteen lyricists. Ewen is an astonishingly prolific author of music history and reference books. His work is not always the most accurate source available for what he reports, and he sometimes retails legends and press-release promotion as biography and history.

Black musicians alone appear in three reference works. Eileen Southern's *Biographical Dictionary of Afro-American and African Musicians* has entries for more than fifteen hundred figures, most born not later than 1945, with bibliographic references to newspaper articles and question-naires, as well as to books, and with references to sources of discography. *Biographical Dictionary of Black Musicians and Music Educators,* volume 1, by Lemuel Berry, Jr., gives brief data entries on classical, jazz, and popular music figures in two alphabetical listings; the second addendum list is about as long as the first and seems to have more jazz and pop figures. Berry gives a bibliography and various appended lists. D. Antoinette Handy's *Black Women in American Bands and Orchestras* has historical surveys and collections of 112 profiles, primarily in symphony orchestras but also with many jazz players. Solo artists, as opposed to ensemble players, are excluded.

General biograpical sources may be useful in the search for music biog-raphy materials, especially of recent or contemporary figures. *Current Biography* has published profiles of all sorts of men and women since 1940; Richard Jackson in his *United States Music* (section A, above) lists about two hundred musical figures, many popular, who had appeared by 1970, and further entries continue to appear. Each feature includes a photograph and references to sources. The *New York Times Biographical Service* is a monthly reprint of biographical features, news items, and obituaries from the paper, running to about 150 pages each month.

GENERAL HISTORY

Gilbert Chase's *American Music: From the Pilgrims to the Present* (1955; second edition, 1966) is a standard history that was an early and influential case of careful musical history interweaving folk and popular forms with its account of the classical tradition. Throughout Chase's book there is strong, primary documentation and frequent illustration with musical examples. The survey does not touch on rock or country music. John Tasker Howard's *Our American Music: A Comprehensive History from 1620 to the Present* (1965) is the fourth edition of a work first published in 1931. It treats both popular and classical strains of early music, devotes most of its effort to the classical tradition over the last century, and returns to a brief survey in the final tenth of the book of popular music since the nineteenth century. There is an excellent bibliography. Ronald L. Davis' *A History of Music in American Life,* in three volumes, is a cultural historical survey of all sorts of American music, more chronicle than analysis. The first volume (up to 1865) includes sentimental songs, the minstrel stage, folk music, and reformers like the Hutchinsons; the second (1865-1920) includes the musical theater of Herbert and Cohan, Tin Pan Alley, blues, ragtime, and early jazz; the third (1920-present) includes musical comedy, jazz, popular songs, country, rock, and soul—along with about equal attention in each volume to classical music. *American Music: A Panorama,* by Daniel Kingman, is a textbook history with illustrations, guides to reading and listening, and an intriguing chart of the interactions of the various American musics.

Histories of popular music by itself are numerous. The best at this writing is *Yesterdays: Popular Song in America* by Charles Hamm, a fully documented account from the eighteenth century to rock, with photographs, musical and verse examples, tables, most-popular lists, and extensive bibliography. Limitations are the exclusion of instrumental music and adherence to sheet music as a primary source, which has been argued to underestimate factors not visible on paper such as black-influenced performance style. David Ewen's *All the Years of American Popular Music* is the largest single history, more popular in tone and less scholarly than Hamm. Two earlier versions of the history by Ewen are his *Panorama of American Popular Music* (1957), emphasizing eclectic breadth of the definition of "popular," and *History of Popular Music* (1961), an unreliable anecdotal chronicle.

Popular histories of popular music have been published in every decade since Helen L. Kaufmann's *From Jehovah to Jazz: Music in America from Psalmody to the Present Day* in 1937. Changes in the way these histories treat various subjects and styles, especially the way they treat whatever is new at the time of the writing, make these older books interesting to a critical reader even when better, or more congenial, perspective is available in a more recent account. Kaufmann's early chronicle passes through ministrelsy and ragtime to a quick treatment of jazz. In 1948 Sigmund Spaeth published *A History of Popular Music in America,* with more than half devoted to music before 1900, the remainder devoted to Tin Pan Alley, Broadway, and Hollywood into the 1940s. Spaeth wrote other books (see chapters 2 and 3) treating popular song with amusement and some scorn. This book by contrast is a serious critical account, emphasizing the relatively sophisticated side of commercial music. Elliot Paul's *That Crazy American Music* (1957) is a light but informed history from colonial times to his own, closing with approving notice of bop jazz and amusement at early rock 'n' roll. John Rublowsky in 1967 published both *Popular Music and Music in America.* The former is a short survey with very brief chapters on Broadway, jazz, country, rock 'n' roll, and various aspects of the big business of music. The latter book is similar but scatters chapters across more time and types: Puritan, colonial, Indian, slave, mountain, minstrel, genteel, New Orleans, modern classical, and a postscript on the last fifty years. In 1972 Ian Whitcomb published *After the Ball: Pop Music from Rag to Rock,* the first history of anything published by a former rock star. The book is a lively but sound and detailed history of modern pop by a British university history student who had brief success as a rock vocalist in the early 1960s. About a quarter of the book is devoted to British pop, the rest to American pop. Tony Palmer's *All You Need Is Love: The Story of Popular Music* (1976) is a large-format and large-scale illustrated history evolved from a series of shows for BBC-TV surveying all twentieth-century branches. Charles Boeckman's *And the Beat Goes On* is a brief survey of the history for younger readers.

Essays with special angles on all or part of the history include the second half of Wilfrid Mellers' *Music in a New Found Land* (the first half is on classical works). Mellers, a critic and musicologist, devotes the later essays in the book to jazz and musical theater from the nineteenth century to the 1950s; appendixes include a large discography by Kenneth W. Dommett. *One Hundred Years of Music in America*, edited by Paul Henry Lang, is an anthology of survey essays. The section "Musical Life" has "Popular Music from Minstrel Songs to Rock 'n' Roll" by Arnold Shaw; the sections "The Business of Music" and "Music, Government, and the Law" have several essays relevant to popular music, for example, "Copyright and the Creative Arts" by Robert J. Burton.

Popular music set in the frame of American popular culture in general makes a chapter in Russel Nye's *The Unembarrassed Muse: The Popular Arts in America.* Nye's book was a pioneering attempt at a history of all American popular culture, and his brief account of popular music and a separate short section on the minstrel stage gain value when read in the setting of the rest of the book. Conversely, Henry Pleasants has written about popular music in the larger, nonpopular musical context. *Serious Music—and All that Jazz!* continues his argument in two earlier books that modern classical music is an exhausted tradition. Pleasants had hailed jazz as the source of new vitality for serious music; in this book he finds jazz also turning away from its audience, and he looks into rock, pop, and country for what they have to offer the future of music in general. Pleasants has brought his interests in classical musicology to bear on popular music in another way in *The Great American Popular Singers,* where he develops a theory of the distinctive art of American popular singing, and in light of that theory examines the performance styles of pop, blues, jazz, country, and rock 'n' roll singers: Jolson, Smith, Waters, Armstrong, Rodgers, Crosby, Bailey, Holiday, Fitzgerald, Sinatra, Jackson, Cole, Williams, Charles, Presley, Garland, Cash, King, Franklin, Merman, Lee, and Streisand. Not biographical but critical in nature, his studies make another sort of composite history of popular music.

The Latin Tinge: The Impact of Latin American Music on the United States by John Storm Roberts is the single full-length study of its subject. Roberts argues a thorough penetration of major forms of American popular music by Brazilian, Argentinian, Cuban, and Mexican sounds from the mid-nineteenth century onward, including *habanera* song; tango, rhumba, and successive dance band styles; mariachi and marimba music; and strands of jazz, rhythm and blues, country, and rock. Influences from other directions are suggested in Theodore C. Grame's *America's Ethnic Music,* which documents and argues for more recognition of a vast diversity of traditional music from Europe and the orient that has survived in this country; Grame attacks the melting-pot ideology that rationalizes the homogenization of commercial popular music.

The Jews on Tin Pan Alley, by Kenneth Kanter, traces the contributions of Jews to American popular music from Henry Russell in the 1830s to Broadway after World War II, with brief historical survey and particular chapters on Russell, Monroe Rosenfeld, Charles K. Harris, the Von Tilzers, Jerome Kern, Irving Berlin, the Gershwins, Hart, and Rodgers and Hammerstein.

Anthologies of songs with introductory material present a history of popular song in glimpses. Except for collections of nineteenth-century sheet music, songbooks are not covered in the present survey, but two books may be mentioned where commentary is emphasized. Maymie R. Krythe's *Sampler of American Songs* gives anecdotal backgrounds for eighteen favorite patriotic, pious, and Christmas songs from "Yankee Doodle" to "Rudolph, the Red-Nosed Reindeer." Irwin Silber's *Songs America Voted By* is a large anthology with historical political commentary on election songs up to a Nixon ditty in 1968. An appendix gives a bibliography of campaign songbooks.

BLACK TRADITIONS

Within and throughout American popular music there has been the significant presence of Afro-American music, both in distinct self-contained styles and markets and as a pervasive ingredient in other styles. Chapter 4 will treat the blues and black popular music; chapter 5 will take up jazz. Materials are mentioned here that bear on the history and influences of black music more broadly than will fit the singular categories of the later chapters.

Dominique-René De Lerma has published a *Bibliography of Black Music.* The first of three volumes, *Reference Materials,* collects books and articles on African as well as Afro-American music: general reference, bibliography, discography, photographic albums, directories, dissertations, and periodicals. There are especially rich collections of individual jazz discographies and of elusive magazines. Volume 2, *Afro-American Idioms,* lists references in nineteenth- and twentieth-century popular idioms, in jazz, and those concerning blacks in classical music. Other jazz bibliographies are larger, and the "Rhythm and Blues" section often sweeps in works not very closely associated with black music. Volume 3, *Geographical Studies,* covers black music studies around the world by geographical area. Only the last fifth treats the United States, with Mexico and Canada, but in this space there are many items not included in the earlier volumes. See in particular the "Northern Americas" section, "Louisiana" and "New York" for jazz, and the concluding section on "Acculturation."

Unlike De Lerma, JoAnn Skowronski gives occasional brief annotations in her *Black Music in America: A Bibliography,* though much of it is assembled from standard book and essay indexes without consulting the materials themselves. Most of the book, twelve thousand references, is a series of bibliographies for various selected artists. A section of general references is ordered by date of publication and for most purposes must be used by means of the index.

The *Music of Black Americans: A History* by Eileen Southern is a scholarly account in 500 pages of African backgrounds and American evolution, especially thorough on the nineteenth century. Covering as much as it does, this authoritative book can, in some sections, only mention names and works, but it is very inclusive and presents photographs and other illustrations, an African map, chronologies, musical and textual examples, and descriptive bibliography and discography by chapters. Southern has also edited *Readings in Black American Music,* a historical anthology of accounts by observers of the music from within and without, from early Africa to the present. Two-thirds of the readings treat black music before the twentieth century. Commentary is given in headnotes. *Black Music of Two Worlds* by John Storm Roberts is a similarly scholarly survey of the encounter of African with European music in the Americas—South, Central, Caribbean, and North—and of west African music before and after the encounter. Roberts also provides photographs and extensive bibliography and discography. John Rublowsky's *Black Music in America* is a brief, illustrated history concentrating on African origins and the eighteenth and nineteenth centuries but, in bulk, only the equivalent of two or three chapters of Southern's work. Hildreth Roach's *Black American Music: Past and Present* is a musicological survey beginning with Africa and touching folk music, spirituals, minstrels, jazz, and black contributions to art music. For minstrels and later subjects Roach concludes each chapter with a series of biographical sketches of composers. Musical examples, maps, and recommendations for readings and recordings are included.

Three recent works of black biographical reference are mentioned under general biography, above. An early book on black American musicians was Maud Cuney-Hare's *Negro Musicians and Their Music* in 1936. Two chapters touch African background, four treat nineteenth-century folk songs, and one covers musical comedy; the remaining half of the book is mostly given to classical music pursuits. Photographs, many of them portraits, are included. In the same year, Alain Locke published *The Negro and His Music,* intended as a textbook, with discussion questions and suggested readings by chapter; the book may have special interest because of Locke's eminence in black scholarship and education. *The Social Implications of Early Negro Music in the United States,* edited by Bernard Katz, is an anthology of "pioneer writings," essays and articles that appeared between 1862 and 1939. A collection of more modern articles is *The Negro in Music and Art* edited by Lindsay Patterson. Half the book is reprints of articles and chapters on such subjects as spirituals, minstrel and "postminstrel" entertainment, ragtime, blues, gospel, jazz, and rock 'n' roll.

The commercial history of black music is reported in Arnold Shaw's *The World of Soul: Black America's Contribution to the Pop Music Scene.* Shaw surveys a background of blues, jazz vocals, and black pop for a foreground of rhythm and blues as recorded from the mid-1940s to the mid-1950s; a final chapter on soul is made up of short sections on six artists. The account is somewhat diffuse because it undertakes to report social context and business history and the careers of recording artists all at the same time. Another distinctive angle on black music is that found in Johannes Riedel's *Soul Music Black and White: The Influence of Black Music on the Churches.* Riedel's main interest is new directions for modern Protestant and Catholic church music, but in tracing back the paths of influence of black forms he gives a good brief history of the evolution of African to Afro-American music.

Essays on the place and meaning of the music include Ortiz Walton's *Music: Black, White, and Blue: A Sociological Survey of the Use and Misuse of Afro-American Music,* a carefully documented polemical history. Beginning with elements of African music, Walton traces the stages of black American music as continuous and as set over against a white society that he sees as controlling and exploiting that music economically. Ben Sidran's *Black Talk* is another essay in cultural history, tracing black music as a central and sustaining factor in the essentially oral culture of black America. He provides a music-and-society bibliography and chronology. Dominique-René De Lerma has edited two volumes of conference proceedings concerned with the music. *Black Music in Our Culture* focuses on curricular ideas and resources for teaching black music in colleges. *Reflections on Afro-American Music* presents some twenty discussants, mainly on black contributions to art music but with two pieces on jazz, one on soul by Phyl Garland, and one on gospel by its eminent proponent Thomas A. Dorsey. De Lerma's preface gives an account of the founding of the Black Music Center at Indiana University, where he was the first director. D. Antoinette Handy's *Black Music: Opinions and Reviews* reprints her articles for the *Richmond Afro-American* from 1972 to 1974.

The Tudors' evaluative discography *Black Music* has been mentioned earlier with its companion volumes.

The journal *Black Perspective in Music,* edited by Eileen Southern, publishes scholarly articles and reviews. *Black Music Newsletter* is published by Fisk University's recently founded Institute for Research in Black American Music.

D. SOCIOLOGY AND TECHNOLOGY

SOCIAL INTERPRETATION

Social and cultural analysis of popular music is closely related to the interpretive history in some of the books described in the previous section, which may be consulted along with the following listing.

Jacques Barzun's *Music in American Life,* published in 1956, consists of severe Gallic reflections on that subject with some disapproving notice of pop. D. Duane Braun's *Toward a Theory of Popular Culture: The Sociology and History of American Music and Dance, 1920-1968* is a smaller work than the title might indicate, a short analytic survey with charts and academic footnotes. *The Sounds of Social Change: Studies in Popular Culture,* edited by R. Serge Denisoff and Richard A. Peterson, is an anthology of scholarly and journalistic essays on the social backgrounds, constraints, uses, and implications of popular music, including jazz, country, soul, Tin Pan Alley, and rock. *The Sounds of People and Places: Readings in the Geography of Music,* edited by George O. Carney, gives an unusual and valuable perspective: the authors are geographers, and their essays explore the spatial dimension of musical phenomena (principally country, pop, and rock), differentiating, for example, the markets of different songs, city to city, or tracing the evolution and diffusion of styles.

A political analysis of English popular song, Dave Harker's *One for the Money: Politics and Popular Song* bears on American study both because it considers some American materials and because its critique may have validity here as well as in England and may be instructive when it applies and when it shows difference. Harker's book is a serious and scholarly polemic committed to an ideal of a possible working-class culture that would speak to and for that class. He analyzes the popular music industry (part 1) and the possibility of "Alternatives" (part 2) derived from folk song and gives some methods for social and historical study of songs (part 3). Dealing with songs themselves, he analyzes mainly the lyrics, especially in an extended section on Bob Dylan.

Politics and economics of the American musicians' union are studied in Robert D. Leiter's *The Musicians and Petrillo,* a scholar's history of the American Federation of Musicians and of its tough president, James C. Petrillo, who in 1942 led the union to a two-year boycott of commercial recording. This book was, at least at one time, distributed by locals of the union to their members.

Music in American Society, 1776-1976: From Puritan Hymn to Synthesizer, edited by George McCue, is a set of papers from a bicentennial music festival in St. Louis, including K. Peter Etzkorn's history of popular music in business and technological terms, Dan Morgenstern's "Jazz as an Urban Music," and Mary Elaine Wallace's essay on musical theater. A social-scholarly anthology by Charles Hamm, Bruno Nettl, and Ronald Byrnside, *Contemporary Music and Music Cultures,* includes (with material not relevant here) essays by Hamm on acculturation of popular music and on the effect of phonograph technology and essays by Byrnside on early rock and on jazz improvisation. *Superculture: American Popular Culture and Europe* edited by C.W.E. Bigsby has an essay on American popular music and one on jazz as encountered by Europe and as Europe has been influenced by them. Study of the exportation of American popular music might be enriched by consideration of the two books by John Storm Roberts cited earlier, dealing with the penetration of influence from Africa and from Latin America as that music has been formed.

Two academic journals published at Bowling Green State University in Ohio have addressed the music from a socioanalytic side: *Popular Music and Society* (from 1971, but recently inactive) and *The Journal of Popular Culture.* The latter has a wide scope but publishes some articles on American popular music.

Social and technical perspectives are combined in Michael Lydon's unusual book *Boogie Lightning,* which deals with the coming together of black music style and the new possibility of electrification as the crucial synthesis of twentieth-century popular music. There are profile chapters on John Lee Hooker, Bo Diddley, producer Ralph Bass, The Chiffons, Aretha Franklin, and Ray Charles.

TECHNOLOGY

The history of musical, recording, broadcasting, and reproducing technology—the technology of sound—is an essential element of the whole history of popular music. Some chapters of technical history are given in works on specific styles and eras of music. Green's *Country Roots* and Wolfe's first chapter in Carr's *The Illustrated History of Country Music* give the history of some popular music instruments (see chapter 6). Pleasants, in *The Great American Popular Singers,* shows the importance of microphone technology for singing styles. Belz' *The Story of Rock* explains the importance of successive sizes and speeds of records associated with stages in pop music becoming rock music; Bennett's *On Becoming a Rock Musician* explains the technology of modern electrified instruments and amplification and their significance to the player and audience of rock (both books in chapter 7).

Home instruments were the heart of music production up through the first two decades of the twentieth century when sheet music outsold phonograph records. Cyril Ehrlich's *The Piano: A History* tells a predominantly European story, but his chapter 7 and appendix 2 give useful facts on American production. Ehrlich gives a long bibliography. Robert F. Gellerman's *The American Reed Organ: Its History; How It Works; How to Rebuild It* is a scrapbook history of text, photographs, drawings, sheet music, and old advertisements. He has a bibliography and a long pictorial catalog. Automatic pianos and similar instruments are the subject of several nostalgic studies. Harvey Roehl's *Player Piano Treasury,* enlarged from his *The Player Piano: An Historical Scrapbook,* is an immense collection of data and photographs with captions. Arthur W.J.G. Ord-Hume's *Player Piano: The History of the Mechanical Piano and How to Repair It* is a long study with photographs, detailed drawings, serial number lists, and bibliography. The same author's *Clockwork Music: An Illustrated History of Mechanical Musical Instruments from the Musical Box to the Pianola, from Automaton Lady Virginal Players to Orchestrion* is a catalog history, the latter part including American commercial devices. Q. David Bowers has produced *Put Another Nickel In: A History of Coin-Operated Pianos and Orchestrions,* similar to Roehl's work on player pianos, and *Encyclopedia of Automatic Musical Instruments,* a thousand-page compendium that is mostly photographs.

Phonograph history is given in *The Fabulous Phonograph, 1877-1977* by Roland Gelatt. As first published in 1955, Gelatt's history ends with the first LP records; the third edition adds a quick three chapters on subsequent developments. The bulk of the book is devoted to history before 1929, and the musical interest throughout is predominantly classical. *From Tin Foil to Stereo* by Oliver Reed and Walter Welch is a large, detailed history through the 1950s with much technical information. Both these books are illustrated with photographs. Two catalogs recall exhibits of recording history: Cynthia A. Hoover's *Music Machines—American Style* presents a Smithsonian display; brief notes on broadcasting and recording introduce a photograph album of recording devices, documents, and performers. James R. Smart and Jon W. Newsom's *"A Wonderful Invention": A Brief History of the Phonograph from Tinfoil to the LP* came out of an exhibit at the Library of Congress; it is a partially illustrated catalog of machines, records, and memorabilia with a twenty-three-page historical introduction. C. A. Schicke's *Revolution in Sound* (see section E, below) includes a survey history of recording technology. H. Wiley Hitchcock has edited *The Phonograph and Our Musical Life: Proceedings of a Centennial Conference 7-10 December 1977,* a collection of brief papers and transcribed discussions on the interactions of recording, music, and society. Topics include Muzak, jazz performance and scholarship, the producer as artist, Stephen Foster recreations, and films. J. Krivine's *Juke Box Saturday Night* is a large scrapbook history, with many of its photographs in color, devoted to the history of coin-operated record players. There are glowing, garishly beautiful photographs with brief commentary in a small catalog called *Jukebox: The Golden Age,* by Vincent Lynch and Bill Henkin.

Music in Modern Media by Robert Emmett Dolan is a technical handbook of recording, film soundtrack, television, and electronic music, with diagrams and tables throughout and a glossary. Technology changes, so the date (1967) must be noted. Lucy Gordon's *Music and the Modern Media of Transmission* (1976) is a brief outline of technology. Some details about modern recording can be found in a technical booklet by David Bird, *From Score to Tape: A Handbook of Mixing and Recording Techniques* (1973), which is accompanied by a demonstration record.

E. BUSINESS AND PROFESSION

HISTORY AND ANATOMY OF THE MUSIC BUSINESS

Music publishing was the main business of popular music through the Tin Pan Alley era, until recording and radio came to dominate some time in the 1920s. Works on music publishing in the nineteenth century by Epstein (Chicago), Harwell (the Confederacy), and Krohn (middle western states), and the 1870 sheet music catalog, will be described in the next chapter. A long span of history but with a narrow focus is shown in *One Hundred and Fifty Years of Music Publishing in the United States* by William Arms Fisher (1933), expanded from his 1918 book *Notes on Music in Old Boston;* both primarily tell the story of the Oliver Ditson company. The 1933 book is still a small work but with many details about the careers of these businessmen and their publications. Paula Dranov surveys the industry today in *Inside the Music Publishing Industry,* which is a collection of information on marketing and the general economic and demographic forces that bear on it; compare the books by Shemel and Krasilovsky mentioned below that include treatment of the legal side of the business. Distinct from the much larger record industry with which it works, the publishing business still deals in printed music and, now more importantly, copyrights and performance royalties. Dranov gives many data tables and a descriptive directory of publishers.

The recording business is now the vast dominating bulk of the business of music. A survey of its history and structure is C. A. Schicke's *Revolution in Sound: A Biography of the Recording Industry,* which recounts the evolution of technology along with some business history through the 1960s, and in a second section describes the workings of a modern record company and the economics and production processes of record making. Brian Rust's *The American Record Label Book* is an encyclopedia of record company label designations, illustrated by reproductions of the center-of-the-record labels and with historical notes on the companies and discographic data about music. R. Serge Denisoff's *Solid Gold: The Popular Record Industry* is a large study of the industry in the rock era, emphasizing business dynamics of the music system. Denisoff supplies documentation and includes a bibliographic chapter at the end. A provocative, less sympathetic analysis is *Rock 'n' Roll Is Here to Pay: The History and Politics of the Music Industry* by Steve Chapple and Reebee Garofalo. Their book is a careful examination and radical critique of the political economics of the big business of rock, including chapters on racism in its structure and on the places women have found in the music, its culture, and its business. Documentation grounds what they have to say in printed sources and interviews; an extra attraction is an intriguing grand chart of musical currents from 1955 to 1974. *Star-Making Machinery: Inside the Business of Rock and Roll* by Geoffrey Stokes is a detailed case study of the corporate economics of rock production and promotion in the history of an album by Commander Cody and His Lost Planet Airmen. Charlie Gillett's *Making Tracks: Atlantic Records and the Growth of a Multi-Billion-Dollar Industry* is a sympathetic corporate biography of Atlantic from its beginnings as a jazz house in the late 1940s through rhythm and blues to rock and pop and major corporate status. The focus is on the personal stories of the founders and then especially on the artists they signed to record.

Earlier accounts contribute perspective on history and the present. Paul S. Carpenter's *Music: An Art and a Business* (1950) is a scholarly protest against the tyranny of business considerations over the growth of American musical art. Carpenter's interest was in "serious" music, but he included a study of film music, the record industry, ASCAP, and unions that is pertinent to popular music. Hazel Meyer's *The Gold in Tin Pan Alley* (1958) is a popular history of the business with emphasis on the working practices of distributors of sheet music and records. *Anything Goes: The World of Popular Music* (1964) by David Dachs is an extensive survey of the popular music industry including Nashville, Broadway, and Hollywood, drawing widely on published material, though without footnotes. His text is enlivened by quoted lyrics of many songs and by photographs. Paul Hirsch's *The Structure of the Popular Music Industry: The Filtering Process by Which Records Are Preselected for Public Consumption* is a sociological monograph on the workings of the top-forty selection system in the radio and record industries. Roger Karshner's *The Music Machine* is a lively insider's expose of subterranean scramblings within the record business. An account of the British record business, Michael Cable's *The Pop Industry Inside Out,* shows in its analysis and brief history how that industry is interconnected with and like the American; appendixes give statistics and sample record charts.

Partial accounts by participants include *John Hammond On Record* and Clive Davis' *Clive: Inside the Record Business.* Hammond's memoirs recall his remarkable career as a nonmusician in music—discovering, reporting, promoting, and producing records for jazz and pop figures beginning in the 1930s and continuing to the present—from Billie Holiday to Bob Dylan and beyond. Davis' book reports on a recording executive's tumultuous career in the late 1960s and early 1970s. *Twenty Years of Service to Music* is a booklet describing and boosting the role in the business of BMI, Broadcast Music Incorporated, since its founding in 1940 as a performance rights society to rival ASCAP. A historical sketch is followed by photographs of performing members and of business operations.

The role of the radio record announcer is traced through the history of records and broadcasting in Arnold Passman's *The Deejays;* Passman places the beginning of the tradition in 1909. Larry Lujack's *Super Jock* is a shrill monologue describing the life of a rock disc jockey.

Essays on the music business appear in the anthologies of Paul Henry Lang (section C, above) and of McCue (section D, above). A historical and bibliographical essay by James Von Schilling, "Records and the Recording Industry," is included in volume 3 of *Handbook of American Popular Culture* edited by M. Thomas Inge.

Current commercial information on the music industry is compiled in *Billboard International Buyer's Guide,* a trade annual of advertising and various listings including record companies, music publishers, jobbers, wholesalers, services, supplies, dealers, and other business categories. The *Billboard International Talent and Touring Directory,* fourth edition (with this new title) 1981-1982, is a magazine directory of artists, management, equipment, facilities, events, and even restaurants. There is also a *Billboard Country Music Sourcebook*; also see in chapter 6 the *Country Music Who's Who* trade annual. *The Musician's Guide* is a directory for classical, popular, and other musicians, and of organizations, competitions, schools, libraries, books, and many other resources and facts. *The Music Yearbook* is a similar British directory. Carol Price Rabin's *A Guide to Music Festivals in America: Classical, Opera, Jazz, Ragtime, and Dixieland, Pops and Light Classical, Folk and Traditional, Bluegrass, Old-Time Fiddlers, and Country* is a descriptive catalog giving history, typical programs, setting, and addresses and telephone numbers. For one year Judith Glassman compiled *The Year in Music 1977,* an eclectic photograph album celebrating a range of music from classical to country, with million-seller record lists and award winners, a section of star biographies, and various other lists and directories. Ronald Zalkind's *Contemporary Music Almanac 1980/81* is a compilation of many kinds of information centering on rock (see chapter 7).

Journals of the industry are, most prominently, *Billboard* and *Cashbox,* similar weekly tabloids, the former begun in 1894 and the latter in 1942. Both print business news, ads, record charts, and review notes on new record releases. A *Billboard Index* was compiled for 1971 and for 1972-1973 but was not continued. *ASCAP Today* and *BMI* are free bulletins for the trade published by those two organizations.

CAREERS IN POPULAR MUSIC

In the late 1970s, a flurry of books appeared calculated to guide people into and through careers in the large and complex industry of popular music. Joseph Csida's *The Music/Record Career Handbook* is a catalog of such careers—creative, commentary, business, educational—treated in eighty minichapters of description, history, and advice, with a directory of unions and other organizations. David Baskerville's *Music Business Handbook and Career Guide* is a large data source and textbook, perhaps the most comprehensive reference work on this subject. It prints many legal forms, a directory of organizations, and a bibliography along with its sections on songwriting, publishing, copyright, business affairs, the record industry, music in broadcasting and film, and career development and planning. Ronald Zalkind's *Getting Ahead in the Music Business* is a book of exhortative advice on what to do and what to think as a beginner in the music business world, in ninety-eight blunt chapters for performers and entrepreneurs. Jean Young and Jim Young's *Succeeding in the Big World of Music* has chapters analyzing and advising about careers as artist, producer, engineer, jingler, deejay, promoter, and various other job titles. Dick Weissman's *The Music Business: Career Opportunities and Self-Defense* has more air of helping than of managing the neophyte, and is recommended by Weissman's collaboration with Larry Sandberg on the outstanding *Folk Music Sourcebook* (see chapter 6). The strengths of Weissman's book include the breadth of its survey of possible careers (for example, music in the armed forces), a long annotated bibliography, and a directory of relevant college programs. *Making It with Music: Kenny Rogers' Guide to the Music Business* is a guide for the performer built around Rogers' career experiences, written before and during his own comeback and achievement of major star status. Detailed advice is combined with considerable display of Rogers in pictures and narrative—self-promotion appears to be the lesson. Herby Harris and Lucien Farrar's *How to Make Money in Music* is a broad and quite general survey for potential performers, with a long appendix of contracts and forms. Sidney Shemel and M. William Krasilovsky have produced *This Business of Music: Revised and Enlarged Copyright Act Edition,* a comprehensive reference book on copyright and contract law as they apply to recording companies and artists (part 1), music publishers and writers (part 2), and other angles—trademarks, privacy, taxation, and so on. Appendixes give text of laws, contracts, and forms. The same authors' *More about This Business of Music* gives additional economic and legal material, with a section on "serious" music and another including production and sale of printed music, background music and transcription, tape cartridges, and live performers at rock concerts and festivals. Like the first volume, it appends many legal forms along with lists and directories. Harvey Rachlin's *The Encyclopedia of the Music Business* (1981) is an alphabetical reference book of 438 brief articles on the business, legal, and technical lore of commercial music.

Books on particular careers include Howard Stein and Ronald Zalkind's *Promoting Rock Concerts.* Drawing on his experience promoting large events in New York, Stein gives advice on securing business, figuring costs, making financial and legal arrangements, and running the concert itself; again, legal documents are included, and a glossary. *Dancing on the Seats: A Step by Step Guide to College Concert Production* by Andrew H. Meyer is a brief course in procedures and pitfalls of that undertaking. Dennis

Lambert and Ronald Zalkind's *Producing Hit Records* is a home study textbook of the business and technical details of the job of record producer, with many diagrams and legal forms. Walter E. Hurst and Don Rico's *How to Be a Music Publisher* is made up of brief outline pages of notes on legal details. (The publishers advertise they also offer books by the authors on a dozen other aspects of entertainment law.) *A Musician's Guide to the Road,* by Gary Burton, a renowned jazz vibraphonist, gives detailed and very practical tips on planning for and surviving professional touring, and includes legal forms, useful addresses, and phone numbers.

The usefulness of these books may extend beyond their advice to people on the threshold of music careers. Both their large generalizations and their practical advice reflect the state of the music business and how it sees itself. A similar use is possible for a related old and large family of books offering tips to the would-be songwriter. Their advice on how to construct hit songs, many of them in styles of song long outmoded, offers glimpses into the structures of those styles, the practical business history of popular music, and the minds of various eras. Furthermore, they remind us that, if we step back, we can get similar perspective, beyond the explicit advice, from the books that tell how to succeed with songs now.

Songwriting manuals are ephemeral and elusive, springing up in odd corners of middle America as well as on Broadway and in Hollywood. To show the durability of the tradition, and because the publication facts themselves are of some interest, I will give here a supplementary bibliography of such manuals I have heard of, whether I have seen them or not. (The facts are from standard bibliographic sources but cannot be attested to in the same way as the other material in this book.)

1906   Harris, Charles K. *How to Write a Popular Song.* New York: C. K. Harris. Harris himself had lived the dream of sudden success with his 1892 hit "After the Ball."

1916   Wickes, Edward M. *Writing the Popular Song.* Springfield, Mass.: Home Correspondence School.

1919   Gordon, Jack. *How to Publish Your Own Music Successfully.* Chicago: Jack Gordon.

1926   Lincoln, Harry V. *How to Write and Publish Music.* Cincinnati: O. Zimmerman and Son.

1927   Green, Abel. *Inside Stuff on How to Write Popular Songs.* New York: Paul Whiteman Publications. Whiteman, the publisher, was the popular orchestra leader, in what the public thought was the jazz style.

1928   Dubin, Al. *The Art of Song Writing.* New York: Jack Mills. Some of Dubin's songs appeared on Broadway.

1931   Wickes, Edward M. *Song Writer's Guide*. New York: Morrison Music.

1933   Autry, Gene. *The Art of Writing Songs and How to Play a Guitar*. Evanston, Ill.: Frontier Publishers. By the cowboy star in his years of radio fame and Sears catalog sales, before his first film.

1935   Lewis, A. *From Rhymes to Riches*. New York: Donaldson, Douglas and Gumble.

1935   McMahon, Jack. *Practical Song Writing and Composition*. South Norwalk, Conn.: Cromat Publishing.

1935   Sherman, Sterling. [John Milton Hager]. *Songwriting and Selling Secrets*. Upland, Ind.: A. D. Freese and Sons.

1936   Gornston, David, and Herscher, Louis. *Practical Songwriting*. New York: Harry Engel.

1938   Adams, Chick. *Song Success*. New York: Chick Adams.

1939   Jones, Arthur, as told to Louise Howard and Jeron Criswell. *How to Crash Tin-Pan Alley: The Authoritative Handbook for a Successful Song Writing Career*. New York: Howard and Criswell. Like several others, self-published.

1939   Spaeth, Sigmund, and Bruce, Robert. *The Fundamentals of Popular Songwriting,* vols. 1-12. New York: Songmart. Spaeth elsewhere wrote with wit and scorn about the foolishness of song lyrics and also wrote the serious history listed in section C, above. See also the next entry.

1939   Bruce, Robert and Silver, Abner. *How to Write and Sell a Song Hit*. New York: Prentice-Hall. The first of these books offered by a major publisher.

1940   Sabas, F. *How to Make a Million Dollars Writing Songs*. New York: Fortuny's.

1941   Hartman, Frank Josef. *A Complete Song-Writing Course for Self-Instruction*. Washington, D.C.: National Song Bureau.

1942   Garland, Wallace Graydon. *Popular Songwriting Methods: The Unit System for Composing Melody, Harmony, Rhythm and Lyrics*. New York: American Music Guild.

Early   Bender, Leta S. *Short Cut Method of Successful Songwriting*.
forties Friend, Nebr.: Studio News.

1945   Knight, George Morgan. *How to Write and Publish That Song in Your Heart*. Leonardtown, Md.: Knight Publishing. A tenth edition was published in 1953. Knight also published his 1948 and 1953 works and the book by Stiner in 1948. He was the author of works on ventriloquism and such titles as *How to Mimeograph Your Way to Fame and Fortune*.

1945 Bruce, Robert. *How to Write a Hit Song and Sell It.* New York: Lexington Press.

1946 Kenny, Nick. *How to Write, Sing and Sell Popular Songs, with Advice and Special Articles by: Irving Berlin, Cole Porter and others. . . .* New York: Heritage Press.

1947 Littig, Frank. *Song-Writing Technic for Lyricists.* Friend, Nebr.: Studio News.

1948 Knight, George Morgan. *How to Construct and Write Song Hits of Today and Tomorrow.* Leonardtown, Md.: Knight Publishing.

1948 Stiner, E. J. *What Every Amateur Songwriter Should Know about Songwriting and Publishing.* Ed. George Morgan Knight, Jr. Leonardtown, Md.: Knight Publishing.

1949 Stoddard, Harry. *Secrets of Successful Song Writing.* Los Angeles: MusiCrest Publications.

1953 Knight, George Morgan. *How and Where to Really Put a Song Over, Once You Have Written and Published It and Its Been Cleared for Radio and Other Performances Use.* Leonardtown, Md.: Knight Publishing.

1957 Korb, Arthur. *How to Write Songs That Sell.* Rev. ed. Boston: Plymouth Publishing.

1958 Stormen, Win. *Your Guide to Playing and Writing Popular Music.* New rev. ed. New York: Arco Publishing.

1960 Willis, S. L. *Turn Professional in Your Lyric Song Writing.* New York: Exposition Press.

1962 Kane, Henry. *How to Write a Song: As Told to Henry Kane by Duke Ellington and Others.* New York: Macmillan.

1963 Herscher, Louis. *Successful Songwriting: The Magic Key to Words and Melody, Including a Handy Rhyming Dictionary.* Beverly Hills, Calif.: Accadia Music Co.

1963 Rolontz, Robert. *How to Get Your Song Recorded.* New York: Watson-Guptill.

1964 Deutsch, Dr. Maury. *The Art of Song Writing.* New York: Charles Colin.

1965 Benner, Jules. *Wanna Write a Song? Why Not?* Philadelphia: M. Lee Publications.

1970 Boyce, Henry. *How to Make Money $elling the $ongs You Write.* New York: Frederick Fell.

1972 Hutchinson, Larry. *Rock and Roll Songwriter's Handbook.* New York: Scholastic Book Service. Books by this publisher are marketed primarily to school students.

1973   Harris, Rolf. *Write Your Own Pop Song*. London: Wolfe Publishing. A British book noted here because Harris had great American success with his novelty record "Tie Me Kangaroo Down."

1973   Decker, Tom W. *So You Wrote a Song, Now What?* Dallas: Mecca Press.

1974   Boyce, Tommy. *How to Write a Hit Song . . . and Sell It*. North Hollywood, Calif.: Melvin Powers, Wilshire Book Company.

1976   Pincus, Lee. *The Songwriters' Success Manual*. New York: Music Press. Illustrated with amateur cartoons.

1976   Hall, Tom T. *How I Write Songs, Why You Can*. New York: Chappell Music. Hall is a Nashville artist.

1978   Rachlin, Harvey. *Songwriters Handbook*. New York: Funk and Wagnalls.

1979   Kasha, Al, and Hirschhorn, Joel. *If They Ask You, You Can Write a Song*. New York: Simon and Schuster.

1979   Rappoport, Victor D. *Making It in Music*. Englewood Cliffs, N.J.: Prentice-Hall.

Issuance of the last three by major publishing houses, and the inclusion in the last book of forms, directory, and lawyer's advice signal the assimilation of this tradition with the recent fashion for music career guidance books mentioned above.

Magazines for songwriters include *Songwriter Magazine, The Songwriter's Review,* and *Songsmith's Journal*. The annual *Songwriter's Market* is an annotated directory of firms employing or publishing songwriters, relevant organizations, and events; an introductory section has six articles of practical career advice.

BIBLIOGRAPHY

Abstracts of Popular Culture: A Quarterly Publication of International Popular Phenomena, vol. 1. Ed. Ray B. Browne. Bowling Green, Ohio: Bowling Green University Popular Press, 1976-1977. Vol. 2 A-B, 1978. Vol. 3 A-B, 1982.

Alternative Press Index. Northfield, Minn., 1969- . (Now Baltimore, Md.)

American Doctoral Dissertations. Ann Arbor, Mich.: University Microfilms, annually.

Armitage, Andrew D., and Tudor, Dean. *Annual Index to Popular Music Record Reviews, 1972-* . Metuchen, N.J.: Scarecrow Press, 1973- . (Compilers vary.)

ASCAP Biographical Dictionary of Composers, Authors and Publishers. 1966 Edition. Compiled and edited by the Lynn Farnol Group, Inc. New York: American Society of Composers, Authors, and Publishers, 1966.

ASCAP Biographical Dictionary. 4th ed. New York: Jaques Cattell Press/R. R. Bowker, 1980.

ASCAP Today. New York, 1967- .

Ash, Lee, ed. *Subject Collections: A Guide to Special Book Collections and Subject Emphases as Reported by University, College, Public, and Special Libraries and Museums in the United States and Canada.* 5th ed. rev. and enlarged. New York: R. R. Bowker, 1978.

Barzun, Jacques. *Music in American Life.* 1956. Reprint. Bloomington: Indiana University Press, 1965.

Baskerville, David. *Music Business Handbook and Career Guide.* Denver: Sherwood, 1979.

Belz, Carl. *The Story of Rock.* 2d ed. New York: Oxford University Press, 1972.

Bennett, H. Stith. *On Becoming a Rock Musician.* Amherst: University of Massachusetts Press, 1980.

Berry, Lemuel, Jr. *Biographical Dictionary of Black Musicians and Music Educators,* vol. 1. Guthrie, Okla.: Educational Book Publishers, 1978.

Bigsby, C.W.E., ed. *Superculture: American Popular Culture and Europe.* Bowling Green, Ohio: Bowling Green University Popular Press, 1975.

Billboard. Los Angeles, 1894- .

Billboard Country Music Sourcebook. Los Angeles, 1977- .

Billboard Index, 1971. Ann Arbor, Mich.: Xerox University Microfilms, 1974.

———, *1972-1973.* Ann Arbor, Mich.: Xerox University Microfilms, 1975.

Billboard International Buyer's Guide. Los Angeles, 1971- .

Billboard International Talent and Touring Directory. 4th ed. Los Angeles: Billboard Publications, 1981.

Bio-Bibliographical Index of Musicians in the United States of America Since Colonial Times. 2d ed. Reprint. New York: AMS Press, 1972.

Bird, David. *From Score to Tape: A Handbook of Mixing and Recording Techniques.* Boston: Berklee Press, 1973.

Black Music Newsletter. Nashville, 1981- .

Black Perspective in Music. Cambria Heights, N.Y., 1973- .

Block, Adrienne Fried, and Neuls-Bates, Carol. *Women in American Music: A Bibliography of Music and Literature.* Westport, Conn.: Greenwood Press, 1979.

BMI: The Many Worlds of Music. New York, 1962- .

Boeckman, Charles. *And the Beat Goes On: A Survey of Pop Music in America.* Washington, D.C.: Robert B. Luce, 1972.

Bowers, Q. David. *Encyclopedia of Automatic Musical Instruments: Cylinder Music Boxes, Disc Music Boxes, Piano Players and Player Pianos, Coin-Operated Pianos, Orchestrions, Photoplayers, Organettes, Fairground Organs, Calliopes, and Other Self-Playing Instruments Mainly of the 1750-1940 Era, Including a Dictionary of Automatic Musical Instrument Terms.* Vestal, N.Y.: Vestal Press, 1972.

———. *Put Another Nickel In: A History of Coin-Operated Pianos and Orchestrions.* Vestal, N.Y.: Vestal Press, 1966.

Braun, D. Duane. *Toward a Theory of Popular Culture: The Sociology and History of American Music and Dance, 1920-1968.* Ann Arbor, Mich.: Ann Arbor Publishers, 1969.

Brohaugh, William, ed. *1979 Songwriter's Market.* Cincinnati: Writer's Digest Books, 1978.

Brooks, Elston. *I've Heard Those Songs Before: The Weekly Top Ten Tunes for the Past Fifty Years.* New York: Morrow Quill Paperbacks, 1981.

Burton, Gary. *A Musician's Guide to the Road.* New York: Billboard Book/Watson-Guptill, 1981.

Burton, Jack. *The Index of American Popular Music: Thousands of Titles Cross-Referenced to Our Basic Anthologies of Popular Song.* Watkins Glen, N.Y.: Century House, 1957.

Cable, Michael. *The Pop Industry Inside Out.* London: W. H. Allen, 1977.

Carney, George O., ed. *The Sounds of People and Places: Readings in the Geography of Music.* Washington, D.C.: University Press of America, 1978.

Carpenter, Paul S. *Music: An Art and a Business.* Norman: University of Oklahoma Press, 1950.

Carr, Patrick, ed. *The Illustrated History of Country Music, by the Editors of "Country Music" Magazine.* Garden City, N.Y.: *Country Music* Magazine Press Book/Doubleday, 1979.

Cashbox: The International Music-Record Weekly. New York, 1942- .

Chapple, Steve, and Garofalo, Reebee. *Rock 'n' Roll Is Here to Pay: The History and Politics of the Music Industry.* Chicago: Nelson-Hall, 1977.

Chase, Gilbert. *America's Music: From the Pilgrims to the Present.* 2d ed. rev. New York: McGraw-Hill, 1966.

Chicorel, Marietta, ed. *Chicorel Bibliography to Books on Music and Musicians.* New York: Chicorel Library Publishing Corporation, 1974.

Chipman, John H. *Index to Top-Hit Tunes (1900-1950).* Boston: Bruce Humphries, 1962.

Claghorn, Charles Eugene. *Biographical Dictionary of American Music.* West Nyack, N.Y.: Parker Publishing, 1973.

Collectors Guide to Sheet Music. Gas City, Ind.: L-W Promotions, 1975.

Country Song Roundup. Derby, Conn., 1947- .

Craig, Warren. *Sweet and Lowdown: America's Popular Song Writers.* Metuchen, N.J.: Scarecrow Press, 1978.

Csida, Joseph. *The Music/Record Career Handbook.* New York: Billboard Publications, 1975.

Cuney-Hare, Maud. *Negro Musicians and Their Music.* 1936. Reprint. New York: Da Capo, 1974.

Current Biography. New York, 1940- .

Dachs, David. *Anything Goes: The World of Popular Music.* Indianapolis: Bobbs-Merrill, 1964.

Davis, Clive, and Willwerth, James. *Clive: Inside the Record Business.* New York: William Morrow, 1975.

Davis, Ronald L. *A History of Music in American Life: The Formative Years, 1620-1865,* vol. 1. Malabar, Fla.: Robert Krieger Publishing, 1981.

_____. *The Gilded Years, 1865-1920,* vol. 2. Malabar, Fla.: Robert Krieger Publishing, 1980.

_____. *The Modern Era, 1920-Present,* vol. 3. Malabar, Fla.: Robert Krieger Publishing, 1981.

De Charms, Desiree, and Breed, Paul F. *Songs in Collections: An Index.* Detroit: Information Service, 1966.

De Lerma, Dominique-René. *Bibliography of Black Music: Reference Materials.* vol. 1. Greenwood Encyclopedia of Black Music. Westport, Conn.: Greenwood Press, 1981.

_____. *Afro-American Idioms,* vol. 2. Westport, Conn.: Greenwood Press, 1981.

_____. *Geographical Studies,* vol. 3. Westport, Conn.: Greenwood Press, 1982.

_____. *Black Music in Our Culture: Curricular Ideas on the Subjects, Materials and Problems.* Kent, Ohio: Kent State University Press, 1970.

_____. *Reflections on Afro-American Music.* Kent, Ohio: Kent State University Press, 1973.

Denisoff, R. Serge. *Solid Gold: The Popular Record Industry.* New Brunswick, N.J.: Transaction Books, 1975.

_____, and Peterson, Richard A., eds. *The Sounds of Social Change: Studies in Popular Culture.* Chicago: Rand McNally, 1972.

Dichter, Harry, and Shapiro, Elliott. *Early American Sheet Music, Its Lure and Lore, 1768-1889. Including a Directory of Early American Music Publishers.* New York: Bowker, 1941.

_____. *Handbook of Early American Sheet Music, 1768-1889.* 1941. Reprint. New York: Dover Publications, 1977.

Dictionary Catalog of the Music Collection: Boston Public Library. 20 vols. Boston: G. K. Hall, 1972.

_____. *First Supplement.* 4 vols. Boston: G. K. Hall, 1977.

Dictionary Catalog of the Music Collection: New York Public Library Reference Department. 33 vols. Boston: G. K. Hall, 1964.

_____. *Bibliographic Guide to Music.* Boston: G. K. Hall, 1975- .

_____. *Cumulative Supplement, 1964-1971.* 10 vols. Boston: G. K. Hall, 1973.

_____. *Supplement, 1974.* Boston: G. K. Hall, 1976.

Dictionary Catalog of the Rodgers and Hammerstein Archive of Recorded Sound: New York Public Library. The Research Libraries. 15 vols. Boston: G. K. Hall, 1981.

Dissertation Abstracts International: A—The Humanities and Social Sciences. Ann Arbor, Mich.: University Microfilms, monthly.

Docks, L. R. *1915-1965 American Premium Record Guide: Identification and Values, 78's, 45's and LP's.* Florence, Ala.: Books Americana, 1980.

Dolan, Robert Emmett. *Music in Modern Media.* New York: G. Schirmer, 1967.

Dranov, Paula. *Inside the Music Publishing Industry.* White Plains, N.Y.: Knowledge Industry Publications, 1980.

Duckles, Vincent. *Music Reference and Research Materials: An Annotated Bibliography.* 3d ed. New York: Free Press, 1974.

Ehrlich, Cyril. *The Piano: A History.* London: J. M. Dent and Sons, 1976.

80 Years of American Song Hits 1892-1972: A Comprehensive Yearly Reference Book Listing America's Major Hit Songs and Their Writers. New York: Chappell, 1973.

Essay and General Literature Index. New York, 1934- .

Ewen, David. *All the Years of American Popular Music.* Englewood Cliffs, N.J.: Prentice-Hall, 1977.

_____. *American Popular Songs from the Revolutionary War to the Present.* New York: Random House, 1966.

_____. *Great Men of American Popular Song: The History of the American Popular Song Told through the Lives, Careers, Achievements, and Personalities of Its Foremost Composers and Lyricists—From William Billings of the Revolutionary War through Bob Dylan, Johnny Cash, and Burt Bacharach.* Rev. and enlarged ed. Englewood Cliffs, N.J.: Prentice-Hall, 1972.

_____. *History of Popular Music.* New York: Barnes and Noble, 1961.

_____. *Panorama of American Popular Music: The Story of Our National Ballads and Folk Songs—The Songs of Tin Pan Alley, Broadway and Hollywood—New Orleans Jazz, Swing and Symphonic Jazz.* Englewood Cliffs, N.J.: Prentice-Hall, 1957.

_____. *Popular American Composers from Revolutionary Times to the Present: A Biographical and Critical Guide.* New York: H. W. Wilson, 1962.

_____. *Popular American Composers from Revolutionary Times to the Present: A Biographical and Critical Guide. First Supplement.* New York: H. W. Wilson, 1972.

Felton, Gary S. *The Record Collector's International Directory.* New York: Crown Publishers, 1980.

Fisher, William Arms. *Notes on Music in Old Boston.* Boston: Oliver Ditson, 1918.

_____. *One Hundred and Fifty Years of Music Publishing in the United States: An Historical Sketch with Special Reference to the Pioneer Publisher, Oliver Ditson Company, Inc., 1783-1933.* 1933. Reprint. St. Clair Shores, Mich.: Scholarly Press, 1977.

Fuld, James J. *American Popular Music (Reference Book) 1875-1950.* Philadelphia: Musical Americana, 1955.

_____. *Supplement to American Popular Music (Reference Book), 1875-1950.* Philadelphia: Musical Americana, 1956.

_____. *The Book of World-Famous Music: Classical, Popular and Folk.* Rev. and enlarged ed. New York: Crown Publishers, 1971.

Gammond, Peter, and Clayton, Peter. *A Guide to Popular Music.* London: Phoenix House, 1960.

Gelatt, Roland. *The Fabulous Phonograph, 1877-1977.* 3d rev. ed. New York: Macmillan, 1977.

Gellerman, Robert F. *The American Reed Organ: Its History; How It Works; How to Rebuild It. A Treatise on Its History, Restoration and Tuning, with Descriptions of Some Outstanding Collections, including a Stop Dictionary and a Directory of Reed Organs.* Vestal, N.Y.: Vestal Press, 1973.

Gillett, Charlie. *Making Tracks: Atlantic Records and the Growth of a Multi-Billion-Dollar Industry.* New York: Sunrise Book/E. P. Dutton, 1974.

Glassman, Judith. *The Year in Music 1977.* New York: Gladstone Book/Columbia House, 1977.

Gordon, Lucy. *Music and the Modern Media of Transmission.* New York: Gordon Press, 1976.

Grame, Theodore C. *America's Ethnic Music.* Tarpon Springs, Fla.: Cultural Maintenance Associates, 1976.

Green, Douglas B. *Country Roots: The Origins of Country Music.* New York: Hawthorn Books, 1978.

Hamm, Charles. *Yesterdays: Popular Song in America.* New York: W. W. Norton, 1979.

_____; Nettl, Bruno; and Byrnside, Ronald. *Contemporary Music and Music Cultures.* Englewood Cliffs, N.J.: Prentice-Hall, 1975.

Hammond, John, and Townsend, Irving. *John Hammond On Record.* New York: Ridge Press, 1977.

Handy, D. Antoinette. *Black Music: Opinions and Reviews.* Ettrick, Va.: BM&M, 1974.

_____. *Black Women in American Bands and Orchestras.* Metuchen, N.J.: Scarecrow Press, 1981.

Harker, Dave. *One for the Money: Politics and Popular Song.* London: Hutchinson, 1980.

Harris, Herby, and Farrar, Lucien. *How to Make Money in Music: A Guidebook for Success in Today's Music Business.* New York: Arco Publishing, 1978.

Havlice, Patricia. *Popular Song Index.* Metuchen, N.J.: Scarecrow Press, 1975.

_____. *First Supplement.* Metuchen, N.J.: Scarecrow Press, 1978.

Hirsch, Paul. *The Structure of the Popular Music Industry: The Filtering Process by Which Records Are Preselected for Public Consumption.* Ann Arbor, Mich.: Institute for Social Research, University of Michigan: n. d.

Hitchcock, H. Wiley, ed. *The Phonograph and Our Musical Life: Proceedings of a Centennial Conference 7-10 December 1977.* New York: Institute for Studies in American Music, 1980.

Hit Parader. Derby, Conn., 1942- .

Hoover, Cynthia A. *Music Machines—American Style: A Catalog of the Exhibition.* Washington, D.C.: Smithsonian Institution Press, 1971.

Horn, David. *The Literature of American Music in Books and Folk Music Collections: A Fully Annotated Bibliography.* Metuchen, N.J.: Scarecrow Press, 1977.

Howard, John Tasker. *Our American Music: A Comprehensive History from 1620 to the Present.* 4th ed. New York: Thomas Y. Crowell, 1965.

Humanities Index. New York, 1975- .

Hurst, Walter E., and Rico, Don. *How to Be a Music Publisher: The Ins and Outs of the Music Publishing Business for Songwriters, Artists, Musicians, Distributors, Teachers, Students, Accountants, Attorneys, Publicists.* Hollywood: Seven Arts Press, 1979.

Index to the Chicago Sun-Times. Wooster, Ohio, 1979- .

Index to the Chicago Tribune. Wooster, Ohio, 1972- .

Index to the Christian Science Monitor. Wooster, Ohio, 1949- .

Index to the Denver Post. Wooster, Ohio, 1979- .

Index to the Detroit News. Wooster, Ohio, 1976- .

Index to the Houston Post. Wooster, Ohio, 1976- .

Index to the Los Angeles Times. Wooster, Ohio, 1972- .

Index to the New Orleans Times-Picayune. Wooster, Ohio, 1972- .

Index to the San Francisco Chronicle. Wooster, Ohio, 1976- .

Index to the Washington Post. Wooster, Ohio, 1972- .

Jackson, Richard. *United States Music: Sources of Bibliography and Collective Biography.* Brooklyn, N.Y.: Institute for Studies in American Music, 1973.

Journal of Popular Culture. Bowling Green, Ohio, 1976- .

Kanter, Kenneth Aaron. *The Jews on Tin Pan Alley: The Jewish Contribution to American Popular Music, 1830-1940.* New York: Ktav Publishing House, 1982.

Karshner, Roger. *The Music Machine.* Los Angeles: Nash Publishing, 1971.

Katz, Bernard, ed. *The Social Implications of Early Negro Music in the United States.* New York: Arno Press/New York Times, 1969.

Kaufmann, Helen L. *From Jehovah to Jazz: Music in America from Psalmody to the Present Day.* 1937. Reprint. Port Washington, N.Y.: Kennikat Press, 1969.

Kingman, Daniel. *American Music: A Panorama.* New York: Schirmer Books, 1979.

Kinkle, Roger D. *The Complete Encyclopedia of Popular Music and Jazz, 1900-1950.* 4 vols. New Rochelle, N.Y.: Arlington House, 1974.

Klamkin, Marian. *Old Sheet Music: A Pictorial History.* New York: Hawthorn Books, 1975.

Krivine, J. *Juke Box Saturday Night.* Secaucus, N.J.: Chartwell Books, 1977.

Krummel, D. W.; Geil, Jean; Dyen, Doris J.; and Root, Deane L. *Resources of American Music History: A Directory of Source Materials from Colonial Times to World War II.* Music in American Life. Urbana: University of Illinois Press, 1981.

Krythe, Maymie R. *Sampler of American Songs.* New York: Harper and Row, 1969.

Lambert, Dennis, and Zalkind, Ronald. *Producing Hit Records.* Zadoc Music Business Series. New York: Schirmer Books, 1980.

Lang, Paul Henry, ed. *One Hundred Years of Music in America.* New York: G. Schirmer, 1961.

Leigh, Robert. *Index to Song Books: A Title Index to Over 11,000 Copies of Almost 6,800 Songs in 111 Song Books Published between 1933 and 1962.* 1964. Reprint. New York: Da Capo, 1973.

Leiter, Robert D. *The Musicians and Petrillo.* New York: Bookman Associates, 1953.

Lenroot-Ernt, Lois. *Directory of Special Libraries and Information Centers.* 7th ed. 3 vols. Detroit: Gale Research, 1982.

Lewine, Richard, and Simon, Alfred. *Songs of the American Theater: A Comprehensive Listing of More Than 12,000 Songs, Including Selected Titles from Film and Television Productions.* New York: Dodd, Mead, 1973.

List-o-Tapes. Los Angeles, 1964- .

Locke, Alain. *The Negro and His Music.* 1936. Reprint. New York: Arno Press, 1969.

Lujack, Larry. *Super Jock: The Loud, Frantic, Nonstop World of a Rock Radio DJ.* Chicago: Henry Regnery, 1975.

Lydon, Michael. *Boogie Lightning.* New York: Dial Press, 1974.

Lynch, Vincent, and Henkin, Bill. *Jukebox: The Golden Age.* Berkeley, Calif.: Lancaster-Miller, 1981.

McCue, George, ed. *Music in American Society, 1776-1976: From Puritan Hymn to Synthesizer.* New Brunswick, N.J.: Transaction Books, 1977.

Marsh, Dave, and Swenson, John, eds. *The Rolling Stone Record Guide: Reviews and Ratings of almost 10,000 Currently Available Rock, Pop, Soul, Country, Blues, Jazz, and Gospel Albums.* New York: Random House/Rolling Stone Press, 1979.

Mattfeld, Julius. *Variety Music Cavalcade, 1620-1969: A Chronology of Vocal and Instrumental Music Popular in the United States.* 3d ed. Englewood Cliffs, N.J.: Prentice-Hall, 1971.

Mead, Rita H. *Doctoral Dissertations in American Music: A Classified Bibliography.* Brooklyn, N.Y.: Institute for Studies in American Music, 1974.

Mellers, Wilfrid. *Music in a New Found Land: Themes and Developments in the History of American Music.* New York: Alfred A. Knopf, 1965.

Meyer, Andrew H. *Dancing on the Seats: A Step by Step Guide to College Concert Production.* Ed. Nat Freedland. New York: Billboard Publications, 1972.

Meyer, Hazel. *The Gold in Tin Pan Alley.* Philadelphia: J. B. Lippincott, 1958.

Miles, Betty T., et al. *The Miles Chart Display: Top 100, 1955-1970,* vol. 1. Boulder, Colo.: Convex Industries, 1971.

Miles, Daniel, and Miles, Martin J. *The Miles Chart Display of Popular Music: Top 100, 1971-1975,* vol. 2. New York: Arno Press, 1977.

Modern Language Association. *MLA International Bibliography of Books and Articles on the Modern Languages and Literatures: General, English, American, Medieval and Neo-Latin, Celtic Literatures; and Folklore,* vol. 1. New York: MLA, annually.

Murrells, Joseph. *The Book of Golden Discs.* London: Barrie and Jenkins, 1974.

Music: Books on Music, and Sound Recordings. Library of Congress Catalogs. Washington, D.C.: Library of Congress, annually in various forms since 1953.

The Musician's Guide: The Directory of the World of Music. 6th ed. Chicago: Marquis Academic Media, 1980.

The Music Index: A Subject-Author Guide to Current Music Periodical Literature. Detroit, 1949- .

The Music Yearbook: A Survey and Directory with Statistics and Reference Articles. New York: St Martin's, 1972- .

NewsBank. New Canaan, Conn., 1975- .

New York Times Biographical Service. New York, monthly.

New York Times Index: A Book of Record. New York, retrospectively to 1851.

Notes: The Quarterly Journal of the Music Library Association. Ann Arbor, Mich., 1934- .

Nye, Russel. *The Unembarrassed Muse: The Popular Arts in America.* New York: Dial Press, 1970.

Ord-Hume, Arthur W.J.G. *Clockwork Music: An Illustrated History of Mechanical Musical Instruments from the Musical Box to the Pianola, From Automaton Lady Virginal Players to Orchestrion.* New York: Crown Publishers, 1973.

_____. *Player Piano: The History of the Mechanical Piano and How to Repair It.* South Brunswick, N.J.: A. S. Barnes, 1970.

Palmer, Tony. *All You Need Is Love: The Story of Popular Music.* Ed. Paul Medlicott. New York: Penguin, 1976.

Passman, Arnold. *The Deejays.* New York: Macmillan, 1971.

Patterson, Lindsay, ed. *The Negro in Music and Art.* International Library of Negro Life and History. New York: Publishers, 1969.

Paul, Elliot. *That Crazy American Music.* 1957. Reprint. Port Washington, N.Y.: Kennikat Press, 1970.

Phono-Log Reporter. Los Angeles, 1948- .

Pleasants, Henry. *The Great American Popular Singers.* New York: Simon and Schuster, 1974.

_____. *Serious Music—And All That Jazz! An Adventure in Music Criticism.* New York: Simon and Schuster, 1969.

Popular Music and Society. Bowling Green, Ohio, 1971- .

Popular Periodical Index. Camden, N.J., 1973- .

A Preliminary Directory of Sound Recordings Collections in the United States and Canada. New York: New York Public Library, 1967.

Priest, Daniel B. *American Sheet Music: A Guide to Collecting Sheet Music from 1775 to 1975, with Prices.* Des Moines, Iowa: Wallace-Homestead Book, 1978.

Rabin, Carol Price. *A Guide to Music Festivals in America: Classical, Opera, Jazz, Ragtime, and Dixieland, Pops and Light Classical, Folk and Traditional, Bluegrass, Old-Time Fiddlers, and Country.* Stockbridge, Mass.: Berkshire Traveller Press, 1979.

Rachlin, Harvey. *The Encyclopedia of the Music Business.* New York: Harper and Row, 1981.

Read, Oliver, and Welch, Walter. *From Tin Foil to Stereo: Evolution of the Phonograph.* Indianapolis: Bobbs-Merrill, 1959.

Readers' Guide to Periodical Literature: An Author and Subject Index. New York, 1905- .

Riedel, Johannes. *Soul Music Black and White: The Influence of Black Music on the Churches.* Minneapolis: Augsburg Publishing House, 1975.

RILM Abstracts of Music Literature. New York, 1967- .

Roach, Hildreth. *Black American Music: Past and Present.* Boston: Crescendo Publishing, 1973.

Roberts, John Storm. *Black Music of Two Worlds.* New York: Praeger Publishers, 1972.

_____. *The Latin Tinge: The Impact of Latin American Music on the United States.* New York: Oxford University Press, 1979.

Rock and Soul Songs. Derby, Conn., 1956- .

Roehl, Harvey. *The Player Piano: An Historical Scrapbook.* Watkins Glen, N.Y.: Century House, n. d.

_____. *Player Piano Treasury: The Scrapbook History of the Mechanical Piano in America as Told in Story, Pictures, Trade Journal Articles, and Advertising.* 2d ed. Vestal, N.Y.: Vestal Press, 1973.

Rogers, Kenny, and Epand, Len. *Making It with Music: Kenny Rogers' Guide to the Music Business.* New York: Harper and Row, 1978.

Rublowsky, John. *Black Music in America.* New York: Basic Books, 1971.

_____. *Music in America.* New York: Crowell-Collier Press, 1967.

_____. *Popular Music.* New York: Basic Books, 1967.

Rust, Brian. *The American Record Label Book.* New Rochelle, N.Y.: Arlington House, 1978.

_____. *Brian Rust's Guide to Discography.* Westport, Conn.: Greenwood Press, 1980.

Sandberg, Larry, and Weissman, Dick. *The Folk Music Sourcebook.* New York: Alfred A. Knopf, 1976.

Schicke, C. A. *Revolution in Sound: A Biography of the Recording Industry.* Boston: Little, Brown, 1974.

Schwann-1 Record and Tape Guide. Boston, 1949- .

Schwann-2 Record and Tape Guide. Boston, 1949- .

Sears, Minnie E. *Song Index: An Index to More Than 12,000 Songs in 177 Song Collections Comprising 262 Volumes.* New York: H. W. Wilson, 1926.

_____. *Song Index Supplement: An Index to More Than 7,000 Songs in 104 Song Collections Comprising 124 Volumes.* 1934. Reprint with the above. Hamden, Conn.: Shoestring Press, 1966.

Shapiro, Nat, ed. *Popular Music: An Annotated Index of American Popular Songs.* 2d ed. 6 vols. New York: Adrian Press, 1964-1973.

Shaw, Arnold. *The World of Soul: Black America's Contribution to the Pop Music Scene.* New York: Cowles Book, 1970.

Shemel, Sidney, and Krasilovsky, M. William. *More about This Business of Music,* 3d ed. Ed. Lee Zhito. New York: Billboard Publications, 1978.

_____. *This Business of Music: Revised and Enlarged Copyright Act Edition.* Ed. Paul Ackerman. New York: Billboard Publications, 1977.

Sibley Music Library Catalog of Sound Recordings: Eastman School of Music, Rochester, New York. 14 vols. Boston: G. K. Hall, 1977.

Sidran, Ben. *Black Talk.* New York: Holt, Rinehart and Winston, 1971.

Silber, Irwin, ed. *Songs America Voted By: with the Words and Music that Won and Lost Elections and Influenced the Democratic Process.* Harrisburg, Pa.: Stackpole Books, 1971.

Simon, George T., and Friends. *The Best of the Music Makers: From Acuff to Ellington to Presley to Sinatra to Zappa and 279 More of the Most Popular Performers of the Last Fifty Years.* Garden City, N.Y.: Doubleday, 1979.

Skowronski, JoAnn. *Black Music in America: A Bibliography.* Metuchen, N.J.: Scarecrow Press, 1981.

_____. *Women in American Music: A Bibliography.* Metuchen, N.J.: Scarecrow Press, 1978.

Slonimsky, Nicolas, ed. *Baker's Biographical Dictionary of Musicians.* Rev. 6th ed. New York: Schirmer Books, 1978.

Smart, James R., and Newsom, Jon W. *"A Wonderful Invention": A Brief History of the Phonograph from Tinfoil to the LP.* Washington, D.C.: Library of Congress, 1977.

Social Sciences and Humanities Index. New York, 1916- .

Social Sciences Index. New York, 1975- .

Sociological Abstracts. San Diego, 1953- .

Soderbergh, Peter A. *Olde Records Price Guide, 1900-1947: Popular and Classical 78 RPM's.* Des Moines, Iowa: Wallace-Homestead Book, 1980.

_____. *78 RPM Records and Prices.* Des Moines, Iowa: Wallace-Homestead Book, 1977.

Song Hits. Derby, Conn., 1942- .

Songsmith's Journal. Northbrook, Ill., 1976- .

Songwriter Magazine. Los Angeles, 1975- .

Songwriter's Market. Cincinnati, 1979- .

The Songwriter's Review: The Guiding Light to Tin Pan Alley. New York: 1946- .

Southern, Eileen. *Biographical Dictionary of Afro-American and African Musicians.* Greenwood Encyclopedia of Black Music. Westport, Conn.: Greenwood Press, 1982.

_____. *The Music of Black Americans: A History.* New York: W. W. Norton, 1971.

_____, ed. *Readings in Black American Music.* New York: W. W. Norton, 1971.

Spaeth, Sigmund. *A History of Popular Music in America.* New York: Random House, 1948.

Stambler, Irwin. *Encyclopedia of Pop, Rock, and Soul.* New York: St. Martin's Press, 1974.

_____. *Encyclopedia of Popular Music.* New York: St. Martin's Press, 1965.

_____, and Landon, Grelun. *Encyclopedia of Folk, Country, and Western Music.* New York: St. Martin's Press, 1969.

Stecheson, Anthony, and Stecheson, Anne. *Stecheson Classified Song Directory.* Hollywood: Music Industry Press, 1961.

_____. *The Supplement to the Stecheson Classified Song Directory.* Hollywood: Music Industry Press, 1978.

Stein, Howard, with Zalkind, Ronald. *Promoting Rock Concerts.* New York: Schirmer Books, 1979.

Stokes, Geoffrey. *Star-Making Machinery: Inside the Business of Rock and Roll.* New York: Vintage Books, 1977.

Taubman, Howard, ed. *The New York Times Guide to Listening Pleasure.* New York: New York Times Book/Macmillan, 1968.

Times (London) *Index.* Reading, England, retrospectively to 1906.

Tudor, Dean, and Tudor, Nancy. *Black Music.* American Popular Music on Elpee. Littleton, Colo.: Libraries Unlimited, 1979.

_____. *Contemporary Popular Music.* American Popular Music on Elpee. Littleton, Colo.: Libraries Unlimited, 1979.

_____. *Grass Roots Music.* American Popular Music on Elpee. Littleton, Colo.: Libraries Unlimited, 1979.

_____. *Jazz.* American Popular Music on Elpee. Littleton, Colo.: Libraries Unlimited, 1979.

_____. *Popular Music Periodicals Index, 1973- .* Metuchen, N.J.: Scarecrow Press, 1974. (Compilers vary.)

Twenty Years of Service to Music. New York: Broadcast Music, Inc., 1960.

Von Schilling, James. "Records and the Recording Industry." In M. Thomas Inge, *Handbook of American Popular Culture,* vol. 3. Westport, Conn.: Greenwood Press, 1981.

Wall Street Journal Index. Princeton, N.J., 1958- .

Walton, Ortiz. *Music: Black, White, and Blue: A Sociological Survey of the Use and Misuse of Afro-American Music.* New York: William Morrow, 1972.

Weissman, Dick. *The Music Business: Career Opportunities and Self-Defense.* New York: Crown Publishers, 1979.

Westin, Helen. *Introducing the Song Sheet: A Collector's Guide with Current Price List.* Nashville: Thomas Nelson, 1976.

Whitburn, Joel. *Joel Whitburn's Pop Annual, 1955-1977.* Menomonee Falls, Wisc.: Record Research, 1978.

_____. *Joel Whitburn's Top Country and Western Records,1949-1971.* Menomonee Falls, Wisc.: Record Research, 1972.

_____. *Joel Whitburn's Top Easy Listening Records, 1961-1974.* Menomonee Falls, Wisc.: Record Research, 1975.

_____. *Joel Whitburn's Top LP's, 1945-1972.* Menomonee Falls, Wisc.: Record Research, 1973.

_____. *Joel Whitburn's Top Pop Records, 1940-1955.* Menomonee Falls, Wisc.: Record Research, 1973.

_____. *Joel Whitburn's Top Rhythm and Blues Records, 1949-1971.* Menomonee Falls, Wisc.: Record Research, 1973.

_____. *Top Pop Records, 1955-1970: Facts about 9800 Recordings Listed in Billboard's "Hot 100" Charts, Grouped Under the Names of the 2500 Recording Artists.* Detroit: Gale Research, 1972.

Whitcomb, Ian. *After the Ball: Pop Music from Rag to Rock.* New York: Simon and Schuster, 1972.

Young, Jean, and Young, Jim. *Succeeding in the Big World of Music.* Boston: Little, Brown, 1977.

Young, Margaret L., and Young, Harold C., eds. *Directory of Special Libraries and Information Centers.* 6th ed. 2 vols. Vol. 1, *Directory of Special Libraries and Information Centers in the United States and Canada.* Detroit: Gale Research, 1981.

Zalkind, Ronald. *Contemporary Music Almanac, 1980/81.* New York: Schirmer Books, 1980.

_____. *Getting Ahead in the Music Business.* New York: Schirmer Books, 1979.

CHAPTER 2

Before the Twentieth Century

A. BIBLIOGRAPHY AND DISCOGRAPHY

A Bibliography of Early Secular American Music by Oscar G. T. Sonneck, revised by William Treat Upton, is the standard, fully descriptive (not annotative) bibliography of known music and books relating to music up to 1800, whether the materials are known to be in existence today or not. The book includes lists of musical articles and essays from the same period, of composers (some with biographical notes), of songsters, of first song lines, of opera libretti, and of publishers. This survey was continued by Richard J. Wolfe in his *Secular Music in America, 1801-1825: A Bibliography,* in three volumes, a larger work for a shorter period as more came to be published then and more survives from the period. Irving Lowens compiled *A Bibliography of Songsters Printed in America before 1821.* A "songster" is an anthology of secular song lyrics. This book is another full, formally descriptive bibliography of 650 such song collections chronologically arranged from the 183 libraries Lowens consulted. The greatest collections are in the American Antiquarian Society in Worcester, Massachusetts, which published the bibliography; at Brown University in Providence, Rhode Island; and at the Library of Congress. Songsters for this early age of the country represent specifically popular music, or the ancestor of what we call popular music. The other bibliographical works described here list many items of music with higher cultural pretensions, along with their song sheets and songsters.

Materials containing musical notation, as opposed to works only concerned with music or that only compile song texts, are cataloged by Donald L. Hixon in *Music in Early America: A Bibliography of Music in Evans.* "Evans" is Charles Evans' *American Bibliography,* the great catalog of early American imprints of all descriptions, the extant body of which has been gradually assembled in a microfilm library by the Readex Corporation. Hixon lists all items containing notation, whether books or separate songs, known to have been printed in America before 1800, separating those available in the microfilm collection from the others. A hundred pages of short biographical notices on the composers and editors are also included. Priscilla S. Heard's *American Music 1698-1800: An Annotated*

Bibliography is another list, partially annotated, of materials containing musical notation, by year, which appears shorter than Hixon's catalog. Heard has an unannotated but descriptive list of other imprints pertaining to music and another of materials not reprinted on microfilm.

Songs of the American Revolution have both a bibliography and an anthology in Gillian B. Anderson's *Freedom's Voice in Poetry and Song;* bibliographical references are given for 1,455 lyrics from newspapers of the time, and texts and tunes are printed for ninety-seven of them.

Bibliography for later decades of the nineteenth century is spotty. One area that has been given attention is the music printed in the south during the Civil War. Marjorie Lyle Crandall's *Confederate Imprints: A Check List Based Principally on the Collection of the Boston Atheneum* includes in its second of two volumes, *Unofficial Publications,* a short section on "Songsters and Musical Instruction" (pp. 553-56) and a larger one on "Sheet Music" (pp. 559-669) compiled by Richard B. Harwell. Harwell later printed a separate volume of *More Confederate Imprints* and a study of Confederate music publishing businesses (see section F, below).

Old music presently available is cataloged in *American Music before 1865 in Print and on Records: A Biblio-Discography,* an inventory of music in print in books or sheet music or on long-playing records as of 1976 when the music has some claim to authenticity.

A historical document of great interest for study of this music is the *Complete Catalogue of Sheet Music and Musical Works, 1870* of the Board of Music Trade of the United States of America, which has been reprinted with an introduction by Dena J. Epstein. The Board was a trade group of twenty publishers. Their catalog, despite its name, is certainly not complete—in fact it is only a members' joint inventory of their wares; but after the period covered by Wolfe's bibliography it is the fullest bibliography that exists of nineteenth-century American music, a massive 575-page list.

One collection of post-Civil War popular music has a printed inventory: *American Song Sheets, Slip Ballads, and Poetical Broadsides 1850-1870: A Catalogue of the Collection of the Library Company of Philadelphia,* compiled by Edwin Wolf, which lists 2,722 pieces with an additional 194 Confederate imprints. Small reproductions of engravings are collected at the beginning. Another collection, at the University of Virginia, is the subject of Lynn McRae's *Computer Catalogue of 19th-Century American-Imprint Sheet Music* on microfiche, an experiment in an economical method of bibliography for such collections, cataloging eight thousand titles in thirty-two retrieval categories.

A Checklist of American Music Periodicals, 1850-1900, by William Weichlein, surveys magazines that covered the musical life of the era, some reflecting the popular taste and some the more genteel species of musical culture. Weichlein includes a chronological list and a geographical tabulation.

Musical phonograph recordings began to be made and sold in 1889. Those produced by the Edison Phonograph Company in the early years are cataloged by artist, title, number, and date in *Edison Cylinder Records, 1889-1912* by Allen Koenigsberg, which includes a brief illustrated history of the phonograph in these years.

B. ANTHOLOGIES

Printed sheets of words and music, which continue to be sold today, were the form in which popular music was sold before there were sound recordings. Such sheets are the records of music before records. Both the sheet music of songs and their illustrated covers have been collected for reprinting in several anthologies, all of which of course can print only tiny samplings from the vast popular song literature.

Words, tunes, and commentary on nearly three hundred songs from the Revolution to the turn of the twentieth century were collected by Sigmund Spaeth in 1926 in *Read 'Em and Weep;* the 1945 revision includes an appendix of sheet music. Spaeth published a second gathering called *Weep Some More, My Lady* with similarly whimsical exposition. Douglas Gilbert compiled *Lost Chords: The Diverting Story of American Popular Songs* with anecdotal commentary around a collection of texts, without music, of songs from the mid-nineteenth century to the first decade of the twentieth.

Lester S. Levy has collected sheet music in four books. *Flashes of Merriment: A Century of Humorous Songs in America, 1805-1905* has ten subject-matter categories with short chapters of introduction. The pictorial covers are reproduced; the music and verse are reprinted (rather than photographically reproduced, as they are in the Dover Publications series described below). *Grace Notes in American History: Popular Sheet Music from 1820 to 1900* concerns social mores and history of nineteenth-century America; some songs are quoted in excerpts, some are reproduced with all words and music, and ninety-four are illustrated with their covers. *Give Me Yesterday: American History in Song, 1890-1920* extends this project, with ten categories of social events and public interest—social history is mixed with vaudeville history. Many songs are quoted in full or part, and fifty-three covers are reproduced. In *Picture the Songs: Lithographs from the Sheet Music of Nineteenth-Century America,* Levy gives a page of annotation for each of a hundred covers, with several in color. This last collection may be compared with David Tatham's *The Lure of the Striped Pig: The Illustration of Popular Music in America, 1820-1870,* a large-format, heavy-paper collection of sixty engravings and lithographs, some in color or half tone, from the "golden age" of this art. Tatham supplies commentary and appends a selected list of works of principal artists and a bibliographic note.

A series of paperback collections of sheet music photographically reproduced, with authoritative but brief introductory matter, has been published by Dover Publications. Richard Jackson edited *Popular Songs of Nine-*

teenth-Century America: Complete Original Sheet Music for 64 Songs, covers included. Jackson also edited the *Stephen Foster Song Book* (see section C, below). Richard Crawford's *The Civil War Songbook: Complete Original Sheet Music for 37 Songs* includes identifying notes on the composers in its historical introduction. Stanley Appelbaum edited *Show Songs from "The Black Crook" to "The Red Mill": Original Sheet Music for 60 Songs from 50 Shows, 1866-1906,* including a few stage photographs. Robert A. Fremont did *Favorite Songs of the Nineties: Complete Original Sheet Music for 89 Songs,* with an introduction by Max Morath, a scholar and performer of the music. Paul Charosh and Robert A. Fremont edited sixty-two *Song Hits from the Turn of the Century;* as a preface they reprint an 1898 article by Theodore Dreiser on the writing of popular songs— Dreiser's brother, who spelled the name Dresser, was a successful practitioner of the art.

Stage songs of the era before 1866 were collected in Grenville Vernon's *Yankee Doodle-Doo,* with selections from the mid-eighteenth century to the Civil War. Vernon gives words and sometimes music for songs from opera, comic opera, and plays but not minstrel or variety show songs; his headnotes introduce the songs with accounts of the writers and the productions.

Among numerous special interest songbooks, three with considerable commentary may be mentioned here. Oscar Brand collected *Songs of '76: A Folksinger's History of the Revolution,* an annotated anthology of sixty-three songs, some set to modern or conjectural tunes and some with conflated texts. (Compare the fuller collection in Anderson's *Freedom's Voice,* section A, above.) Vera Brodsky Lawrence's *Music for Patriots, Politicians, and Presidents: Harmonies and Discords of the First Hundred Years* is a large scrapbook, history, and anthology of political songs from 1765 to 1876. Verses and music appear in varying formats with many illustrations; compare this book to the Irwin Silber anthology of election songs listed in chapter 1. *The Singing Sixties: The Spirit of Civil War Days* by Willard A. Heaps and Porter W. Heaps is an anthology-survey of Civil War songs from both sides, grouping them chronologically and thematically. Texts of several hundred songs are presented, with commentary, and music is given for some.

C. BIOGRAPHY AND MATERIALS RELEVANT TO PARTICULAR FIGURES

COLLECTIVE BIOGRAPHY

A nineteenth-century reference book, F. O. Jones' *A Handbook of American Music and Musicians* (1886) is largely devoted to classical music but includes entries on several composers, artists, and songs "for the masses." It was reprinted in 1971. Biographical chapters on women who starred on the musical stage are included in *They All Had Glamour,* described below in section D. *Monarchs of Minstrelsy, from "Daddy" Rice to*

Date, compiled by Edw. Le Roy Rice in 1911, is a biographical lore book on some thousand men and women associated with the blackface stage.

INDIVIDUAL FIGURES

Stephen Foster (1826-1864) has been given more study than any other figure in early American music. The standard biography is John Tasker Howard's *Stephen Foster, America's Troubadour,* revised in 1953, which draws on many family interviews and other primary material and prints numerous letters, reviews, and song manuscripts. A large resource is the two-volume *Chronicles of Stephen Foster's Family* edited by Evelyn Foster Morneweck, containing letters, personal recollections, and scraps of fact; appendixes give genealogical data, maps, and a catalog of memorial tributes. Another family contribution was Morrison Foster's *My Brother Stephen,* a brief memoir and family history published in 1896. Raymond Walters' *Stephen Foster: Youth's Golden Gleam—A Sketch of His Life and Background in Cincinnati, 1846-1850* is a short, documented monograph illustrated with old photographs. Richard Jackson's *Stephen Foster Song Book: Original Sheet Music of 40 Songs* has an introduction and brief end notes. James J. Fuld's *A Pictorial Bibliography of the First Editions of Stephen C. Foster* is a folio catalog and album of sheet covers, some printed in color. William W. Austin has written an unusual detailed critical study, *"Susanna," "Jeanie," and "The Old Folks at Home": The Songs of Stephen C. Foster from His Time to Ours.* The songs of the title are taken as examples of comic, poetic, and pathetic-plantation songs and those varieties are analyzed in the contexts of Foster's life, career, contemporaries, public, and successors. Austin includes full scholarly notes. There is a library of Foster materials, the Foster Hall Collection, at the University of Pittsburgh.

The Hutchinson family—originally a quartet of the brothers Judson, John, Asa, and sister Abby, and later various other family members—were reformists and entertainers who crusaded for abolition, temperance, and women's suffrage through the 1840s and 1850s; some members continued to be active after the Civil War. John, in his old age, wrote and narrated a mass of recollections compiled in the two volumes of *Story of the Hutchinsons (Tribe of Jesse)* (1896, now reprinted); a fully analytic table of contents gives access to the material. A section of letters and reminiscences from others is also included. Two popular biographies of the family appeared almost simultaneously fifty years later. Philip D. Jordan's *Singin' Yankees* has illustrations and quotes lyrics from many of their songs. Carol Brink's *Harps in the Wind: The Story of the Singing Hutchinsons* (now reprinted, with modified subtitle) is similar to Jordan, but without the reconstructed conversations; a selected song list and bibliography are added.

Bandmaster and composer John Philip Sousa (1854-1932) became in his long career the symbol of the brass band strain of American music and perhaps the most successful American musician. He published his own story in

1928, *Marching Along: Recollections of Men, Women, and Music,* composed of complacent anecdotes of the kinds that fill many other entertainers' autobiographies. A list of his works is given at the end. Ann M. Lingg wrote a popular biography, *John Philip Sousa,* in 1954. Much fuller is Paul E. Bierly's *John Philip Sousa: American Phenomenon,* a lovingly researched tribute-biography with photographs, lists of compositions and other writings, genealogy, residences, military career chronology, and bibliography. Bierly published separately at the same time *John Philip Sousa: A Descriptive Catalog of His Works.* This extensively annotated catalog is a volume in the distinguished scholarly series of Music in American Life volumes issued by the University of Illinois Press. James R. Smart compiled *The Sousa Band: A Discography* of records by Sousa's bands and also by the Marine Band from 1890 to 1892, the last three years Sousa led that official ensemble. There are separate cylinder and disc lists and various indexes. Oddly, Sousa himself led only a few of these recording sessions of his band; he despised records. (See also the book by Schwartz on the tradition of military bands in section D, below.)

Several composers of nineteenth-century popular songs are remembered in biographies and autobiographies. James Bland (1854-1911), a black songwriter, is the subject of *A Song in His Heart* by John Jay Daly, a short illustrated biography and songbook. E. J. Kahn, Jr., wrote *The Merry Partners: The Age and Stage of Harrigan and Hart,* a history of the musical comedy personalities Ned Harrigan (1845-1911) and Tony Hart (pseudonym of Anthony J. Cannon, 1857?-1891); Hart performed, and Harrigan performed, wrote, and produced. John Hill Hewitt (1801-1890) wrote his own *Shadows on the Wall: or, Glimpses of the Past* (1877), grandiloquent notes on his life and his friends in the literary and musical circles of Baltimore, along with his long historical poem on the conquest of Florida. A book on the theater personality and entrepreneur Tony Pastor is listed below in section E. George F. Root (1820-1895), composer of many popular songs during the Civil War, including "The Battle Cry of Freedom" and "Tramp, Tramp, Tramp," wrote *The Story of a Musical Life: An Autobiography* (1891, now reprinted). Some of his songs are included. Oliver Shaw (1779-1818), the first American songwriter to be widely appreciated, has *A Discourse on the Life and Death of Oliver Shaw* by Thomas Williams (1851), and, deriving its facts from that book, a *Memorial of Oliver Shaw* by Denison, Stanley, and Glezen (1884). This second booklet includes critical appreciation as well as biography. Septimus Winner (1827-1902) is recalled in *The Mocking Bird: The Life and Diary of Its Author, Sep. Winner* by Charles Eugene Claghorn; prosaic diary entries and Claghorn's narrative surround lyrics and composition anecdotes of such songs as "Whispering Hope" and "Ten Little Injuns" as well as the enormously popular "Listen to the Mocking Bird." A partial song list is included.

D. HISTORY AND COMMENTARY

The general histories cited in chapter 1, section C, may be supplemented by some studies devoted particularly to the beginnings of American music.

The musicologist Irving Lowens collected his essays on American musical subjects before 1850 in *Music and Musicians in Early America,* including essays on the shaped-note tune books, biographical pieces about composers, and more general essays on music in American life.

Music in New Orleans: The Formative Years, 1791-1841 by Henry A. Kmen is a social historian's study of that city's early balls, bands, and operas, which, especially with its final chapter "Negro Music," establishes the distant background for the rise of jazz. Kmen provides notes and extensive bibliography.

Some particular types of early music have been given separate attention. Nicholas E. Tawa's *Sweet Songs for Gentle Americans: The Parlor Song in America, 1790-1860* is a careful analysis of the evolving forms of music Americans bought to play and sing at home through three generations. Tawa analyzes the bound collections of such sheet music accumulated by many families: over five hundred such collections—in the Brown Collection of the Boston Public Library and in Houghton Library at Harvard—from the east, midwest, and south. The history is explored also through reference to contemporary books, journals, and periodicals. Sixteen of the most popular songs are reproduced. George W. Ewing's *The Well-Tempered Lyre: Songs and Verse of the Temperance Movement* is a scholarly but light-hearted history and anthology of antidrinking verse from the early nineteenth century to the repeal of prohibition; music is printed for about two dozen songs.

Military Music of the American Revolution by Raoul F. Camus is a history from primary sources, with illustrations, musical examples, and a table of the British regimental bands. *Bands of America* by H. W. Schwartz is a history of the military-style concert bands popular from before the Civil War into the 1920s, which peaked around 1910. About a third of the book is devoted to Sousa (see also the works on Sousa in section C, above), the rest to his predecessors and competitors.

The early musical stage, including light opera, is displayed in *They All Had Glamour, from the Swedish Nightingale to the Naked Lady* by Edward B. Marks, with chapters of history, short biographical chapters on female leading singers, and 150 pages of various reference materials, including a chronology, a biographical encyclopedia, and song lists. Marks also includes many photographs, music for some songs, sheet music covers, and posters. Deane L. Root's *American Popular Stage Music: 1860-1880* is a critical history of those two formative decades with a broad survey of types of stage production, much detailed study of particular show and musical examples, and thorough documentation (it had been a doctoral thesis).

Two books specifically treat the minstrel show stage. Robert C. Toll's *Blacking Up: The Minstrel Show in Nineteenth-Century America* is an analytic history. Toll approaches the question of the social meaning and function of this entertainment by survey of the contents of songs, joke books, playbills, and playlet texts. Posters and covers supply illustrations. An earlier book was Hans Nathan's *Dan Emmett and the Rise of Early Negro Minstrelsy*. Tracing the origins of Negro impersonation from eighteenth-century England to America, Nathan picks up the life and career of Dan Emmett as a thread through the history of minstrelsy up to the Civil War. Nathan gives words and music for sixty-five songs by Emmett and others. A chapter is devoted to Emmett's most famous song, "Dixie," and a bibliography of Emmett's works is included. See *Monarchs of Minstrelsy,* above, section C, and *A Minstrel Town,* below, section E.

Patriotic songs have commanded more comment as songs than have any others. At the end of the last century Colonel Nicholas Smith wrote *Stories of the Great National Songs,* giving accounts of the backgrounds, and authors when known, of various patriotic songs, including some of the Confederacy—such as "Columbia, the Gem of the Ocean"; "My Country, 'Tis of Thee"; "Home, Sweet Home"; and "The Bonnie Blue Flag." The Society of the Colonial Dames of America collected *American War Songs* giving texts and historical background for 136 songs, including an interesting selection for the Spanish-American and First World Wars, the latter recent when the book was first published.

A succession of official and semiofficial studies have been made of the national anthem. The librarian and bibliographer Oscar G. T. Sonneck published in 1914 *"The Star Spangled Banner" (Revised and Enlarged from the "Report" on the Above and Other Airs, Issued in 1909),* a ponderously scholarly investigation of its history, with twenty-three plates of music and documents. Joseph Muller compiled in 1935 *The Star Spangled Banner: Words and Music Issued between 1814-1864,* an annotated bibliography of fifty-four items, fifteen more added in a 1973 reprinting. George J. Svejda compiled a *History of the Star Spangled Banner from 1814 to the Present* for the Department of the Interior in 1969, over five hundred pages of narrative, extensive bibliography, and manuscript and print exhibits. P. W. Filby and Edward G. Howard's *Star-Spangled Books* (1972) is a history and a bibliographical catalog.

E. BUSINESS

Some studies of the early period of American music business may be added here to the historical works cited in chapter 1, section E. Richard J. Wolfe, the compiler of the standard bibliography of early nineteenth-century music, has written *Early American Music Engraving and Printing: A History of Music Publishing in America from 1787 to 1825,* a large and learned study of the social, economic, and technical history of the business, with photographs, engravings, tables, and notes. Three other books cover regional publishing activities. Dena J. Epstein's *Music Publishing in Chicago before 1871: The Firm of Root and Cady, 1858-1871* gives history, biographies of the partners Root and Cady, a checklist of published music, and a directory of people and firms in the music trade in Chicago before the great fire. Ernst C. Krohn's *Music Publishing in the Middle Western States before the Civil War* is another small book in the same series of music bibliographies; it is a survey of early music publishing in St. Louis, Cincinnati, Louisville, Detroit, Cleveland, and Chicago prior to the time considered in Epstein. Richard B. Harwell, whose Confederate bibliographies are listed in section A, above, also wrote *Confederate Music*, a history of music publishing in the Confederacy and a listing of the known sheet music.

Popular music before the electronic media, when it was not local, was the business of publishing and also was a closely interlinked business of touring live entertainment. The musical stage and minstrel histories listed in section D recover some of this story. Another perspective is given by Marion S. Revett in *A Minstrel Town,* a chronicle of traveling and local entertainment appearing in Toledo, Ohio, in the last two-thirds of the nineteenth century. The first part is concerned with traveling minstrels; the second, theater; the third, circus; and the fourth, local music. Don B. Wilmeth's *American and English Popular Entertainment: A Guide to Information Sources* is a resource for study of this broad range of nineteenth-century entertainments, including music.

. *Tony Pastor: Dean of the Vaudeville Stage* by Parker Zellers is the story of the career of a singer and songwriter (1837-1908) who became a theater manager in New York after the Civil War and, during the remainder of the century, crusaded to make variety stage entertainment respectable. Zellers documents the story from research in the news sources of the time and brightens the narrative with photographs and theater posters.

BIBLIOGRAPHY

American Music before 1865 in Print and on Records: A Biblio-Discography. Preface by H. Wiley Hitchcock. ISAM Monographs, no. 6. Brooklyn, N.Y.: Institute for Studies in American Music, 1976.

American War Songs. Published under Supervision of National Committee for the Preservation of Existing Records of the National Society of the Colonial Dames of America. 1925. Reprint. Ann Arbor, Mich.: Gryphon Books, 1971.

Anderson, Gillian B., comp. *Freedom's Voice in Poetry and Song: An Inventory of Political and Patriotic Lyrics in Colonial American Newspapers 1773-1783,* part 1. *Song Book,* part 2. Wilmington, Del.: Scholarly Resources, 1977.

Appelbaum, Stanley, ed. *Show Songs from "The Black Crook" to "The Red Mill":*

Original Sheet Music for 60 Songs from 50 Shows, 1866-1906. New York: Dover Publications, 1974.

Austin, William W. *"Susanna," "Jeanie," and "The Old Folks at Home": The Songs of Stephen C. Foster from His Time to Ours*. New York: Macmillan, 1975.

Bierley, Paul E. *John Philip Sousa: A Descriptive Catalog of His Works*. Music in American Life. Urbana: University of Illinois Press, 1973.

————. *John Philip Sousa: American Phenomenon*. Englewood Cliffs, N.J.: Prentice-Hall, 1973.

Board of Music Trade of the United States of America. *Complete Catalogue of Sheet Music and Musical Works, 1870*. 1871. Reprint. New York: Da Capo, 1973.

Brand, Oscar. *Songs of '76: A Folksinger's History of the Revolution*. New York: M. Evans, 1972.

Brink, Carol. *Harps in the Wind: The Singing Hutchinsons of New Hampshire*. 1947. Reprint. New York: Da Capo, 1980.

Camus, Raoul F. *Military Music of the American Revolution*. Chapel Hill: University of North Carolina Press, 1976.

Charosh, Paul, and Fremont, Robert A., eds. *Song Hits from the Turn of the Century: Complete Original Sheet Music for 62 Songs*. New York: Dover Publications, 1975.

Claghorn, Charles Eugene. *The Mocking Bird: The Life and Diary of Its Author, Sep. Winner*. Philadelphia: Magee Press, 1937.

Crandall, Marjorie Lyle. *Confederate Imprints: A Check List Based Principally on the Collection of the Boston Atheneum*. 2 vols. *Unofficial Publications*, vol. 2. Boston: Boston Atheneum, 1955.

Crawford, Richard, ed. *The Civil War Songbook: Complete Original Sheet Music for 37 Songs*. New York: Dover Publications, 1977.

Daly, John Jay. *A Song in His Heart*. Philadelphia: John C. Winston, 1951.

Denison, Frederic; Stanley, Albert A.; and Glezen, Edward K., eds. *Memorials of Oliver Shaw, Prepared and Published under the Auspices of the Rhode Island Veteran Citizens' Historical Association*. Providence: J. A. and R. A. Reid, 1884.

Epstein, Dena J. *Music Publishing in Chicago before 1871: The Firm of Root and Cady, 1858-1871*. Detroit Studies in Music Bibliography 14. Detroit: Information Coordinators, 1969.

Evans, Charles. *American Bibliography: A Chronological Dictionary of all Books, Pamphlets and Periodical Publications Printed in the United States of America from the Genesis of Printing in 1639 down to and including the year 1820, with Bibliographical and Biographical Notes*. 12 vols. New York: Peter Smith, 1941-42. (Two more volumes and a supplement added later by others.)

Ewing, George W. *The Well-Tempered Lyre: Songs and Verse of the Temperance Movement*. Dallas: Southern Methodist University Press, 1977.

Filby, P. W., and Howard, Edward G. *Star-Spangled Books: Books, Sheet Music, Newspapers, Manuscripts, and Persons Associated with "The Star-Spangled Banner."* Baltimore: Maryland Historical Society, 1972.

Foster, Morrison. *My Brother Stephen.* 1896. Reprint. Indianapolis: Hollenbeck Press, 1932.

Fremont, Robert A., ed. *Favorite Songs of the Nineties: Complete Original Sheet Music for 89 Songs.* New York: Dover Publications, 1973.

Fuld, James J. *A Pictorial Bibliography of the First Editions of Stephen C. Foster.* Philadelphia: Musical Americana, 1957.

Gilbert, Douglas. *Lost Chords: The Diverting Story of American Popular Songs.* 1942. Reprint. New York: Cooper Square Publishers, 1970.

Harwell, Richard B. *Confederate Music.* Chapel Hill: University of North Carolina Press, 1950.

_____. *More Confederate Imprints.* Richmond: Virginia State Library, 1957.

Heaps, Willard A., and Heaps, Porter W. *The Singing Sixties: The Spirit of Civil War Days Drawn from the Music of the Times.* Norman: University of Oklahoma Press, 1960.

Heard, Priscilla S. *American Music, 1698-1800: An Annotated Bibliography.* Waco, Tex.: Baylor University Press, 1975.

Hewitt, John Hill. *Shadows on the Wall; or, Glimpses of the Past. A Retrospect of the Past Fifty Years. Sketches of Noted Persons Met with by the Author.* 1877. Reprint. New York: AMS Press, 1971.

Hixon, Donald L. *Music in Early America: A Bibliography of Music in Evans.* Metuchen, N.J.: Scarecrow Press, 1970.

Howard, John Tasker. *Stephen Foster, America's Troubadour.* Rev. ed. New York: Thomas Y. Crowell, 1953.

Hutchinson, John Wallace. *Story of the Hutchinsons (Tribe of Jesse).* Compiled and edited by Charles E. Mann. 2 vols. 1896. Reprint. New York: Da Capo, 1977.

Jackson, Richard, ed. *Popular Songs of Nineteenth-Century America: Complete Original Sheet Music for 64 Songs.* New York: Dover Publications, 1976.

_____. *Stephen Foster Song Book: Original Sheet Music of 40 Songs by Stephen Collins Foster.* New York: Dover Publications, 1974.

Jones, F. O., ed. *A Handbook of American Music and Musicians, Containing Biographies of American Musicians, and Histories of the Principal Musical Institutions, Firms, and Societies.* 1886. Reprint. New York: Da Capo, 1971.

Jordan, Philip D. *Singin' Yankees.* Minneapolis: University of Minnesota Press, 1946.

Kahn, E. J., Jr. *The Merry Partners: The Age and Stage of Harrigan and Hart.* New York: Random House, 1955.

Kmen, Henry A. *Music in New Orleans: The Formative Years, 1791-1841.* Baton Rouge: Louisiana State University Press, 1966.

Koenigsberg, Allen. *Edison Cylinder Records, 1889-1912; with an Illustrated History of the Phonograph.* New York: Stellar Productions, 1969.

Krohn, Ernst C. *Music Publishing in the Middle Western States before the Civil War.* Detroit Studies in Music Bibliography 23. Detroit: Information Coordinators, 1972.

Lawrence, Vera Brodsky. *Music for Patriots, Politicians, and Presidents: Harmonies and Discords of the First Hundred Years.* New York: Macmillan, 1975.

Levy, Lester S. *Flashes of Merriment: A Century of Humorous Songs in America, 1805-1905.* Norman: University of Oklahoma Press, 1971.

_____. *Give Me Yesterday: American History in Song, 1890-1920*. Norman: University of Oklahoma Press, 1975.

_____. *Grace Notes in American History: Popular Sheet Music from 1820 to 1900*. Norman: University of Oklahoma Press, 1967.

_____. *Picture the Songs: Lithographs from the Sheet Music of Nineteenth-Century America*. Baltimore: Johns Hopkins University Press, 1976.

Lingg, Ann M. *John Philip Sousa*. New York: Henry Holt, 1954.

Lowens, Irving. *A Bibliography of Songsters Printed in America before 1821*. Worcester, Mass.: American Antiquarian Society, 1976.

_____. *Music and Musicians in Early America*. New York: W. W. Norton, 1964.

McRae, Lynn T., comp. *Computer Catalogue of 19th-Century American-Imprint Sheet Music*. 13 microfiche. Charlottesville: University of Virginia Library, 1977.

Marks, Edward B. *They All Had Glamour, from the Swedish Nightingale to the Naked Lady*. 1944. Reprint. Westport, Conn.: Greenwood Press, 1972.

Morneweck, Evelyn Foster, ed. *Chronicles of Stephen Foster's Family*. 2 vols. 1944. Reprint. Port Washington, N.Y.: Kennikat Press, 1973.

Muller, Joseph, comp. *The Star Spangled Banner: Words and Music Issued between 1814-1864. An Annotated Bibliographical List with Notices of the Different Versions, Texts, Variants, Musical Arrangements, and Notes of Music Publishers in the United States. Illustrated with 108 Portraits, Facsimiles, etc.* 1935. Reprint. New York: Da Capo, 1973.

Nathan, Hans. *Dan Emmett and the Rise of Early Negro Minstrelsy*. Norman: University of Oklahoma Press, 1962.

Revett, Marion S. *A Minstrel Town*. New York: Pageant Press, 1955.

Rice, Edw. Le Roy, comp. *Monarchs of Minstrelsy, from "Daddy" Rice to Date*. New York: Kenny Publishing, 1911.

Root, Deane L. *American Popular Stage Music: 1860-1880*. Studies in Musicology. Ann Arbor, Mich.: UMI Research Press, 1981.

Root, George F. *The Story of a Musical Life: An Autobiography*. 1891. Reprint. New York: AMS Press, 1972.

Schwartz, H. W. *Bands of America*. 1957. Reprint. New York: Da Capo, 1975.

Smart, James R., comp. *The Sousa Band: A Discography*. Washington, D.C.: Library of Congress, 1970.

Smith, Nicholas. *Stories of the Great National Songs*. Milwaukee: Young Churchman, 1899.

Sonneck, Oscar G. T. *A Bibliography of Early Secular American Music (18th Century)*. Rev. and enlarged by William Treat Upton. 1945. Reprint. New York: Da Capo, 1964.

_____. *"The Star Spangled Banner" (Revised and enlarged from the "Report" on the Above and Other Airs, Issued in 1909)*. Washington, D.C.: U.S. Government Printing Office, 1914.

Sousa, John Philip. *Marching Along: Recollections of Men, Women, and Music*. Boston: Hale, Cushman and Flint, 1928.

Spaeth, Sigmund. *Read 'Em and Weep: A Treasury of American Songs—The Songs You Forgot to Remember—Some Sad, More Merry, Some Sentimental; with a Wealth of Amiable Anecdote, Comment and Fascinating Folk-lore—A Flavorful Feast of Melodious Music*. 1926. Rev. ed., 1945. New York: Arco Publishing, 1959.

_____. *Weep Some More, My Lady*. Garden City, N.Y.: Doubleday, Page, 1927.

Svejda, George J. *History of the Star Spangled Banner from 1814 to the Present*. Springfield, Va.: National Technical Information Service/U.S. Department of the Interior, 1969.

Tatham, David. *The Lure of the Striped Pig: The Illustration of Popular Music in America, 1820-1870*. Barre, Mass.: Imprint Society, 1973.

Tawa, Nicholas E. *Sweet Songs for Gentle Americans: The Parlor Song in America, 1790-1860*. Bowling Green, Ohio: Bowling Green University Popular Press, 1980.

Toll, Robert C. *Blacking Up: The Minstrel Show in Nineteenth-Century America*. New York: Oxford University Press, 1974.

Vernon, Grenville, ed. *Yankee Doodle-Doo: A Collection of Songs of the Early American Stage*. 1927. Reprint. New York: Benjamin Blom, 1972.

Walters, Raymond. *Stephen Foster: Youth's Golden Gleam—A Sketch of His Life and Background in Cincinnati, 1846-1850*. Princeton, N.J.: Princeton University Press, 1936.

Weichlein, William. *A Checklist of American Music Periodicals, 1850-1900*. Detroit Studies in Music Bibliography 16. Detroit: Information Coordinators, 1970.

Williams, Thomas. *A Discourse on the Life and Death of Oliver Shaw*. Boston: Charles C. P. Moody, 1851.

Wilmeth, Don B. *American and English Popular Entertainment: A Guide to Information Sources*. Performing Arts Information Guide Series 7. Detroit: Gale Research Co., 1980.

Wolf, Edwin 2d, comp. *American Song Sheets, Slip Ballads, and Poetical Broadsides 1850-1870: A Catalogue of the Collection of the Library Company of Philadelphia*. Philadelphia: Library Company of Philadelphia, 1963.

Wolfe, Richard J. *Early American Music Engraving and Printing: A History of Music Publishing in America from 1787 to 1825, with Commentary on Earlier and Later Practices*. Music in American Life. Urbana: University of Illinois Press, 1980.

_____. *Secular Music in America, 1801-1825: A Bibliography*. 3 vols. New York: New York Public Library, Astor, Lennox, and Tilden Foundations, 1964.

Zellers, Parker. *Tony Pastor: Dean of the Vaudeville Stage*. Ypsilanti: Eastern Michigan University Press, 1971.

CHAPTER 3

Tin Pan Alley, Dance Bands, Broadway, and Hollywood

The main stream of American popular music in the first half of the twentieth century flowed from New York City, with a subsidiary spring in Hollywood. Beginning around 1890 and especially flourishing between the First and Second World Wars, songwriting and song publishing were centered in New York. Beginning in the 1920s, network radio broadcasting and, later, television were based there. The live musical stage meant Broadway, and of course Broadway meant New York. Filmmakers established their separate base in California, and when the sound era brought musical films, Hollywood musicals became a prominent part of America's music entertainment. But much of this music came from the New York stage or from the established New York songwriters. The music produced from these sources was played around America over the airwaves, on records, and in live performances by dance bands.

I. TIN PAN ALLEY

Twenty-eighth Street in Manhattan became, late in the nineteenth century, the center of American music publishing. This physical localization was reflected in the emergence of a dominant style for popular songs over a half a century—with diversity and room for great creativity, but also with definite conventions of form and content, and often with a definite New York flavor, whether sophisticated or immigrant or Harlem. The style came to be called, after the nickname of its neighborhood, Tin Pan Alley. Materials in this section of the chapter will be those relevant to Tin Pan Alley music and also to some inheritors of its traditions, the writers and singers of middle-ground pop in the age of rock.

IA. TIN PAN ALLEY BIBLIOGRAPHY AND DISCOGRAPHY

The master discographer Brian Rust has produced with Allen G. Debus *The Complete Entertainment Discography from the mid-1890s to 1942*. His large companion work on the dance bands of the same period will be mentioned below. This book covers minstrel, vaudeville, film, radio, and stage performers, American or those popular in America, who made records. (It excludes jazz, blues, dance bands, and certain major stars who have or who merit separate treatment.) There are short biographical notices of performers and full discographic data. One major company's issues are cataloged in another discography, Fred J. Karlin's *Edison Diamond Discs 50001-52651, 1912-1929,* a numerical listing with titles, composers, and performers. There are also some special category lists—medleys, film songs, stage songs—which are also numerical, a fact that can make access difficult since the book has no index to locate a writer, performer, or song. The music is predominantly nonjazz pop, including some early country performers. Karlin's work makes a sequel to Koenigsberg's cylinder catalog of the same company 1889-1912, mentioned in chapter 2. A curious byway in the history of popular music records is presented in Richard S. Sears' *V-Discs: A History and Discography.* A brief illustrated history introduces a vast annotated discography of the records produced in a special program to bring music to the armed forces during and after World War II (1943 to 1949). All kinds of music are represented.

Modern recordings of music in the mainstream pop tradition, Tin Pan Alley, and its descendants are selected and critically annotated in the first half of *Contemporary Popular Music,* one of four volumes of the Tudors' discographies for librarians and consumers. (The second half is rock.)

1B. TIN PAN ALLEY GENERAL REFERENCE

The Blue Book of Tin Pan Alley by Jack Burton is part of a set of reference volumes containing the biographies of song composers and catalogs of their works; there are companion volumes for Broadway and Hollywood (see below). Of the two Tin Pan Alley volumes, the first covers the years before 1910; the second, 1910-1950, with a supplement up to 1965. The set also includes Burton's *The Index of American Popular Music: Thousands of Titles Cross-Referenced to Our Basic Anthologies of Popular Song.* The subtitle is quoted here to correct its misleading word "anthologies," by which Burton means these biographically organized reference books. The *Index* gathers titles of songs; information about them must be pursued in the relevant volume.

A scrapbook history for the same period, the first half of the twentieth century, is Larry Freeman's *The Melodies Linger On.* Decade by decade Freeman presents commentary and a rich and unusual collection of photographs, sketches, music covers, and other souvenirs. A hit song list by years is given at the end. Warren E. Colbert's *Who Wrote That Song?* is a hobbyist's survey of the composers of Tin Pan Alley songs; he includes a song list, but covers only a corner of the data in the larger systematic "songographies" and encyclopedias such as Kinkle, Shapiro, Mattfeld (chapter 1, above), and Burton (above). Elizabeth Rider Montgomery's *The Story behind Popular Songs* gives brief popular sketches of thirty-three songwriters from Foster to Rodgers and Hammerstein, alleging the stories of composition of each writer's principal hit. *This Was "Your Hit Parade"* by John R. Williams is a book of tabulations from the radio and television show that broadcast the weekly top hits from 1935 to 1958.

The Song List: A Guide to Contemporary Music from Classical Sources by James L. Limbacher consists of two extended tables: one of popular songs, including band, radio, and television theme songs, deriving from classical pieces; the other of composers whose works have been used in these songs.

Sheet music covers and the music of a few songs are displayed in Max Wilk's *Memory Lane: The Golden Age of American Popular Music, 1890 to 1925*. The anthologies edited by Robert A. Fremont *(The Nineties)* and by Paul Charosh and Fremont *(Turn of the Century)* are listed in chapter 2.

IC. TIN PAN ALLEY BIOGRAPHY AND MATERIALS RELEVANT TO PARTICULAR FIGURES

Collective biography mostly limited to the Tin Pan Alley tradition can be found in two of David Ewen's books. *Men of Popular Music* includes sketches of Berlin, Whiteman, George Gershwin, Kern, Rodgers and Hart, and Porter, along with jazz figures. *Great Men of American Popular Song* selects writers and stars from the whole course of American history for thirty-two admiring biographical chapters, some on two or three figures, emphasizing Tin Pan Alley and Broadway (no jazz, one blues, one country, one rock). *Sinatra and the Great Song Stylists* by Ken Barnes and others is a book on pop and jazz singers from Al Jolson to Andy Williams, with annotated lists of recommended records for Jolson, Armstrong, Crosby, Fitzgerald, Garland, Sinatra, Lee, Cole, Day, Torme, Vaughan, and Bennett, and briefer treatment of as many others.

The most comprehensive sources, mentioned in chapter 1, are Kinkle's *Complete Encyclopedia,* volumes 2 and 3, and the *ASCAP Biographical Dictionary.*

Individual figures—composers, authors, and artists associated with Tin Pan Alley and kindred music to the 1980s—are gathered in the remainder of this section into one alphabetical list. Persons missing can be found in the similar lists for dance bands, Broadway, and Hollywood, below in this chapter; for jazz in chapter 5; or for rock in chapter 7. Placement in one list or another is in some cases undoubtedly arbitrary.

Pearl Bailey has published two volumes of reminiscences. *The Raw Pearl,* edited from taped conversations, recalls her singing and acting life in the 1940s and 1950s. *Talking to Myself* consists of poetic and prose ruminations about the performing life, looking back from 1971.

Pat Boone's career in nonrock teenage pop has led to the production of several books. *Twixt Twelve and Twenty* was a best seller of advice to teen-agers. *A New Song* is a strongly religious, short autobiography, and

Together: 25 Years with the Boone Family is a personal, career, and family album of stories and photographs.

Sammy Cahn's *I Should Care* is the recollections of a songwriter from the 1930s to the 1970s, with an anthology of thirty of his lyrics, a song list, and photographs.

Rosemary Clooney's *This for Remembrance* tells the personal story behind her career and her life after her career as a pop singer in the 1950s.

Bing Crosby was given a full length but early biography in Barry Ulanov's *The Incredible Crosby* in 1948, including a long discography up to that date. Ted Crosby's *The Story of Bing Crosby* (1937) is a brother's biography of the early career, with photographs and film and record lists. *The One and Only Bing* by Bob Thomas is a photographic and journalistic retrospective published quickly after Crosby's death in the fall of 1977. It includes a survey of his film roles by Norm Goldstein and of his records by Mary Campbell. *Bing Crosby: The Hollow Man* by Donald Shepherd and Robert F. Slatzer is a jaundiced account of Crosby's personal life ironically seen as contrary to his likeable public image. The reader of Crosby's publicity autobiography *Call Me Lucky* (1953) may have his own doubts in the face of the author's enormous self-satisfaction. *The Crosby Years* by Ken Barnes (1980) is a brief history with many pictures, an elaborate discography from 1926 to 1977, and a short anthology of sheet music. See Bookbinder's *The Films of Bing Crosby* under Hollywood, section IV, below. There also has been a fan magazine called *Bing* published in Wales.

Borrowed Time: The 37 Years of Bobby Darin by Al DiOrio is a heavily illustrated story of the life and singing and acting career of Darin, born Walden Robert Cassotto, up to his death in 1973 from lifelong heart disease. Included at the end are a discography illustrated with record jacket photographs, a list of the 153 songs Darin wrote, and a film list.

Eddie Fisher's career as a vocalist is reported in Myrna Greene's *The Eddie Fisher Story,* a surprisingly objective biography by a longtime fan and professional publicist—not for Fisher—of Fisher as singing star and as barometer of the American 1950s.

Charles K. Harris, an early songwriter in this market, wrote *After the Ball: Forty Years of Melody* in 1926. His story of life and business often sounds as if it had been written ironically by Sinclair Lewis, boosting the system and the code of self-made success. The title comes from that of his first and greatest hit song in 1892.

Pinky Herman was a songwriter and ASCAP activist beginning in the 1930s. *Showbiz and "me"* is his self-published memoir scrapbook.

Lena Horne is a black singer who began her career with bands in the 1930s and also performed in films and on Broadway; her one-woman show made a grammy-winning record in 1981. Her book *Lena* brings her into the 1960s and her performance benefits for civil rights.

Al Jolson's huge success as stage singer and the first movie singer is reported in Michael Freedland's *Jolson,* an undocumented but thorough biography. Close attention is paid to Jolson and his personal relationships and triumphs rather than his art or the theatrical context of his work. Barrie Anderton's *Sonny Boy! The World of Al Jolson* is a lively scrapbook-style tribute, with a list of his records and a fuller catalog of films. Pearl Sieben's *The Immortal Jolson* is a short, popular biography. Harry Jolson wrote *Mistah Jolson:* Harry, Al's brother and fellow vaudevillian, is the Jolson in that title; the reminiscences are of both. The theme is Al overshadowing Harry: "There were two Jolson brothers appearing on the stage, and Al was both of them." Robert Oberfirst's *Al Jolson: You Ain't Heard Nothin' Yet* is an overdramatized biography, imagining details and restructuring relationships; it does include lists of Jolson's records and of his shows on stage, screen, and radio. A *Jolson Journal* is published in Quebec.

Bette Midler's 1970s song and stage celebrity is reflected in her spoof scrapbook, *A View from a Broad,* a collection of color photographs and tongue-in-cheek narrative episodes.

Dinah Shore, singer and television personality, has been given a short, popular biography in Bruce Cassiday's *Dinah! A Biography,* with press-release photographs and promotional text.

Bobby Short's *Black and White Baby* is an autobiography of only the pre-adult years of the stylish cabaret pianist and singer of pop songs.

Frank Sinatra has a substantial archive in Albert I. Lonstein and Vito R. Marion's *The Revised Compleat Sinatra: Discography, Filmography, Television Appearances, Motion Picture Appearances, Radio Appearances, Concert Appearances, Stage Appearances,* a huge, 700-page illustrated compendium. Brief chapters introduce the periods of his recording career. In 1947 E. J. Kahn, Jr., published *The Voice: The Story of an American Phenomenon,* a short book of *New Yorker* journalism on Sinatra at age twenty-nine, with a section of photographs. There are two later and more substantial biographies. Earl Wilson's *Sinatra: An Unauthorized Biography* (1976) is a large book in quick journalistic paragraphs by a prominent gossip columnist and sometime friend of Sinatra. Arnold Shaw's *Sinatra: Twentieth-Century Romantic* (1968) is a full-scale story, though of course there has been more of Sinatra since it appeared. Shaw includes a short essay on "Sinatra as a Recording Artist," with some listing of records and films. Alan Frank's *Sinatra* is a British souvenir-book history with photographs, some in color. The Sinatra Music Society of London published a substantial fan tabloid called *Perfectly Frank* which had run to 126 issues through 1973.

Kate Smith has had a singing and stage career over at least five decades. In 1938 she published *Living in a Great Big Way,* a cheery early-mid-career story at the height of her radio and concert success. *Upon My Lips a Song*

(1960) gathers recollections from the 1920s on, from stage and radio into television. Fans began publishing a magazine called *Our Kate* in 1968.

Tiny Tim by Harry Stein is described on the cover as "an unauthorized biography," but it has extended interview statements woven into its story of the long career and brief stardom of this eccentric recreator of old recorded songs.

Sophie: The Sophie Tucker Story by Michael Freedland is a brief popular biography of the brassy stage singer who performed from 1907 to 1965. She had published an autobiography called *Some of These Days* in 1945, which, in light of her reputation for wily self-promotion, is not to be trusted too much.

Rudy Vallée has published three books about himself. *Vagabond Dreams Come True* (1930) was a preening self-portrait in the first year of his radio show success. A collaboration with Gil McKean produced *My Time Is Your Time* in 1962, again very celebratory. Both are more connected and more temperate than *Let the Chips Fall . . .* (1975), a collection of remembered personal and career conquests and squabbles as bandleader, crooner, and playboy.

Bobby Vinton's *The Polish Prince* tells the story of his stardom in the 1960s in such a way as to highlight and promote a later role as Polish-American spokesman-singer.

ID. TIN PAN ALLEY HISTORY AND COMMENTARY

Two song publishers have told their stories in large books that take in so much of the business and performing worlds that they are significant histories of Tin Pan Alley. Isidore Witmark and Isaac Goldberg's *The Story of the House of Witmark: From Ragtime to Swingtime* is an important source of facts on the industry, with photographs, a good index, and lists of songs, acts, and theaters. Edward B. Marks, a rival publisher, wrote *They All Sang: From Tony Pastor to Rudy Vallée* (beginning a tradition of "They All . . ." titles for popular music histories). Marks' story runs from 1894 to the end of the 1920s, through minstrel, vaudeville, and Tin Pan Alley, with many illustrations, a list of 1,545 hit songs with years, writers and singers, a list of about two hundred minstrel performers, a list of other variety acts, and a catalog of New York entertainment spots of the period.

Witmark's collaborator, Isaac Goldberg, also wrote *Tin Pan Alley: A Chronicle of the American Popular Music Racket* in 1930. A new edition in 1961 includes a supplement by Edward Jablonski assertedly continuing the story to the age of rock in a cursory thirty-one pages, but the book remains a history from nineteenth-century origins to the late 1920s: minstrelsy, ragtime, Tin Pan Alley, and an early view of jazz. Maxwell F. Marcuse's *Tin Pan Alley in Gaslight* is a large chronicle from 1880 to 1910, tracing the careers of songwriters and describing and sometimes quoting the succession of most popular songs, with sheet music covers and composer photographs. David Ewen's *The Life and Death of Tin Pan Alley* is a popular chronicle of songwriting from the 1880s through the 1920s, including lists of a hundred standard songs, of lyricists and composers, and of reference sources.

Criticism of the songs was offered in Sigmund Spaeth's *The Facts of Life in Popular Song* (1934), an amused and scornful survey of the sentiments and techniques of Tin Pan Alley songs, elaborated into a short book from a magazine essay of the same title, which is also reprinted elsewhere in that shorter form. Spaeth, in other moods, deals with some of this same material in his *Read 'Em and Weep* and *Weep Some More* anthologies (chapter 2) and in his *History of Popular Music in America* (chapter 1). For a major work of musical criticism of the New York songwriting tradition see Alec Wilder's *American Popular Song,* below under Broadway (Section IIID). Two monuments of Tin Pan Alley, Harris' "After the Ball" and Berlin's "White Christmas," are given extended study in chapters of this author's *The Experience of Songs.*

Criticism of modern song stylists whose repertories include older pop songs is given in a collection of profile essays by Whitney Balliett, whose collections of jazz essays are described in chapter 5. His *American Singers* argues for a "body of classic American song," both pop and jazz, and characterizes as its interpreters Teddi King, Mary Mayo, Barbara Lea, Alberta Hunter, Joe Turner, Helen Humes, Ray Charles, Tony Bennett, Sylvia Syms, Hugh Shannon, Blossom Dearie, Bobby Short, Mabel Mercer, and Anita Ellis.

Performance techniques for the mainstream pop tradition have a detailed textbook, *The Singing Entertainer: A Contemporary Study of the Art and Business of Being a Professional* by singer John Davidson and Cort Casady. With some overlap, this book provides, along with the handbooks for various music careers described in chapter 1, interesting analysis of style and performer's stage manner from the angle of calculating audience response. It is derived from Davidson's Singers' Summer Camp school.

The broadcasting industry in relation to music is the subject of two survey memoirs. Ernest La Prade's *Broadcasting Music* (1947) is a detailed, sometimes technical account by the director of music research for the NBC radio network, touching on composing, programming, and producing music for radio. Dave Dexter, Jr., wrote *Playback: A Newsman/Record Producer's Hits and Misses from the Thirties to the Seventies,* casually organized reminiscences of a Los Angeles recording business insider.

II. DANCE BANDS

The music of Tin Pan Alley, Broadway, and some that was properly jazz was played around America in the first half of the twentieth century by an immense proliferation of various kinds of dance bands. By one estimate there were sixty thousand such bands in the mid-1920s. The jazz bands appear in chapter 5; in this section separate attention is given to the tradition of bands playing "sweet" dance music, though in varying degrees many of these aggregations showed or claimed some jazz influence.

IIA. BAND DISCOGRAPHY

Brian Rust's massive *The American Dance Band Discography 1917-1942* collects in two volumes the data on 78 rpm records of well over two thousand bands, omitting, because they are covered elsewhere, Benny Goodman (see Russ Connor's book in chapter 5), Glenn Miller (see John Flower, below under particular leaders), and the black, jazz-oriented ensembles such as Duke Ellington's (see Rust's *Jazz Records, 1897-1942* and other discographies under jazz discography in chapter 5).

IIB. BAND GENERAL REFERENCE

Leo Walker's *The Big Band Almanac* has entries for 267 bandleaders, with photographs, a few paragraphs of history, and a listing of known sidemen and vocalists, recording companies, and other data. An appendix gives scraps of fact about many other bands. The book has a name index. George T. Simon's *The Big Bands* has historical chapters and a band-biographical encyclopedia for the years 1935 to 1946, with a reprise on the surviving leaders and bands in the 1970s. There are illustrated articles on seventy-two bands and a separate section of shorter entries on many more. There also is a selective discography of available long-playing albums.

IIC. PARTICULAR LEADERS AND BANDS

Desi Arnaz has written *A Book,* memoirs of a Cuban childhood and of a Cuban-American career singing, acting, and bandleading, which came to be absorbed in the *I Love Lucy* industry when he and his wife Lucille Ball began their remarkably successful television comedy series.

Xavier Cugat's *Rumba Is My Life* (1948) is a memoir of the Latin dance band leader, enlivened by his own cartoons.

Tommy and Jimmy: The Dorsey Years, by their friend and fellow musician Herb Sanford, recalls the Dorseys' joint careers. Appendixes list prominent band members and give a 1935 itinerary. There are many photographs.

Guy Lombardo has both a biography and an autobiography. His own *Auld Acquaintance* recalls his ensembles from 1927 to the time of his writing in the mid-1970s. Booton Herndon's *The Sweetest Music This Side of Heaven,* written a decade earlier, is an authorized journalistic story. Both books have photographs.

Vincent Lopez wrote his own *Lopez Speaking,* a large book of memoirs and philosophizing.

Glenn Miller and His Orchestra by George T. Simon recounts Miller's swing career in the 1930s and that of his swing Army Air Force band in the war years up to Miller's death in a military plane crash in 1944. John Flower has collected a mass of fact in *Moonlight Serenade: A Bio-Discography of the Glenn Miller Civilian Band.* Flower lists Miller's recording dates chronologically with full discographic detail, interspersed with a chronicle of life and career.

Lawrence Welk has been the dance-style band leader to achieve the latest broad success, with great impact in the television era. Mary Lewis Coakley wrote an admiring popular biography, *Mister Music Maker,* which includes a roster of his band in the mid-1950s. Welk himself produced a string of homely books promulgating his conservative social and religious ideas with reference to his musical career. *Wunnerful, Wunnerful! The Autobiography of Lawrence Welk* came out in 1971; *Ah-One, Ah-Two! Life with My Musical Family* in 1974; *My America, Your America* in 1976; and *This I Believe* in 1979. *Lawrence Welk's Musical Family Album* (1977) displays Welk and the members of his band and his family, sometimes in color. The musical family also appear in *The Lennon Sisters: Sweethearts of Song,* by A. H. Parr, a cheerful-to-saccharine profile of young singers with the group, and in *Norma* by Norma Zimmer, a vocalist who also has toured with Billy Graham.

IID. BAND HISTORY AND COMMENTARY

There are several heavily illustrated historical surveys of dance bands. Brian Rust's *The Dance Bands,* not a discography this time, covers bands in England and in America. Similar transatlantic coverage is given in Albert McCarthy's *The Dance Band Era* and in Arthur Jackson's *The World of Big Bands.* Jackson devotes nearly half of his book to bands that continued after the war, some to as late as the 1970s. He includes a mostly British bibliography. Gene Fernett's *A Thousand Golden Horns . . . The Exciting Age of America's Greatest Dance Bands* includes a theme-song list and a key to band personnel in some of his photographs. Leo Walker, whose *Almanac* is mentioned above, also produced one of these history-and-photograph albums, *The Wonderful Era of the Great Dance Bands.*

Critical journalism from the middle age of dance bands makes up George T. Simon's collection of his own writings, *Simon Says: The Sights and Sounds of the Swing Era, 1935-1955.* Articles originally published in *Metronome Magazine,* with original illustrations, are supplied with a new marginal commentary. In an appendix, Simon lists band reviews the magazine published from 1935 to 1946.

III. BROADWAY

Early musical theater sprang up in several colonial American cities, including Charleston, Baltimore, Philadelphia, and Boston, as well as in New

York. Operas and ballad operas played in the same theaters as nonmusical drama throughout the country. As various uses of music on stage evolved through the nineteenth century toward the modern musical comedy in the twentieth century, New York clearly came to be the center of American stage culture, some of it in theaters on Broadway, until that street came to name American musical theater.

IIIA. BROADWAY BIBLIOGRAPHY AND DISCOGRAPHY

James M. Salem's *A Guide to Critical Reviews: Part II, The Musical, 1909-1974,* is a bibliography of reviews of Broadway musical shows, grouping reviews by show. (Other volumes of the same main title deal with other forms of drama.)

The Broadway Musical: A Complete LP Discography by Gordon W. Hodgins catalogs 424 albums from 331 shows. The main listing, by show, gives albums, cast, credits, and songs; numerous indexes follow. Hodgins includes records by major North American companies, leaving out several small categories of existing records—British and European, limited editions, mail-order records, and pirated issues.

The New York Public Library's Lincoln Center Branch houses not only the huge Archive of Recorded Sound and the Music Division with its Americana Collection but also the General Library and Museum of the Performing Arts and the special Billy Rose Theatre Collection. An independent Institute of the American Musical, Incorporated, formerly located in New York, is now in Los Angeles, with six thousand books and thirty-five thousand records. A smaller collection of musical theater materials is housed in the Yale Library in New Haven, Connecticut.

IIIB. BROADWAY GENERAL REFERENCE

The best overall reference work about Broadway is Gerald Bordman's *The American Musical Theatre: A Chronicle,* which tells the story from Broadway's beginnings, season by season from 1867-1868 to 1977-1978. Every musical to appear on Broadway and some from other cities are noticed. Bold-face type locates show titles and names of some theater figures who are given brief biographical notes. For plays, plots are summarized with comment; sometimes a bit of dialogue is given, but few lyrics and no music are quoted. There are indexes to shows, songs, and people. David Ewen's *New Complete Book of the American Musical Theater* is an encyclopedia of show and biographical entries: part one, musical shows; part two, librettists, lyricists, and composers. Appendixes give a chronology and a selection of titles of outstanding songs. Stanley Green's *Encyclopedia of the Musical Theatre* is a "ready-reference" book, less detailed than Ewen, with entries for people, productions, and songs of the New York and London stages; production entries list only selected songs. The same author's *Ring Bells! Sing Songs! Broadway Musicals of the 1930s* covers that single decade, first in an illustrated history and then in a show-per-page catalog listing credits, cast, musical numbers, theater, and performance run.

Songs of the American Theater by Richard Lewine and Alfred Simon indexes twelve thousand songs, from all Broadway and off-Broadway productions between 1925 and 1971, with a few earlier songs and a few songs written for films or television. This book triples their earlier listing which was called *Encyclopedia of Theatre Music.* Jack Burton's *The Blue Book of Broadway Musicals* is with the Tin Pan Alley, Hollywood, and index volumes part of a song reference set. This volume gives shows, with cast and song list, by composers, grouped into decades. In 1958 ASCAP published *40 Years of Show Tunes: The Big Broadway Hits from 1917-1957,* intended for the use of broadcasters, which lists about seventeen hundred recorded songs chronologically by year, with an index.

The Theatre Student Guide to Broadway Musical Theatre by Tom Tumbusch is principally a catalog of 114 shows for the use of performers and producers, with descriptive data such as cast requirements, plot digest, and critical notes on how a given show should be staged.

Anthologies of show song lyrics by Coward, the Gershwins, Hammerstein, and Porter are listed in the following section. A selected anthology of lyrics by many writers is Lehman Engel's *Their Words Are Music,* with critical afternotes to many of the songs and illustrative photographs and posters. The principal selections are from seventeen masters from 1925 to 1972, but there are shorter sections on the beginning of the Broadway era, on the Kurt Weill collaborators, on miscellaneous successful shows, and on writers of the early 1970s. Stanley Richards has edited three volumes anthologizing the books and lyrics of about thirty shows, in *Ten Great Musicals of the American Theatre, Great Musicals of the American Theatre,* and *Great Rock Musicals.* Production details are included in brief introductions, and there are some photographs.

IIIC. BROADWAY BIOGRAPHY AND MATERIALS RELEVANT TO PARTICULAR FIGURES

Collective biographic materials appear in two books in addition to the encyclopedias cited above. *Men and Melodies* by Leonard A. Paris gives brief stories of eighteen Broadway lyricists and composers from De Koven to Lerner and Loewe. Max Wilk's *They're Playing Our Song* is an "oral history" of twenty-one songwriters from Kern to Sondheim.

Individual figures identified with Broadway are arranged alphabetically in the following paragraphs.

Harold Arlen, most famous now for composing the music for *The Wizard of Oz,* is given a biography in Edward Jablonski's *Harold Arlen: Happy with the Blues.* It includes a catalog of his work in revues, musicals, and films from the 1920s to the 1950s and a discography.

Abe Barrows, writer of books for Broadway shows, wrote his own story in *Honest, Abe: Is There Really No Business Like Show Business?* The book gives much attention to production details of his hit *Guys and Dolls.*

Irving Berlin, in his nineties at the present writing, has had a career that is astonishing in many ways. His "White Christmas" is the most successful song ever recorded. It is nearly as remarkable for any celebrity to be able to look back on a biography of himself written more than half a century earlier: Alexander Woolcott's *The Story of Irving Berlin,* an illustrated biography, closes with a list of Berlin's greatest hits through 1924 and was published the following year. David Ewen's *The Story of Irving Berlin* had another quarter century of the story to tell in 1950; it is aimed at younger readers. In 1974 Michael Freedland brought out *Irving Berlin,* with Berlin's limited cooperation, a popular biography in journalistic style.

Noël Coward's career was primarily English rather than American, but his work ran on Broadway in the 1920s, 1930s, 1940s, and 1960s. His *Lyrics of Noël Coward* is a large but still selected anthology of his verse to 276 theater and revue songs. Coward's early autobiography *Present Indicative* (1937) includes American episodes. The sequel *Future Indefinite* covers the years of the Second World War which brought him here only very briefly.

Howard Dietz wrote *Dancing in the Dark,* witty reminiscences of a long Broadway and Hollywood career: he first collaborated with Jerome Kern in 1924, and published this book fifty years later. Many informal photographs of show business personalities are included along with a catalog of Dietz's stage shows.

Lehman Engel, the composer whose books on the theater and critical anthology of the works of Broadway lyricists are noted elsewhere, was music director for 164 Broadway shows from the 1930s to the 1960s. His *This Bright Day: An Autobiography* offers recollections of a wide circle of acquaintances in the arts and show business.

George Gershwin's career as a composer included collaboration with his brother Ira Gershwin as his lyricist in Broadway productions until his death in 1937. Ira continued lyrical collaborations with other composers. George Gershwin, and the two brothers in collaboration, have been given extensive chronicle, tribute, and scholarship. *George Gershwin: A Selective Bibliography and Discography* by Charles Schwartz collects 654 printed items on or by Gershwin, not including his published music; the discography lists "commendable" records. Schwartz also published a documented critical biography, based on his doctoral dissertation, with appendixes of musical analysis, composition list, film list, and shorter bibliography and discography. The first biography had been Isaac Goldberg's authorized *George Gershwin: A Study in American Music* in 1931, later reprinted with additional chapters by Edith Garson. Merle Armitage's *George Gershwin: Man and Legend* includes Ira's tribute to his brother, reprinted from a 1938 volume Armitage edited, but the body of this book is Armitage's own reminiscences of George from 1919 to his death, with analysis and defense of his place in American and western music. David Ewen has published two versions of a large popular biography. *A Journey to Greatness* includes a bibliography and discography which Ewen dropped in the revised *George Gershwin: His Journey to Greatness.* Photographs include reproductions of Gershwin's paintings. Ewen also wrote *The Story of George Gershwin* for younger readers.

George and Ira Gershwin's joint careers have two scrapbook-style histories. Edward Jablonski and Lawrence D. Stewart wrote *The Gershwin Years,* with a thread of narrative and a mass of photographs, manuscripts of music and lyrics, sketches, and memorabilia, ending with a catalog of the works of both together and of their separate works. A revision of the book was printed the same year (1973) that Robert Kimball and Alfred Simon's *The Gershwins* came out. After a historical introduction by John S. Wilson, they assemble a large set of private and public photographs, letters, verse, and paintings organized around successive shows from 1919 to 1970. Lawrence D. Stewart's *The Gershwins: Words upon Music* is the separate publication of a short book of notes written to accompany a record, *Ella Fitzgerald Sings the George and Ira Gershwin Song Books.* A few paragraphs comment on the background of each of fifty-three songs. Ira Gershwin has published *Lyrics on Several Occasions,* a selection of his song texts with whimsical reminiscent essays prefixed to each.

Oscar Hammerstein II, like Ira Gershwin, has been chronicled in his most famous collaboration—see the books below under Richard Rodgers—but he also has a full biography in *Getting to Know Him* by Hugh Fordin, which benefits from family archives to quote some unpublished lyrics; there is an introductory appreciation of Hammerstein by Stephen Sondheim, for whom Hammerstein was an early mentor. Hammerstein himself published a book of *Lyrics,* seventy-one texts for show music by Rodgers, Kern, Romberg, and Bizet's *Carmen* in its Broadway translation as *Carmen Jones.* Hammerstein wrote a preface of reflections and memories.

Lorenz Hart's brilliant lyrics are printed with memorabilia in *Thou Swell, Thou Witty* edited by his sister-in-law, Dorothy Hart. Short memoirs by colleagues, candid and Broadway production photographs, and data on shows are deployed around Dorothy's narrative of his life and the texts of his lyrics. (See also under Rodgers, below).

Jerome Kern was one of the creators of the American musical. Gerald Bordman's *Jerome Kern: His Life and Music* is a large-scale biography incorporating Kern's life story, full accounts of his stage productions, and semitechnical analysis of his music. (For further such analysis see the chapter on Kern in Wilder's *American Popular Song* listed below in section IIID.) Michael Freedland's *Jerome Kern* is a popular biography drawing on material provided by Kern's daughter and on interviews of Freedland's with show business people of the era while he prepared this and his five previous biographies of entertainment figures. David Ewen's *The World of Jerome Kern* was an earlier popular biography; Ewen's *The Story of*

Jerome Kern, like several of his similar titles, is a small book for young or casual readers, with short, selected lists of Kern's works of various kinds.

Eartha Kitt, actress and night club singer, wrote a publicity autobiography in 1956 called *Thursday's Child.* Twenty years later her *Alone with Me: A New Autobiography* was a fuller and franker, as well as longer, story, including her period of semiexile in Europe in the 1950s and her involvement in political controversy in the 1960s.

Alan Jay Lerner's *The Street Where I Live* is a chronicle of the decade from the early 1950s to the early 1960s in which Lerner collaborated as lyricist with composer Frederick Lowe to create *My Fair Lady, Gigi,* and *Camelot.* An introduction gives a brief autobiography up to 1952, and an appendix prints the lyrics he wrote for the three shows.

Mary Martin's *My Heart Belongs* is a book of recollections of her acting career on Broadway, with photographs.

Ethel Merman's performing career has been recalled in two autobiographical collaborative books. *Who Could Ask for Anything More* in 1955 was a mid-career self-profile. *Merman* in 1978 consists of chatty reminiscences of her life, with a selection of pictures and a catalog of shows and films in which she played.

Helen Morgan was a singing star of revues, musicals, and films in the 1920s and 1930s. Gilbert Maxwell wrote her biography in *Helen Morgan: Her Life and Legend.*

Cole Porter fascinated his contemporaries and later audiences, writers, and readers by the dazzling wit of his lyrics (for which he also wrote the music) and by his life in fashionable society. *The Life That Late He Led* by George Eells is a large biography, without documentation but including a forty-page list of Porter's works. The title paraphrases a Porter song but there is little quotation from other lyrics. Charles Schwartz' *Cole Porter: A Biography* has more interest in intimate revelations and psychology than does Eells. A bibliography and discography are included. Richard G. Hubler published *The Cole Porter Story as Told to Richard G. Hubler* after Porter's death. The first two chapters of this brief book are Porter's reminiscences from interviews given in 1954, which he broke off and declined to continue or have published while he lived. Hubler finishes the story in four chapters of highly laudatory narrative. David Ewen's *The Cole Porter Story* is another of the young readers' books, including a film and television show list, selected song and record lists, and a bibliography. Porter's lyrics are printed in a book edited by Robert Kimball, *Cole* [with] *a Biographical Essay by Brendan Gill.* The "essay" is a few pages reprinted from *The New Yorker;* the book is a large scrapbook-format collection, interspersing photographs and other souvenirs with lyrics from 1910 to 1958. Kimball also edited *The Unpublished Cole Porter,* a songbook of twenty-three of the finished songs left unpublished at Porter's death; Kimball provides brief headnotes.

The composer Richard Rodgers, like his most prominent collaborators

Oscar Hammerstein II and Lorenz Hart, has been given both separate and shared consideration by writers about the Broadway stage. David Ewen's *Richard Rodgers* (1957) uses interviews and material supplied by Rodgers and adds appendixes listing his music in various categories. *With a Song in His Heart* is Ewen's slightly later small book for adolescents. Rodgers himself published *Musical Stages: An Autobiography* at the age of seventy-two, career memories decorated with photographs and playbills.

Together, Rodgers and Hammerstein have the *Rodgers and Hammerstein Fact Book: A Record of Their Works Together and with Other Collaborators* edited by Stanley Green. It is principally a catalog of shows, detailing story, cast, musical numbers, performance runs, and excerpts from reviews through 1979, with a notice of Rodgers' death in that year. Among the appendix materials is a listing of songs by subject categories. Green had written *The Rodgers and Hammerstein Story* in 1963, a short, popular dual biography. A decade earlier, Deems Taylor wrote *Some Enchanted Evenings: The Story of Rodgers and Hammerstein* in the midst of both their careers, through *The King and I* but before *The Sound of Music.* Frederick Nolan's *The Sound of Their Music* is the last narrative in Rodgers' lifetime, a documented chronicle with notes and a chronology that includes some critical commentary on productions. Some attention is also given to their other partners.

Rodgers together with Hart is treated in *Rodgers and Hart: Bewitched, Bothered and Bedeviled* by Samuel Marx and Jan Clayton, which collects gossip and recollections by the authors and others associated with the careers of the subjects. There are small reproductions of stage photographs.

Stephen Sondheim, perhaps the outstanding craftsman on Broadway in the 1970s, has a mid-career portrait in *Sondheim and Co.* by Craig Zadan. Much of this book consists of interview statements by Sondheim and others. Photographs, a production catalog, and a list of original-cast records are included in an appendix.

Jule Styne, a composer for Broadway and Hollywood shows, is the subject of a full popular biography, *Jule,* by Theodore Taylor.

Kurt Weill was an established European composer and collaborator with Bertolt Brecht *(The 3-Penny Opera)* when he came to New York in flight from Nazi Germany in 1935. He then began extensive work writing music for Broadway lyricists, which lasted until his death in 1950. His biography is *The Days Grow Short: The Life and Music of Kurt Weill* by Ronald Sanders, with extensive documentation, composition list, and discography.

IIID. BROADWAY HISTORY AND COMMENTARY

The best history of Broadway is Bordman's *The American Musical Theatre,* also listed above under general reference. David Ewen's *The Story of America's Musical Theater* is an uncritical popular history, showing the haste of its prolific author in the reporting of various legends about Broadway personalities that other writers have investigated and rejected.

Ethan Mordden's *Better Foot Forward* is a breezy critical history up to
Follies in 1977, with a short critical bibliography. Cecil Smith's *Musical
Comedy in America* is a history from *The Black Crook* to *South Pacific*,
but the bulk of it is devoted to the stage from the 1860s to the 1920s, with
only two short chapters covering shows after the 1930s. Robert Baral's
Revue: A Nostalgic Reprise of the Great Broadway Period is a history-
scrapbook centering on a year-by-year catalog of Ziegfeld and other follies
and a show-by-show catalog of other productions. There are some
illustrated historical chapters and a list of shows, with casts, from 1903 to
1945. Henry T. Sampson's *Blacks in Blackface: A Source Book on Early
Black Musical Shows* assembles facts on the black shows in black theaters
from the 1890s to the 1930s. Much information is taken from the black
newspapers of the time; Sampson includes histories of the entrepreneurs,
producers, and theaters, show synopses, and biographies of performers.
Martin Gottfried's *Broadway Musicals* is a large and lavish artbook of the
theater. The text surveys topics and people, but the main thing is the photographs, in large, high-quality color prints.

Analysis of the art and business of Broadway is undertaken in three
books by Lehman Engel. *The American Musical Theater: A Consideration*
was written to be a companion to a set of records chosen from the catalog of
Columbia releases; it has a history section that is mostly a photograph
album. A revision produced *The American Musical Theater,* a fuller
attempt to draw on Engel's career as composer and conductor to describe
the basics of the art of musicals. The long central chapter breaks down the
contemporary musical into its components for study: "subplot," "scene
and act endings," and so on. *The Making of a Musical* is a short practical
guide for aspiring professionals and the kibitzing general reader, with many
examples cited under music, lyrics, libretto, and assignments (from his BMI
Musical Theatre Workshops), and with final comments. Richard Kislan's
The Musical: A Look at the American Musical Theater is comparable,
described by its author as a book of fundamentals for beginners. Kislan
gives a brief, illustrated survey of topics in the history of Broadway; of the
work of Kern, Rodgers and Hammerstein, and Sondheim; and of the
anatomy of a modern Broadway show.

Critical histories include Arthur Jackson's *The Best Musicals: From
Show Boat to A Chorus Line, Broadway—Off-Broadway—London.* Production photographs predominate over text; appendixes give data on
people, shows, songs, plot classifications, long runs, and lists of films,
records, and books. Abe Laufe, in *Broadway's Greatest Musicals,* gives a
history of "hit" shows defined as those running more than five hundred
performances, mostly from the 1950s and 1960s.

Corners of the history of Broadway include the memoir by P. G. Wodehouse and Guy Bolton, *Bring on the Girls! The Improbable Story of Our
Life in Musical Comedy,* a chatty and witty evocation of the authors'
careers writing book and lyrics in the teens and the 1920s, mostly anecdote

and dialogue, but, for reference, indexed. *Show Boat: The Story of a Classic American Musical* by Miles Kreuger is a critical history of the many incarnations, after Ferber's novel in 1926, of the 1927 Kern-Hammerstein musical in its first form and, later, in films and revivals. Lorrie Davis gives a performer's account of the 1967 sensation *Hair* in *Letting Down My Hair: Two Years with the Love Rock Tribe.*

Musical analysis of the Broadway and Tin Pan Alley song tradition makes a unique and valuable book of Alec Wilder's *American Popular Song: The Great Innovators, 1900-1950.* Wilder, a songwriter and oracle of the show-song culture, treats the compositions of Kern, Berlin, George Gershwin, Rodgers, Porter, Arlen, Youmans, and Schwartz in separate chapters, with shorter notice of many others. Many musical examples are printed for analysis and critical pronouncement—except for Berlin's, who does not permit such quotations from either his words or his music.

IV. HOLLYWOOD

Music has been part of the entertainment that films have offered Americans from the earliest silent films accompanied by live piano to the London Symphony Orchestra sound tracks for the *Star Wars* movies. This commercial musical entertainment sometimes has been strictly music of the theater and sometimes has found its way out into other channels of popular music, as with the songs of the Hollywood musicals and the record albums of orchestral soundtracks. This section will touch on the varieties of music associated with films in America.

IVA. HOLLYWOOD BIBLIOGRAPHY AND DISCOGRAPHY

The great industry and subculture of American film has a vast literature. A recent guide to it is Robert A. Armour's *Film: A Reference Guide* in the same series as this book.

A Handbook of Film, Theatre, and Television Music on Record, 1948-1969 compiled by Steven Smolian is a pair of pamphlets—the first, an album discography by title; the second, indexes of manufacturers and composers. Comparable discography is included in Limbacher's *Violins to Video* and *Keeping Score,* listed in the following section. Limbacher's books present a fuller inventory in slightly less discographic detail. *Hollywood on Record: The Film Stars' Discography* by Michael R. Pitts and Louis H. Harrison lists LP and some 45 rpm records from 1948 on, including records made apart from the film career as well as soundtrack and other film-related records. Dates are not included. See also Brian Rust's *Complete Entertainment Discography* (section IA), which includes film stars and covers the years up to 1942.

IVB. HOLLYWOOD GENERAL REFERENCE

The fullest reference sources are two books by James L. Limbacher that make a set (a combined edition is planned): *Film Music: From Violins to*

Video and *Keeping Score: Film Music 1972-1979.* In the former book part 1 is an anthology of reprinted articles of the history and criticism of film music; part 2 is a 600-page series of reference listings, including lists of films with dates, of films with composers, of composers with films, and of recorded musical scores. The second volume continues the lists. Despite its title, about a third of the entries come from earlier years supplementing, rather than merely continuing, the earlier book. Limbacher has also compiled several editions of a directory called *Feature Films on 8 mm and 16 mm,* which may be consulted for the rental, lease, or purchase of such films. The films make a valuable record of this music in its designed setting, although rental of films does not make a very practical mode of research reference. Data about both the films and their music is compiled in the reference section of Taylor and Jackson's *The Hollywood Musical,* which can be found below in section IVD.

An older guide is Jack Burton's Hollywood volume, *The Blue Book of Hollywood Musicals,* whose Tin Pan Alley, Broadway, and common index companion volumes have already been cited. Covering the years from 1927 to 1952, Burton lists films in briefly introduced annual divisions, by categories, with credits and songs. A list of albums from those years and a short directory of stars are given at the end.

Songs from Hollywood Musical Comedies, 1927 to the Present (1976) by Allen L. Woll is a "dictionary" of seven thousand songs keyed to a film list with credits, songs, and recordings. There is a chronology of the 1,187 films by year and an index by composers and lyricists. Reference from composer to works can also be pursued in Clifford McCarty's *Film Composers in America: A Checklist of Their Work* (1953). Films to that early date are ordered under each of 164 composers, by year and in generic groupings. McCarty also compiles Academy Awards, and that list is brought up to 1971 in the reprinted edition.

There is a scholarly and professional *Filmmusic Notebook,* a quarterly journal published by the Film Music Collective in Los Angeles. An older journal, called *Film Music Notes,* then *Film Music,* then *Film & TV Music,* ran from 1941 to 1957 as a newsletter printing many extracts from score manuscripts.

IVC. HOLLYWOOD BIOGRAPHY AND MATERIALS RELEVANT TO PARTICULAR FIGURES

The Great Songwriters of Hollywood by Warren Craig profiles thirty-two writers. Each is given a portrait photograph, a still from a film, and a few sheet music covers to decorate a biographical sketch and a chronological song list.

The Films of Bing Crosby by Robert Bookbinder is a scrapbook survey of Crosby's Hollywood career with a few pages of data, comment, and stills for each movie. A list of songs from these films that were nominated for Academy Awards is included, and a list of those that won.

The Films of Jeanette MacDonald and Nelson Eddy by Philip Castanza is similar to the Crosby book, tracing their series of romantic co-starring features from 1929 to 1949. A list of duets with discography is included.

Vincent Minnelli and the Film Musical by Joseph Andrew Casper is a study of the films directed by Minnelli from 1941 to 1970. The text is balanced by stills from the films in chapters that, after brief background, divide the art and techniques of his work.

Elvis in Hollywood by Paul Lichter is a picture catalog of Presley's films with credits, long synopses, and a fan's criticism; a discography of the songs from the films is included. Similar material is found in the Zmijewskys' *Elvis: The Films and Career of Elvis Presley.* See also other materials on Presley in chapter 7, section C.

Barbra Streisand: An Illustrated Biography by Frank Brady has a dwindling text running through a gallery of publicity shots.

Pinky Tomlin has written an autobiography named for his most famous song, *The Object of My Affection.* Besides songwriting, his career in the 1930s took in movie roles and stage shows, featuring singing and Oklahoma folksiness, scoring of films, and bandleading.

Harry Warren and the Hollywood Musical by Tony Thomas is a large-format illustrated history and songbook for Warren, who wrote songs for about sixty film musicals. Excerpts of words and music are scattered throughout the text, and twenty-five complete songs are also included.

IVD. HOLLYWOOD HISTORY AND COMMENTARY

Limbacher's *Film Music: From Violins to Video* (above, section IVB) begins with an anthology of essays on the art. John Russell Taylor and Arthur Jackson's *The Hollywood Musical* has historical essays by Taylor, illustrated, for its first third, followed by Jackson's reference section. The latter includes a catalog of 277 films with singers and songs, a biographical directory with credits, an index of songs, and a list of the dates of 1,437 films.

The largest historical compendium is Clive Hirshhorn's *The Hollywood Musical,* a heavily illustrated chronicle from 1927 to 1980. Each film describable as a musical is given a long paragraph of summary, comment, and facts, including a song list; appendixes list related kinds of films, and there are five specialized indexes. A brief history is Douglas McVay's *The Musical Film* (1967), a critical chronicle of American and European productions. John Kobal's *Gotta Sing, Gotta Dance: A Pictorial History of Film Musicals* tells its story through text and a large array of film stills.

Specialized histories include Michael B. Druxman's *The Musical: From Broadway to Hollywood,* which examines the production histories of twenty-five successful or unsuccessful films adapted from Broadway plays from 1949 to 1977, with numerous stills. Hugh Fordin's *The World of Entertainment! Hollywood's Greatest Musicals* is a detailed history of the production career of Arthur Freed and his "Freed Unit" at MGM, from *The Wizard of Oz* in 1939—Freed was associate producer—to 1970. There are many production photographs, massive documentation supplied by Freed and the company, a tone of admiration, and heavy emphasis on the glamor of it all. *The MGM Years* by Lawrence B. Thomas has a two-page spread for each of forty musicals from 1939 to 1971, with data and bits of critics' comments. A directory of stars at the end is illustrated with caricature drawings, and there are directory listings also for producers, directors, and music people. Contemporary reception of the first musicals is collected by Miles Kreuger in *The Movie Musical from Vitaphone to 42nd Street,* a large scrapbook of articles and advertisements from *Photoplay* magazine between 1926 and 1933, including a final section that gathers the monthly record reviews of film music in those years. At the other end of the history of musicals, Philip Jenkinson and Alan Warner's *Celluloid Rock: Twenty Years of Movie Rock* gives a quick, illustrated survey of rock music movies in the United States and Britain; a list at the end catalogs about three hundred films with the musical performers they featured.

Technical and critical analysis of movie music includes a body of material on the music that was provided live in theaters to accompany silent films. A scholarly inquiry is Charles Merrell Berg's *An Investigation of the Motives for and Realization of Music to Accompany the American Silent Film, 1896-1927.* Berg's doctoral dissertation (University of Iowa, 1973), printed in an Arno Press film study series, considers the value such music had as a weapon against distracting noise and against silence itself, the use of music to give a film continuity and expressiveness, and the economic value the music had as an added commercial attraction. There are valuable bibliographic notes in his introduction as well as a long bibliography at the end. Charles Hofmann's *Sounds for Silents* is a history in the scrapbook style with sheet music, score pages, stills, quotations, and commentary. An accompanying record demonstrates Hofmann's idea of music samples for five films (but such records are often missing from library copies of books). Two examples may be offered here of the manuals that were published in the 1920s for film accompanists. Edith Lang and George West's *Musical Accompaniment of Moving Pictures: A Practical Manual for Pianists and Organists and an Exposition of the Principles Underlying the Musical Interpretation of Moving Pictures* (1920, with a modern reprint) suggests how the theater musician might identify tone colors, produce special effects, and adapt music to such challenges as flashbacks, cartoons, and weekly newsreels. A cue sheet from the film *Rose of the World* is included. George W. Beynon's *Musical Presentation of Motion Pictures* (1921) affirms that forty thousand musicians were employed at the time in this business, and surveys its history and science. He includes biographical sketches of seven leading theater music directors.

The cinema organ was a prominent voice of musical entertainment until the coming of talkies, and some of its virtuosos and fans kept it alive in radio and television accompaniment and in a few theaters after soundtracks made them obsolete for their former employment. Reginald Foort's *The Cinema Organ: A Description in Non-Technical Language of a Fascinating Instrument and How It Is Played* was first published in 1932 and expanded in 1970. It has discussion of the instrument, many photographs, reminiscences, and a discography of Foort's own numerous recordings.

In the sound era, the place of music in films has not been limited to song numbers sung by stars. The continuous or intermittent accompaniment of the action, which had grown up as an art of theater performance, became arts of composing, performing, and recording soundtrack. Roy M. Prendergast's *A Neglected Art: A Critical Study of Music in Films* is a musicological history and analysis, focusing on major examples for close study. Some examples are reproduced from manuscript, vividly demonstrating the complexity and also the haste of the music's production. There is a full bibliography. *Soundtrack* by Mark Evans is a critical history. The early chapters include biographical subsections on major figures. *Music for the Movies* by Tony Thomas is a lively history of the art of scoring films, much of it told in biographical subchapters, including several interviews. There are photographs, a discographic chapter, and a score catalog by Clifford McCarty (see his separate book, above, in section IVB).

A very early study was *Film Music: A Summary of the Characteristic Features of Its History, Aesthetics, Techniques; and Possible Developments* by Kurt London, published in 1936 and now reprinted. This serious musicianly and technological essay set a precedent for such later studies as Hanns Eisler's *Composing for the Films* (1947), a composer's analysis of the pitfalls and resources of such music; and composer Irwin Bazelon's *Knowing the Score: Notes on Film Music* (1975), a history and analysis with extended musical examples and a long section of interviews with other composers. A collection of professional opinions is also found in *Film Score: The View from the Podium* edited by Tony Thomas, an anthology of articles by twenty composers.

A technical survey of the field is *The Technique of Film Music* by Roger Manvell and John Huntley for the British film academy in 1957, revised by Richard Arnell and Peter Day in 1975. A more specialized book is Milton Lustig's *Music Editing for Motion Pictures,* a detailed technical guide with charts, diagrams, score pages, and pictures of equipment.

Hollywood Studio Musicians: Their Work and Careers in the Recording Industry by Robert R. Faulkner is a sociological research study of this elite circle of performers and of the conditions and patterns of their careers. The approach is social-scientific rather than human interest or historiographic;

analytic methods are carefully defined, and informants are quoted anonymously in an effort to define the social system in which they live.

BIBLIOGRAPHY

Anderton, Barrie. *Sonny Boy! The World of Al Jolson.* London: Jupiter, 1975.

Armitage, Merle. *George Gershwin: Man and Legend.* 1958. Reprint. Freeport, N.Y.: Books for Libraries, 1970.

Armour, Robert A. *Film: A Reference Guide.* Westport, Conn.: Greenwood Press, 1980.

Arnaz, Desi. *A Book.* New York: William Morrow, 1976.

Bailey, Pearl. *The Raw Pearl.* New York: Harcourt, Brace and World, 1968.

_____. *Talking to Myself.* New York: Harcourt Brace Jovanovich, 1971.

Balliett, Whitney. *American Singers.* New York: Oxford University Press, 1979.

Baral, Robert. *Revue: A Nostalgic Reprise of the Great Broadway Period.* New York: Fleet Publishing, 1962.

Barnes, Ken. *The Crosby Years.* New York: St. Martin's Press, 1980.

_____. *Sinatra and the Great Song Stylists.* With contributions from Stan Britt, Arthur Jackson, Fred Dellar, and Chris Ellis. London: Ian Allan, 1972.

Barrows, Abe. *Honest, Abe: Is There Really No Business Like Show Business?* Boston: Little, Brown, 1980.

Bazelon, Irwin. *Knowing the Score: Notes on Film Music.* New York: Van Nostrand Reinhold, 1975.

Berg, Charles Merrell. *An Investigation of the Motives for and Realization of Music to Accompany the American Silent Film, 1896-1927.* New York: Arno Press, 1976.

Beynon, George W. *Musical Presentation of Motion Pictures.* New York: G. Schirmer, 1921.

Bing. Cwmbran, Gwent, Wales, 1950- .

Bookbinder, Robert. *The Films of Bing Crosby.* Secaucus, N.J.: Citadel Press, 1977.

Boone, Pat. *A New Song.* Carol Stream, Ill.: Creation House, 1970.

_____. *Together: 25 Years with the Boone Family.* Nashville, Tenn.: Thomas Nelson Publishers, 1979.

_____. *Twixt Twelve and Twenty.* Englewood Cliffs, N.J.: Prentice-Hall, 1960.

Booth, Mark W. *The Experience of Songs.* New Haven, Conn.: Yale University Press, 1981.

Bordman, Gerald. *The American Musical Theatre: A Chronicle.* New York: Oxford University Press, 1978.

_____. *Jerome Kern: His Life and Music.* New York: Oxford University Press, 1980.

Brady, Frank. *Barbra Streisand: An Illustrated Biography.* New York: Grosset and Dunlap, 1979.

Burton, Jack. *The Blue Book of Broadway Musicals.* 3d ed. Watkins Glen, N.Y.: Century House, 1976.

_____. *The Blue Book of Hollywood Musicals: Songs from the Sound Tracks and the Stars Who Sang Them since the Birth of the Talkies a Quarter-Century Ago.* Watkins Glen, N.Y.: Century House, 1953.

_____. *The Blue Book of Tin Pan Alley: A Human Interest Encyclopedia of American Popular Music.* 2 vols. Watkins Glen, N.Y.: Century House, 1962, 1965.

_____. *The Index of American Popular Music: Thousands of Titles Cross-Referenced to Our Basic Anthologies of Popular Song.* Watkins Glen, N.Y.: Century House, 1957.

Cahn, Sammy. *I Should Care: The Sammy Cahn Story.* New York: Arbor House, 1974.

Casper, Joseph Andrew. *Vincent Minnelli and the Film Musical.* South Brunswick, N.J.: A. S. Barnes, 1977.

Cassiday, Bruce. *Dinah! A Biography.* New York: Franklin Watts, 1979.

Castanza, Philip. *The Films of Jeanette MacDonald and Nelson Eddy.* Secaucus, N.J.: Citadel Press, 1978.

Clooney, Rosemary, with Raymond Strait. *This for Remembrance: The Autobiography of Rosemary Clooney, an Irish-American Singer.* Chicago: Playboy Press, 1977.

Coakley, Mary Lewis. *Mister Music Maker, Lawrence Welk.* Garden City, N.Y.: Doubleday, 1958.

Colbert, Warren E. *Who Wrote That Song? or, Who in the Hell Is J. Fred Coots? An Informal Survey of American Popular Songs and Their Composers.* New York: Revisionist Press, 1975.

Coward, Noël. *Future Indefinite.* Garden City, N.Y.: Doubleday, 1954.

_____. *The Lyrics of Noël Coward.* Woodstock, N.Y.: Overlook Press, 1973.

_____. *Present Indicative.* Garden City, N.Y.: Doubleday, Doran, 1937.

Craig, Warren. *The Great Songwriters of Hollywood.* San Diego, Calif.: A. S. Barnes, 1980.

Crosby, Bing, as told to Pete Martin. *Call Me Lucky.* New York: Simon and Schuster, 1953.

Crosby, Ted. *The Story of Bing Crosby.* 1937 Rev. ed. Cleveland, Ohio: World Publishing, 1946.

Cugat, Xavier. *Rumba Is My Life.* New York: Didier, 1948.

Davidson, John, and Casady, Cort. *The Singing Entertainer: A Contemporary Study of the Art and Business of Being a Professional.* N.p.: Alfred Publishing, 1979.

Davis, Lorrie, with Rachel Gallagher. *Letting Down My Hair: Two Years with the Love Rock Tribe—from Dawning to Downing of Aquarius.* New York: Arthur Fields Books, 1973.

Dexter, Dave, Jr. *Playback: A Newsman/Record Producer's Hits and Misses from the Thirties to the Seventies.* New York: Billboard Publications, 1976.

Dietz, Howard. *Dancing in the Dark: Words by Howard Dietz.* New York: Quadrangle/New York Times Book, 1974.

DiOrio, Al. *Borrowed Time: The 37 Years of Bobby Darin.* Philadelphia: Running Press, 1981.

Druxman, Michael B. *The Musical: From Broadway to Hollywood.* South Brunswick, N.J.: A. S. Barnes, 1980.

Eells, George. *The Life That Late He Led: A Biography of Cole Porter.* New York: G. P. Putnam's Sons, 1967.

Eisler, Hanns. *Composing for the Films.* New York: Oxford University Press, 1947.

Engel, Lehman. *The American Musical Theater*. Rev. ed. New York: Macmillan, 1975.

———. *The American Musical Theater: A Consideration*. New York: CBS Legacy Collection/Macmillan, 1967.

———. *The Making of a Musical*. New York: Macmillan, 1977.

———. *Their Words Are Music: The Great Theatre Lyricists and Their Lyrics*. New York: Crown Publishers, 1975.

———. *This Bright Day: An Autobiography*. New York: Macmillan, 1974.

Evans, Mark. *Soundtrack: The Music of the Movies*. New York: Hopkinson and Blake, 1973.

Ewen, David. *The Cole Porter Story*. New York: Holt, Rinehart and Winston, 1965.

———. *Complete Book of the American Musical Theatre*. Rev. ed. New York: Henry Holt, 1959.

———. *George Gershwin: His Journey to Greatness*. Englewood Cliffs, N.J.: Prentice-Hall, 1970.

———. *Great Men of American Popular Song: The History of the American Popular Song Told through the Lives, Careers, Achievements, and Personalities of Its Foremost Composers and Lyricists—From William Billings of the Revolutionary War through Bob Dylan, Johnny Cash, and Burt Bacharach*. Rev. and enlarged ed. Englewood Cliffs, N.J.: Prentice-Hall, 1972.

———. *A Journey to Greatness: The Life and Music of George Gershwin*. New York: Henry Holt, 1956.

———. *The Life and Death of Tin Pan Alley: The Golden Age of American Popular Music*. New York: Funk and Wagnalls, 1964.

———. *Men of Popular Music*. 1944. Reprint. Freeport, N.Y.: Books for Libraries, 1972.

———. *New Complete Book of the American Musical Theater*. New York: Holt, Rinehart and Winston, 1970.

———. *Richard Rodgers*. New York: Henry Holt, 1957.

———. *The Story of America's Musical Theater*. Philadelphia: Chilton Book, 1961.

———. *The Story of George Gershwin*. New York: Henry Holt, 1943.

———. *The Story of Irving Berlin*. New York: Henry Holt, 1950.

———. *The Story of Jerome Kern*. New York: Henry Holt, 1953.

———. *With a Song in His Heart: The Story of Richard Rodgers*. New York: Holt, Rinehart and Winston, 1963.

———. *The World of Jerome Kern*. New York: Henry Holt, 1960.

Faulkner, Robert R. *Hollywood Studio Musicians: Their Work and Careers in the Recording Industry*. Chicago: Aldine/Atherton, 1971.

Fernett, Gene. *A Thousand Golden Horns . . . The Exciting Age of America's Greatest Dance Bands*. Midland, Mich.: Pendell, 1966.

Filmmusic Notebook. Los Angeles, 1974- .

Film Music Notes. (Later *Film Music* and *Film & TV Music*.) Hollywood (later New York), 1941-1957.

Flower, John. *Moonlight Serenade: A Bio-Discography of the Glenn Miller Civilian Band*. New Rochelle, N.Y.: Arlington House, 1972.

Foort, Reginald. *The Cinema Organ: A Description in Non-Technical Language of a Fascinating Instrument and How It Is Played*. London: Sir I. Pitman and Sons, 1932.

_____. 2d ed. Vestal, N.Y.: Vestal Press, 1970.

Fordin, Hugh. *Getting to Know Him: A Biography of Oscar Hammerstein II.* New York: Random House, 1977.

_____. *The World of Entertainment! Hollywood's Greatest Musicals.* Garden City, N.Y.: Doubleday, 1975.

40 Years of Show Tunes: The Big Broadway Hits from 1917-1957. New York: ASCAP, 1958.

Frank, Alan. *Sinatra.* London: Hamlyn, 1978.

Freedland, Michael. *Irving Berlin.* New York: Stein and Day, 1974.

_____. *Jerome Kern.* New York: Stein and Day, 1978.

_____. *Jolson.* New York: Stein and Day, 1972.

_____. *Sophie: The Sophie Tucker Story.* London: Woburn Press, 1978.

Freeman, Larry. *The Melodies Linger On: 50 Years of Popular Song.* Watkins Glen, N.Y.: Century House, 1951.

Gershwin, Ira. *Lyrics on Several Occasions: A Selection of Stage and Screen Lyrics Written for Sundry Situations; and Now Arranged in Arbitrary Categories. To Which Have Been Added Many Informative Annotations and Disquisitions on Their Why and Wherefore, Their Whom-for, Their How; and Matters Associative.* 1959. Reprint. New York: Viking Press, 1973.

Goldberg, Isaac. *George Gershwin: A Study in American Music.* New York: Simon and Schuster, 1931.

_____. *Tin Pan Alley: A Chronicle of American Popular Music, with a supplement "From Sweet and Swing to Rock 'n' Roll" by Edward Jablonski.* New York: Frederick Ungar, 1961.

_____. *Tin Pan Alley: A Chronicle of the American Popular Music Racket.* New York: John Day, 1930.

Gottfried, Martin. *Broadway Musicals.* New York: Harry N. Abrams, 1979.

Green, Stanley. *Encyclopedia of the Musical Theatre.* New York: Dodd, Mead, 1976.

_____. *Ring Bells! Sing Songs! Broadway Musicals of the 1930s.* New Rochelle, N.Y.: Arlington House, 1971.

_____. *The Rodgers and Hammerstein Story.* New York: John Day, 1963.

_____. *The World of Musical Comedy: The Story of the American Musical Stage as Told through the Careers of Its Foremost Composers and Lyricists.* 3d ed. Rev. and enlarged. South Brunswick, N.J.: A. S. Barnes, 1974.

_____, ed. *Rodgers and Hammerstein Fact Book: A Record of Their Works Together and with Other Collaborators.* New York: Lynn Farnol Group, 1980.

Greene, Myrna. *The Eddie Fisher Story.* Middlebury, Vt.: Paul S. Eriksson, 1978.

Hammerstein, Oscar. *Lyrics.* New York: Simon and Schuster, 1949.

Harris, Charles K. *After the Ball: Forty Years of Melody.* New York: Frank-Maurice, 1926.

Hart, Dorothy, ed. *Thou Swell, Thou Witty: The Life and Lyrics of Lorenz Hart.* New York: Harper and Row, 1976.

Herman, Pinky. *Showbiz and "me."* Lauderdale Lakes, Fla.: Manor Music Book, 1977.

Herndon, Booton. *The Sweetest Music This Side of Heaven: The Guy Lombardo Story.* New York: McGraw-Hill, 1964.

Hirschhorn, Clive. *The Hollywood Musical.* New York: Crown Publishers, 1981.

Hodgins, Gordon W. *The Broadway Musical: A Complete LP Discography.* Metuchen, N.J.: Scarecrow Press, 1980.

Hofmann, Charles. *Sounds for Silents.* New York: Drama Book Specialists, 1970.

Horne, Lena, and Schickel, Richard. *Lena.* Garden City, N.Y.: Doubleday, 1965.

Hubler, Richard G. *The Cole Porter Story as Told to Richard G. Hubler.* Cleveland, Ohio: World Publishing, 1965.

Jablonski, Edward. *Harold Arlen: Happy with the Blues.* Garden City, N.Y.: Doubleday, 1961.

_____, and Stewart, Lawrence D. *The Gershwin Years.* 1958. Rev. ed. Garden City, N.Y.: Doubleday, 1973.

Jackson, Arthur. *The Best Musicals: From Show Boat to A Chorus Line, Broadway—Off-Broadway—London.* New York: Crown Publishers, 1977.

_____. *The World of Big Bands: The Sweet and Swinging Years.* New York: Arco Publishing, 1977.

Jenkinson, Philip, and Warner, Alan. *Celluloid Rock: Twenty Years of Movie Rock.* London: Lorrimer Publishing, 1974.

Jolson, Harry, as told to Alban Emley. *Mistah Jolson.* Hollywood: House-Warven, 1951.

Jolson Journal. Brownsburg, Quebec. No. 46, 1973.

Kahn, E. J., Jr. *The Voice: The Story of an American Phenomenon.* New York: Harper and Brothers, 1947.

Karlin, Fred J. *Edison Diamond Discs 50001-52651, 1912-1929,* vol. 1. Santa Monica, Calif.: Bona Fide Publishing, 1972.

Kimball, Robert, ed. *Cole* [with] *a Biographical Essay by Brendan Gill.* New York: Holt, Rinehart and Winston, 1971.

_____. *The Unpublished Cole Porter.* New York: Simon and Schuster, 1975.

_____, and Simon, Alfred. *The Gershwins.* New York: Atheneum, 1973.

Kislan, Richard. *The Musical: A Look at the American Musical Theater.* Englewood Cliffs, N.J.: Prentice-Hall, 1980.

Kitt, Eartha. *Alone with Me: A New Autobiography.* Chicago: Henry Regnery, 1976.

_____. *Thursday's Child.* New York: Duell, Sloan and Pearce, 1956.

Kobal, John. *Gotta Sing, Gotta Dance: A Pictorial History of Film Musicals.* London: Hamlyn, 1971.

Kreuger, Miles, ed. *The Movie Musical from Vitaphone to 42nd Street: As Reported in a Great Fan Magazine.* New York: Dover Publications, 1975.

_____. *Show Boat: The Story of a Classic American Musical.* New York: Oxford University Press, 1977.

Lang, Edith, and West, George. *Musical Accompaniment of Moving Pictures: A Practical Manual for Pianists and Organists and an Exposition of the Principles Underlying the Musical Interpretation of Moving Pictures.* 1920. Reprint. New York: Arno Press, 1970.

La Prade, Ernest. *Broadcasting Music.* New York: Rinehart and Co., 1947.

Laufe, Abe. *Broadway's Greatest Musicals.* New York: Funk and Wagnalls, 1973.

Lerner, Alan Jay. *The Street Where I Live.* New York: W. W. Norton, 1978.

Lewine, Richard, and Simon, Alfred. *Encyclopedia of Theatre Music: A Comprehensive Listing of More Than 4000 Songs from Broadway and Hollywood: 1900-1960.* New York: Random House, 1961.

_____. *Songs of the American Theater: A Comprehensive Listing of More Than 12,000 Songs, Including Selected Titles from Film and Television Productions.* New York: Dodd, Mead, 1973.

Lichter, Paul. *Elvis in Hollywood.* New York: Simon and Schuster, 1975.

Limbacher, James L., comp. and ed. *Feature Films on 8 mm and 16 mm.* New York: R. R. Bowker, 1977.

_____. *Film Music: From Violins to Video.* Metuchen, N.J.: Scarecrow Press, 1974.

_____. *Keeping Score: Film Music 1972-1979.* Metuchen, N.J.: Scarecrow Press, 1981.

_____, ed. *The Song List: A Guide to Contemporary Music from Classical Sources.* Ann Arbor, Mich.: Pierian Press, 1973.

Lombardo, Guy, with Jack Altshul. *Auld Acquaintance.* Garden City, N.Y.: Doubleday, 1975.

London, Kurt. *Film Music: A Summary of the Characteristic Features of Its History, Aesthetics, Techniques; and Possible Developments.* Trans. Eric S. Bensinger. 1936. Reprint. New York: Arno Press, 1970.

Lonstein, Albert I., and Marion, Vito R. *The Revised Compleat Sinatra: Discography, Filmography, Television Appearances, Motion Picture Appearances, Radio Appearances, Concert Appearances, Stage Appearances.* Ellenville, N.Y.: Sondra M. Lonstein, 1979.

Lopez, Vincent. *Lopez Speaking: An Autobiography.* New York: Citadel Press, 1960.

Lustig, Milton. *Music Editing for Motion Pictures.* New York: Communication Arts Books/Hastings House, 1980.

McCarthy, Albert. *The Dance Band Era: The Dancing Decades from Ragtime to Swing, 1910-1950.* Philadelphia: Chilton Book, 1971.

McCarty, Clifford. *Film Composers in America: A Checklist of Their Work.* 1953. Reprint. New York: Da Capo, 1972.

McVay, Douglas. *The Musical Film.* International Film Guide Series. London: A. Zwemmer, 1967.

Manvell, Roger, and Huntley, John. *The Technique of Film Music.* 1957. Rev. and enlarged by Richard Arnell and Peter Day. New York: Hastings House, 1975.

Marcuse, Maxwell F. *Tin Pan Alley in Gaslight: A Saga of the Songs That Made the Gray Nineties "Gay."* Watkins Glen, N.Y.: Century House, 1959.

Marks, Edward B., as told to Abbott J. Liebling. *They All Sang: From Tony Pastor to Rudy Vallée.* New York: Viking Press, 1934.

Martin, Mary. *My Heart Belongs.* New York: William Morrow, 1976.

Marx, Samuel, and Clayton, Jan. *Rodgers and Hart: Bewitched, Bothered and Bedevilled. An Anecdotal Account.* New York: G. P. Putnam's Sons, 1976.

Maxwell, Gilbert. *Helen Morgan: Her Life and Legend.* New York: Hawthorn Books, 1974.

Merman, Ethel, with George Eells. *Merman.* New York: Simon and Schuster, 1978.

_____, as told to Pete Martin. *Who Could Ask for Anything More.* Garden City, N.Y.: Doubleday, 1955.

Midler, Bette. *A View from a Broad*. New York: Fireside Book/Simon and Schuster, 1980.

Montgomery, Elizabeth Rider. *The Story behind Popular Songs*. New York: Dodd, Mead, 1958.

Mordden, Ethan. *Better Foot Forward: The History of American Musical Theatre*. New York: Grossman Publishers, 1976.

Nolan, Frederick. *The Sound of Their Music: The Story of Rodgers and Hammerstein*. London: J. M. Dent and Sons, 1978.

Oberfirst, Robert. *Al Jolson: You Ain't Heard Nothin' Yet*. San Diego: A. S. Barnes, 1980.

Our Kate: Honoring Kate Smith, America's First Lady of Song. Scotia, N.Y., 1968- .

Paris, Leonard A. *Men and Melodies*. Rev. ed. New York: Thomas Y. Crowell, 1959.

Parr, A. H. *The Lennon Sisters: Sweethearts of Song*. Garden City, N.Y.: Doubleday, 1960.

Perfectly Frank. London. No. 126, 1973.

Pitts, Michael R., and Harrison, Louis H. *Hollywood on Record: The Film Stars' Discography*. Metuchen, N.J.: Scarecrow Press, 1978.

Prendergast, Roy M. *A Neglected Art: A Critical Study of Music in Films*. New York: New York University Press, 1977.

Richards, Stanley, ed. *Great Musicals of the American Theatre*, vol. 2. Radnor, Pa.: Chilton Book, 1976.

_____. *Great Rock Musicals*. New York: Stein and Day, 1979.

_____. *Ten Great Musicals of the American Theatre*. Radnor, Pa.: Chilton Book, 1973.

Rodgers, Richard. *Musical Stages: An Autobiography*. New York: Random House, 1975.

Rust, Brian. *The American Dance Band Discography 1917-1942*. 2 vols. New Rochelle, N.Y.: Arlington House, 1975.

_____. *The Dance Bands*. New Rochelle, N.Y.: Arlington House, 1974.

_____, with Allen G. Debus. *The Complete Entertainment Discography from the mid-1890s to 1942*. New Rochelle, N.Y.: Arlington House, 1973.

Salem, James M. *A Guide to Critical Reviews: The Musical, 1909-1974*, part 2. 2d ed. Metuchen, N.J.: Scarecrow Press, 1976.

Sampson, Henry T. *Blacks in Blackface: A Source Book on Early Black Musical Shows*. Metuchen, N.J.: Scarecrow Press, 1980.

Sanders, Ronald. *The Days Grow Short: The Life and Music of Kurt Weill*. New York: Holt, Rinehart and Winston, 1980.

Sanford, Herb. *Tommy and Jimmy: The Dorsey Years*. 1972. Reprint. New York: Da Capo Press, 1980.

Schwartz, Charles. *Cole Porter: A Biography*. New York: Dial Press, 1977.

_____. *George Gershwin. A Selective Bibliography and Discography*. Bibliographies in American Music 1. Detroit: Information Coordinators, 1974.

_____. *Gershwin: His Life and Music*. Indianapolis: Bobbs-Merrill, 1973.

Sears, Richard S. *V-Discs: A History and Discography*. Westport, Conn.: Greenwood Press, 1980.

Shaw, Arnold. *Sinatra: Twentieth-Century Romantic*. New York: Holt, Rinehart and Winston, 1968.

Shepherd, Donald, and Slatzer, Robert F. *Bing Crosby: The Hollow Man.* New York: St. Martin's Press, 1981.

Short, Bobby. *Black and White Baby.* New York: Dodd, Mead, 1971.

Sieben, Pearl. *The Immortal Jolson: His Life and Times.* New York: Frederick Fell, 1962.

Simon, George T. *The Big Bands.* Rev. ed. New York: Macmillan, 1974.

_____. *Glenn Miller and His Orchestra.* New York: Thomas Y. Crowell, 1974.

_____. *Simon Says: The Sights and Sounds of the Swing Era, 1935-1955.* New Rochelle, N.Y.: Arlington House, 1971.

Smith, Cecil. *Musical Comedy in America.* New York: Theatre Arts Books/Robert M. MacGregor, 1950.

Smith, Kate. *Living in a Great Big Way.* New York: Blue Ribbon Books, 1938.

_____. *Upon My Lips a Song.* New York: Funk and Wagnalls, 1960.

Smolian, Steven, comp. *A Handbook of Film, Theatre, and Television Music on Record, 1948-1969.* 2 vols. New York: Record Undertaker, 1970.

Spaeth, Sigmund. *The Facts of Life in Popular Song.* New York: Whittlesey House/ McGraw-Hill, 1934.

Stein, Harry. *Tiny Tim.* Chicago: Playboy Press, 1976.

Stewart, Lawrence D. *The Gershwins: Words upon Music.* N.p.: Verve Records, 1959.

Taylor, Deems. *Some Enchanted Evenings: The Story of Rodgers and Hammerstein.* 1953. Reprint. Westport, Conn.: Greenwood Press, 1972.

Taylor, John Russell, and Jackson, Arthur. *The Hollywood Musical.* New York: McGraw-Hill, 1971.

Taylor, Theodore. *Jule: The Story of Composer Jule Styne.* New York: Random House, 1979.

Thomas, Bob. *The One and Only Bing.* New York: Grosset and Dunlap, 1977.

Thomas, Lawrence B. *The MGM Years.* New York: Columbia House, 1972.

Thomas, Tony, ed. *Film Score: The View from the Podium.* South Brunswick, N.J.: A. S. Barnes, 1979.

_____. *Harry Warren and the Hollywood Musical.* Secaucus, N.J.: Citadel Press, 1975.

_____. *Music for the Movies.* South Brunswick, N.J.: A. S. Barnes, 1973.

Tomlin, Pinky, with Lynette Wert. *The Object of My Affection: An Autobiography.* Norman: University of Oklahoma Press, 1981.

Tucker, Sophie, with Dorothy Giles. *Some of These Days: The Autobiography of Sophie Tucker.* Garden City, N.Y.: Doubleday, 1945.

Tudor, Dean, and Tudor, Nancy. *Contemporary Popular Music.* American Popular Music on Elpee. Littleton, Colo.: Libraries Unlimited, 1979.

Tumbusch, Tom. *The Theatre Student Guide to Broadway Musical Theatre.* New York: Richards Rosen Press, 1972.

Ulanov, Barry. *The Incredible Crosby.* New York: Whittlesey House/McGraw-Hill, 1948.

Vallée, Rudy. *Let the Chips Fall . . .* Harrisburg, Pa.: Stackpole Books, 1975.

_____. *Vagabond Dreams Come True.* New York: Grosset and Dunlap, 1930.

_____, with Gil McKean. *My Time Is Your Time: The Story of Rudy Vallée.* New York: Ivan Obolensky, 1962.

Vinton, Bobby. *The Polish Prince.* New York: M. Evans, 1978.

Walker, Leo. *The Big Band Almanac.* Pasadena, Calif.: Ward Ritchie Press, n.d.

_____. *The Wonderful Era of the Great Dance Bands*. Berkeley, Calif.: Howell-North Books, 1964.

Welk, Lawrence, with Bernice McGeehan. *Ah-One, Ah-Two! Life with My Musical Family*. Englewood Cliffs, N.J.: Prentice-Hall, 1974.

_____. *Lawrence Welk's Musical Family Album*. Englewood Cliffs, N.J.: Prentice-Hall, 1977.

_____. *My America, Your America*. Englewood Cliffs, N.J.: Prentice-Hall, 1976.

_____. *This I Believe*. Englewood Cliffs, N.J.: Prentice-Hall, 1979.

_____. *Wunnerful, Wunnerful! The Autobiography of Lawrence Welk*. Englewood Cliffs, N.J.: Prentice-Hall, 1971.

Wilder, Alec. *American Popular Song: The Great Innovators, 1900-1950*. Ed. James T. Maher. New York: Oxford University Press, 1972.

Wilk, Max, ed. *Memory Lane: The Golden Age of American Popular Music, 1890 to 1925*. 1973. Reprint. New York: Ballantine Books, 1976.

_____. *They're Playing Our Song: From Jerome Kern to Stephen Sondheim—The Stories behind the Words and Music of Two Generations*. New York: Atheneum, 1973.

Williams, John R. *This Was "Your Hit Parade."* Camden, Maine: John R. Williams, 1973.

Wilson, Earl. *Sinatra: An Unauthorized Biography*. New York: Macmillan, 1976.

Witmark, Isidore, and Goldberg, Isaac. *The Story of the House of Witmark: From Ragtime to Swingtime*. 1939. Reprint. New York: Da Capo, 1976.

Wodehouse, P. G., and Bolton, Guy. *Bring on the Girls! The Improbable Story of Our Life in Musical Comedy, with Pictures to Prove It*. New York: Simon and Schuster, 1953.

Woll, Allen L. *Songs from Hollywood Musical Comedies, 1927 to the Present: A Dictionary*. New York: Garland Publishing, 1976.

Woolcott, Alexander. *The Story of Irving Berlin*. New York: G. P. Putnam's Sons, 1925.

Zadan, Craig. *Sondheim and Co*. New York: Macmillan, 1974.

Zimmer, Norma. *Norma*. Wheaton, Ill.: Tyndale House Publishers, 1976.

Zmijewsky, Steven, and Zmijewsky, Boris. *Elvis: The Films and Career of Elvis Presley*. Secaucus, N.J.: Citadel Press, 1976.

CHAPTER *4*

The Blues and Black Popular Music

The Afro-American quality that has imbued almost all American popular music, joining English, German, Jewish, Irish, Latin, and several other vital infusions in many generations of recombinations from Stephen Foster to disco, has flowed in a continuous but diverse stream of music of the black American community itself. It is a folk music belonging to black Americans and a popular music made by black artists to entertain black Americans, especially as they found themselves collecting in cities. Secular and sacred folk music moved from country to city and onto records. Country blues became city blues; spirituals gave rise to something called *gospel*. Both went into the making of *rhythm and blues* and successor forms of black pop, some of them called *soul*. The diversity of these forms makes it convenient to treat them in this chapter in the following short sections; within each section the order of reference materials mentioned will be the order followed in other full chapters: first bibliography and discography, then general reference, then biography, and history and commentary. More general works on black music have been grouped in a portion of chapter 1, section C. Ragtime and jazz are treated in chapter 5.

I. ORIGINS

The beginnings of Afro-American music lie in slave culture, and the roots of slave culture were in various African tribal cultures as they existed in the years when the slaves were taken to the New World. Two books have been written, both by established scholars of the blues, seeking to trace surviving examples of the music as it must have existed in those cultures. Paul Oliver's *Savannah Syncopators: African Retentions in the Blues* is a short, illustrated survey of what is known on the subject and of Oliver's own trip to Ghana, outlining questions and evidence about the link between African traditional forms and American blues. Oliver provides notes, a record list, a glossary, and an index of tribes and peoples. A decade later in 1981, Samuel Charters published *The Roots of the Blues: An African Search,* recording his investigative journey through West Africa. Charters' account remains inconclusive about actual origins of the blues, but it is informative and reflective about traditional solo singing and playing and the part such performance has in those cultures that can now be observed.

Afro-American music as it existed among the slaves themselves—already a mixture and no longer purely African, though full of the memory of that past—can be glimpsed in a gathering of *Slave Songs of the United States* made in 1867 by William Francis Allen, Charles Pickard Ware, and Lucy McKim Garrison. This vital document for the history of black music contains songs, mostly transcribed by the editors from singing heard on southern plantations. The transcriptions are spare by modern folkloristic standards; some further sense of the music can be gleaned from the editorial comments printed with them. More than half a century later, Henry Edward Krehbiel published *Afro-American Folksongs: A Study in Racial and National Music.* His pioneering book of musical analysis printed words and music of many songs and investigated the music in terms of western musicology—modes, scales, rhythms—and uses of the music, with some attention also paid to the verses. Miles Mark Fisher's *Negro Slave Songs in the United States* (1953) is a black scholar's study of the mind and life of slave men and women through analysis of the words of their songs. *Negro Folk Music, U.S.A.* by Harold Courlander is a survey, analysis, and anthology. In chapters on various musical forms, Courlander quotes many sets of verses and prints occasional music. A last section prints another fifty pages of music in simple transcription. There are notes, bibliography, and discography. Dena J. Epstein's *Sinful Tunes and Spirituals: Black Folk Music to the Civil War* is the most recent major study, a scholarly assemblage and analysis of the evidence about the place music had in slave society and its acculturation through the nineteenth century. The book gives detailed attention to the various instruments, occasions, and forms of the music. Part 3 studies white awareness of black music during the Civil War. The bibliography is extensive; illustrations include engravings of old sheet music and book pages, as well as photographs.

Frederic Ramsey, Jr.'s *Been Here and Gone* is an exercise in what might be called photographic archaeology, a photograph album with commentary of the author's journeys through the south in the early 1950s in search of traces of black musical culture of the past.

(Several books also relevant to this section are described in chapter 1.)

II. BLUES

There is some difficulty in drawing the line between blues as folk music and blues as commercial entertainment; blues as the voice of a people or as a performance; as southern or northern; as rural or urban. The vitality of the popular music called blues derives from its immediate contact and sometimes its complete identity with the music of obscure and scattered local blues makers. Bessie Smith sang blues with bands in northeastern cities and recorded extensively in the early 1920s; blues revival enthusiasts were still finding aging practitioners of the folk blues four decades later (see, for example, Oster's *Living Country Blues,* in section IID, below). The following survey of writings about the blues will span the whole of blues from folk song to the borders of rock 'n' roll.

IIA. BLUES BIBLIOGRAPHY AND DISCOGRAPHY

For blues bibliography see the books by De Lerma and Skowronski under "Black Traditions" in chapter 1. The chronicle of the recording of the blues is divided between two books. *Blues and Gospel Records, 1902-1942* compiled by John Godrich and Robert M. W. Dixon is a huge, 912-page discography with occasional annotations. *Blues Records: January, 1943 to December, 1966* by two young English hobbyists, Mike Leadbitter and Neil Slaven, is more selective. It drops the coverage of gospel and also excludes city blues. The Tudors' *Black Music* evaluative discography volume covers blues as well as rhythm and blues, gospel, soul, and reggae. Godrich and Dixon have written *Recording the Blues,* a brief, illustrated history from 1920 to 1945 of singers and companies producing the early blues records.

IIB. BLUES GENERAL REFERENCE

The richest single reference source on blues is *Blues Who's Who: A Biographical Dictionary of Blues Singers* by Sheldon Harris. This large and highly detailed encyclopedia of blues singers packs notes of the life, known performing appearances, artists influencing and influenced, and source references for each singer into telegraphic data entries—that is, even in nearly 800 large pages it is a concentrated file of facts that might make many volumes in the press format of most biographical reference works. Many photographs are included. Each entry has, when relevant, a bibliography, but appendixes give a selected common bibliography along with a record company directory, a film list, radio and television program lists, theater appearance list, and an index of sixty-eight hundred songs of the singers, as well as a thorough general index. Some students will find also Karel Bogaert's *Blues Lexicon: Blues, Cajun, Boogie Woogie, Gospel,* but fewer will be able to make full use of this Flemish-language book; still, some of its data can be puzzled out even by the American not familiar with Flemish or its close cognate languages. As in some other titles of European reference books, "lexicon" here does not mean a wordbook but rather a biographical reference work. Bogaert includes blues artists and also some jazz, rock, and other near-blues performers, with discographies.

A striking anthology is Eric Sackheim's *The Blues Line: A Collection of Blues Lyrics,* an imaginative and luxurious book printed in Japan. The 270 transcribed texts of country blues and a few city blues are presented sparely on large pages with a layout of print that attempts to convey something of the rhythm and emphasis of the performance. The book also presents sketch portraits of the singers by Jonathan Shahn and a fifty-page anthology of passages from world literature as comparative commentary on the blues. Harry Oster's *Living Country Blues,* containing 230 folk blues lyrics, is listed below in section IID.

A curious special reference source is Eric Townley's *Tell Your Story: A Dictionary of Jazz and Blues Recordings, 1917-1950,* an explanatory dictionary of the expressive *titles* of twenty-seven hundred recordings.

IIC. BLUES BIOGRAPHY

Collective biography is best represented by *Blues Who's Who* described in the preceding section. Several books gather profiles of small selections of blues artists. Paul Oliver's *Conversation with the Blues* consists of interviews with sixty-eight blues singers, with capsule biographies gathered separately at the end. The interviews were taped in 1960, and a selection from them is available on record. Robert Neff and Anthony Connor's *Blues* is a skein of interwoven interviews with fifty-five blues performers in 1973 and 1974. There are photographs, and bare data on each are given in a listing at the back. Hettie Jones' *Big Star Fallin' Mama: Five Women in Black Music* reaches from blues to soul in brief, illustrated biographies of Ma Rainey, Bessie Smith, Mahalia Jackson, Billie Holiday, and Aretha Franklin. Samuel Charters' *The Legacy of the Blues . . . Twelve Great Bluesmen* profiles Big Joe Williams, J. D. Short, Bukka White, Snooks Eaglin, Champion Jack Dupree, Mighty Joe Young, Lightnin' Hopkins, Memphis Slim, Robert Pete Williams, Juke Boy Bonner, Sunnyland Slim, and Eddie Boyd. A middle chapter examines the language and the poetics of blues lyrics, and another prints the words of sixteen songs by these singers.

Leonard "Baby Doo" Caston, a blues pianist, appears in a pamphlet of interview recollections edited by Jeff Todd Titon called *From Blues to Pop.* Titon also prints brief musical transcriptions and four photographs.

W. C. Handy was the first musician to publish a significant amount of blues material—he is most famous for "St. Louis Blues." His autobiography, *Father of the Blues,* came out in 1941 and has been reprinted. It tells the story of his career as a prejazz cornet player, leader of a syncopated band, and music publisher, and it also prints music for a few of his pieces and lyrics of others. A list of his works is included in an appendix.

Billie Holiday's *Lady Sings the Blues* is the blunt and bitter telling of the difficult life of a great blues singer. She is also portrayed in a chapter of Hettie Jones' *Big Star Fallin' Mama,* mentioned above.

Tommy Johnson by David Evans is one of the series of short books on blues artists and schools published by Studio Vista in London. Johnson, who died in 1956, was a Mississippi guitarist and singer. Evans includes photographs, some lyrics, and a list of reissued records.

The Arrival of B. B. King: The Authorized Biography by Charles Sawyer is a full-scale story and study of King, whose popular success has been so broad that he now appears on billboards advertising a food store chain. Sawyer undertakes a "social rather than musical" biography, though he includes a chapter on King's style and an appendix analyzing a guitar solo. The book is documented with economic data on sharecropping and an essay on the historiography of oral history. There are many photographs and a full annotated discography. See also the chapter on King in Keil's *Urban Blues* in section IID, below.

Little Brother Montgomery, a blues pianist, collaborated with Karl Gert zur Heide on another of the Studio Vista booklets called *Deep South Piano:*

The Story of Little Brother Montgomery. A sketchy narrative covers the 1920s and 1930s around the south and up to Chicago, mentioning other artists that Montgomery encountered—those people mentioned are given data entries at the end. There are photographs of people and places and the words to twenty-four blues songs.

Charley Patton is a Studio Vista book by John Fahey, himself a popular guitarist, about an influential Mississippi blues guitarist of the 1920s and early 1930s. Fahey gives a short biography and extended analysis of the music and words of Patton's blues. Tunes are transcribed, and there are discography and bibliography.

Ma Rainey and the Classic Blues Singers by Derrick Stewart-Baxter, in the same series, is another brief, illustrated history. Like the piano book, it covers several figures: the classic singers of the title include Mamie Smith, Lucille Hegamin, Edith Wilson, Bessie Smith, Ida Cox, Victoria Spivey, Clara Smith, Sippie Wallace, Bertha Hill, Maggie Jones, and Alberta Hunter. On these figures, consult also Harris' *Blues Who's Who* in section IIB, above. Ma Rainey has one of the chapters in Jones' *Big Star Fallin' Mama* as well.

Bessie Smith appears in all three of those books and in others where she is the whole subject. *Bessie,* by Chris Albertson, is carefully researched from interviews and other primary sources and includes a selective discography of Bessie Smith and other women blues singers. Albertson's *Bessie Smith: Empress of the Blues* is a separate book, a songbook of transcriptions from her singing prefaced by a sketch of her life, a collection of pictures, and an essay "Bessie's Singing Style" by musician and musicologist Gunther Schuller. The empress of the blues also appears among the Kings of Jazz, another profile series, in a short *Bessie Smith* by Paul Oliver.

Muddy Waters, an electric bluesman who has achieved widespread popular recognition, is given half of James Rooney's *Bossmen: Bill Monroe and Muddy Waters,* which claims for him a standing in his kind of blues equal to that of Monroe in bluegrass. See also the chapters on Waters in Peter Guralnick's *Feel Like Going Home* and Robert Palmer's *Deep Blues* in section IID, below.

Peetie Wheatstraw was a guitar and piano bluesman who died in 1941; he had been a popular and influential figure in the 1930s. *The Devil's Son-in-Law* by Paul Garon is a Studio Vista biography, gleaned from scanty materials, giving an account of the St. Louis and Chicago blues ambience of the time and an interpretive discussion of Wheatstraw's songs, many of which are printed.

IID. BLUES HISTORY AND COMMENTARY

The first history of the Mississippi, Alabama, and Texas country blues as they are preserved in commercial recordings was *The Country Blues* by Samuel Charters (1959). Charters combines biographies of the singers with passages from the song lyrics and history of the recording business that distributed their records to southern black listeners beginning in the early 1920s. Appendixes give information on records and reissues. A corrected version was published in 1967 as *The Bluesmen;* a successor volume with a different regional focus is listed below. Giles Oakley's *The Devil's Music: A History of the Blues* is a survey history with many striking photographs of singers and of the life behind their music, with quoted lyrics, notes, and selected discography. Paul Oliver's *The Story of the Blues* is a large-format illustrated paperback history, from an exhibition the author assembled for the U.S. Information Service. Pictures from Oliver's own collection and from other sources support a historical text covering origins and periods; at the end are ten transcribed musical examples, bibliography, and discography. Albert Murray's *Stomping the Blues* is a scrapbook history of blues and a good deal of jazz.

Regional varieties of the blues have some separate histories. William Ferris, Jr., has written two versions of a book called *Blues from the Delta.* The first (1970) was in the Studio Vista series, a brief folkloric study of the culture of the Mississippi delta country artists and an analysis of their lyrics, including an interesting transcript of a field recording session, photographs, and source notes, all grounded in the author's folklore doctoral dissertation. A later version (1978) with the same title is twice as long, with fifteen short topical chapters, a long transcription of a talking and singing house party, and some reproduced letters from the singers. The expanded appendix data now include a filmography.

Memphis Blues and Jug Bands by Bengt Olsson (also Studio Vista) is a brief and avowedly incomplete illustrated survey of performers in the Memphis tradition. Sixteen lyrics are transcribed. Memphis blues have an extended study in *Beale Black and Blue: Life and Music on Black America's Main Street* by Margaret McKee and Fred Chisenhall, a journalistic and oral-historical study of that city's blues musicians, supported by an attempt to reconstruct the history of their community from the few surviving documents. Eleven biographical chapters profile such singers as Furry Lewis, Booker "Bukka" White, and Lillie Mae Glover, up to the urban and pop successes of Bobby Blue Bland and B. B. King (these last treated briefly).

Louisiana blues are the *Living Country Blues* in Harry Oster's book, a large, annotated anthology of 230 folk blues lyrics collected by the author in Louisiana between 1955 and 1961, many in the state penitentiary. Introductory essays analyze setting, history, themes and function, and poetics. There is a section of photographs, bibliography, and a discography of performances, many on the Folk-Lyric label produced by Oster himself.

Eastern blues are the subject of Bruce Bastin's *Crying for the Carolines,* a Studio Vista history of the blues of the piedmont region centered in north Georgia and South and North Carolina. The survey begins with Blind Boy Fuller in the 1930s and touches his contemporaries and successors city by city, with references. A sequel to Samuel Charters' *Bluesmen* is *Sweet as the*

Showers of Rain: The Bluesmen, volume 2, devoted to blues of the Atlantic coast region, Georgia, and Tennessee in the 1930s, with history, interviews, and some lyrics and music.

Blues criticism and interpretive analysis—social, musical, and literary— have produced a variety of thoughtful books that can be grouped here although they often overlap the concerns of the more historically intended works just mentioned.

Big Road Blues: Tradition and Creativity in the Folk Blues, by David Evans, is a painstaking literary-folkloric study of the folk blues centering on the tradition of singers in and around the town of Drew in the delta region of Mississippi, which includes Tommy Johnson, Charley Patton, and Howlin' Wolf, along with many singers unknown to the outside world. In particular, Evans studies the way blues "songs" shift and change in creative recomposition from singer to singer and from performance to performance. He gives musical or textual transcriptions for eighty examples; the book has full scholarly apparatus and numerous photographs. Jeff Todd Titon's *Early Downhome Blues: A Musical and Cultural Analysis* is another credit- able volume of the scholarly University of Illinois series, Music in American Life. Titon's is a study of the cultural setting of the country blues as they were recorded in the 1920s (part 1), musical and poetic analysis from detailed transcriptions (part 2), and consideration of aspects of the record- ing and marketing of this music (part 3 and appendix A). Photographs and advertisements illustrate, and a record distributed with the book carries the sound itself. Robert Palmer's *Deep Blues* delves into the delta blues through local history and the lives of singers, dwelling especially on Muddy Waters.

The Poetry of the Blues by Samuel Charters is a short book on the mean- ing and techniques of blues verse, about half the text being composed of quotations from blues. *Blues Fell This Morning: The Meaning of the Blues,* by Paul Oliver, studies the content and context of lyrics, quoting 350 examples and sympathetically interpreting them in the light of social fact. Oliver's *Aspects of the Blues Tradition* (originally *Screening the Blues*) is a collection of his studies of the history and evolutionary processes of blues, with some of the pieces reprinted from jazz periodicals. There are some musical examples, but Oliver's main concern is the critical and comparative study of the words. Bruce Cook's *Listen to the Blues* is a first-person jour- nalistic investigation of blues people, their history, and their influence on other American music. More significant investigations are recalled in John A. Lomax's *Adventures of a Ballad Hunter* (1947). Lomax was a great col- lector and editor of several kinds of American folk music. These memoirs tell, with many quotations from the songs, of his early investigation of blues and prison work songs. Paul Garon's *Blues and the Poetic Spirit* analyzes the themes and psychology of blues lyrics from the author's point of view as an adherent of surrealism and a wary critic of "bourgeois-Christian" cul- ture. Charles Keil's *Urban Blues* is a sociological role study of the city blues man, but includes technical description of blues styles, interviews, and some lyrics. There are chapters on B. B. King and Bobby Blue Bland. At the end there is a short essay applying Erik Erikson's identity psychology to blues men, another raising anthropological issues about music analysis, and an "annotated outline" of blues styles. The history to go with this social science is in Mike Rowe's *Chicago Breakdown,* a careful history of Chicago blues from the mid-1930s to about 1970, in the context of population data, pictures of the artists and of the city, and such further exhibits as record labels and death certificates.

The Blues Revival by Bob Groom is another short, illustrated Studio Vista book, this time an account of the 1950s and 1960s with emphasis on the British concert and recording scene.

British enthusiasm for this deeply American music, evidenced throughout this section in scholarly and critical books produced by English writers, shows once more in a general book on *Pop Music and the Blues* by Richard Middleton, a British musician's careful analysis, with sociological perspective as well, of the connection of country and city blues to rock 'n' roll, soul, and early rock (the late 1960s). An American evaluation of these connections is Peter Guralnick's *Feel Like Going Home: Portraits in Blues and Rock 'n' Roll.* Guralnick presents a succession of profiles of blues singers—Muddy Waters, Johnny Shines, Skip James, Robert Pete Williams, Howlin' Wolf—extended by chapters on Sun Records, Jerry Lee Lewis, Charlie Rich, and Chess Records to assert a continuity of the two musics. See also Michael Lydon's *Boogie Lightning* in chapter 1, section D.

Blues Unlimited magazine, published in Britain, is the leading journal of blues. There have been two books published collecting articles from the magazines. Simon A. Napier's *Back Woods Blues* gathers brief biographical, autobiographical, and tribute articles on thirteen artists. A considerably larger set is Mike Leadbitter's *Nothing but the Blues* with much information on dozens of artists, unfortunately without an index or even a table of contents. *Living Blues* is an American quarterly journal, which concentrates its attention on living performers. The power of the voice of the black American blues is testified by the roster of blues magazines scattered across the world: Sheldon Harris lists publications in Japan, Austria, Canada, Finland, the Netherlands, Australia, Germany, France, and Sweden.

III. SPIRITUALS AND GOSPEL

Black spirituals and white spirituals seem to have interchanged much material—which is the main contributor has been vigorously disputed—and there are flourishing separate black and white gospel musics derived from them, which have evolved in the direction of professional entertainment for audiences with certain religious-cultural interests. Each is called just "gospel" by its people, but white gospel is close to modern country music and will be surveyed in chapter 6. The black gospel tradition and its antecedent spirituals are the business of this section.

Blues and Gospel Records, 1902-1942 by Godrich and Dixon is mentioned above as the blues discography for that period. The book that takes up the blues listing after 1942 drops gospel. (See Tudor and Tudor, *Black Music,* for currently available recordings.) A catalog of the composed music itself, as opposed to a discography of the recordings of such music, exists along with a bibliography of materials about it in Irene V. Jackson's *Afro-American Religious Music,* an 873-item list of books and articles and a similar-sized list, by composer, of gospel music from 1938 to 1965.

Biographies of gospel performers can be found in Tony Heilbut's *The Gospel Sound: Good News and Bad Times.* Heilbut has chapters on principal performers, including Sallie Martin, Thomas A. Dorsey, Ira Tucker, Mahalia Jackson, and others, along with a historical introduction, photographs, and selected discography. There are separate books by and about two stars of the popular performance of older spirituals. Mahalia Jackson wrote *Movin' on Up* in 1966, telling her own story. In 1975 Laurraine Goreau published *Just Mahalia, Baby,* a widely researched but unfootnoted large biography, written after Jackson's death but using interviews and materials Jackson had supplied. Jackson has a chapter in *Big Star Fallin' Mama* (section IIC, above). Ethel Waters wrote *His Eye Is on the Sparrow: An Autobiography* in 1951, with the title of the spiritual that had become her signature performance, tracing her story up to her Broadway appearance in the play *A Member of the Wedding* in 1949. In 1972 she published *To Me It's Wonderful,* reminiscences with emphasis on her religious crisis at about the time of the earlier book and her subsequent work with the Billy Graham crusades. A career summary and partial discography are included. Twila Knaack's *Ethel Waters: I Touched a Sparrow* is an account by one who shared those Billy Graham tours in the last two decades of her life. Juliann De Korte's *Ethel Waters: Finally Home* is a brief memoir by a companion who nursed her in her last illness.

History and commentary are found in *Black Song: The Forge and the Flame. The Story of How the Afro-American Spiritual Was Hammered Out* by John Lovell, Jr., a large-scale scholarly study of the development, functions, content, and influence of the spirituals, arguing for their autonomy from other hymn traditions. Apparatus includes a useful analytic table of contents and an index to the five hundred songs cited in the text. Wyatt Tee Walker's *"Somebody's Calling My Name": Black Sacred Music and Social Change* treats more music somewhat less fully. Walker divides black religious song into a background of slave traditions and the eras of spirituals, meter music, hymns of improvisation, and gospel. He studies the history and provides many passages of text, music, and graphic displays. Walker, a prominent black clergyman, popularized this version from his academic dissertation but retains documentation and bibliography. The particular story of the Fisk University choral group that brought attention and admiration to the spirituals from outside their own congregations is told in an old book by J.B.T. Marsh, *The Story of the Jubilee Singers, with*

Their Songs (1881, now reprinted), in part condensed from earlier histories by the Rev. G. D. Pike; the last third is a hymnal of 112 of the jubilee songs. Christa K. Dixon's *Negro Spirituals: From Bible to Folk Song* is a set of analytic and inspirational essays on the texts of twenty-three spirituals. *The Progress of Gospel Music: From Spirituals to Contemporary Gospel,* by Mancel Warrick and others, is only brief and scattered notes on gospel with some musical examples and suggestions for teachers who wish to introduce the material to school classrooms. James H. Cone's *The Spirituals and the Blues: An Interpretation* is a consideration of spirituals themselves and also of blues as secular spirituals, by a theologian.

IV. RHYTHM AND BLUES

Before, beside, and overlapping the rock 'n' roll music of white American teenagers of the 1950s, there was a style of black singers and vocal groups called *rhythm and blues.* A few loyal fans have made themselves scholars of this music, and although their reference compilations and histories usually treat it together with other related music, those books can be gathered here for their common interest.

Fernando L. Gonzalez has compiled the most recent of three self-published discographies. His is called *Disco-File: The Discographical Catalog of American Rock & Roll and Rhythm & Blues, Vocal Harmony Groups—1902 to 1976: Race, Rhythm & Blues, Rock & Roll, Soul,* and tabulates thirty-one thousand records by artist. Robert D. Ferlingere has compiled *A Discography of Rhythm & Blues and Rock 'n' Roll Vocal Groups, 1945 to 1965,* a large tab-indexed looseleaf catalog, by groups, in about 700 pages citing about twenty thousand songs. Similar but smaller is Albert Leichter's *A Discography of Rhythm & Blues and Rock & Roll, circa 1946-1964: A Reference Manual,* a list by song title, then by artist under each song, in 189 sheets printed on one side; a supplement adds another eighty-seven sheets. See also the record collecting guides by Propes and by Edwards in chapter 7, section A. One of Joel Whitburn's Record Research volumes is *Joel Whitburn's Top Rhythm and Blues Records 1949-1971: Facts about 4,000 Recordings Listed in Billboard's "Best Selling Rhythm and Blues (Soul) Singles" Charts—Grouped under the Names of the 1,200 Recording Artists* (see chapter 1, section B). See also, again, the Tudor's *Black Music* for review-listings of currently available long-playing records.

A large history of the musicians, the music, and the business of rhythm and blues from 1945 to 1960 is Arnold Shaw's *Honkers and Shouters,* which includes many interviews with performers and businessmen and an extensive discography. Philip Groia's *They All Sang on the Corner: New York City's Rhythm & Blues Vocal Groups of the 1950s* is a study from interviews and trade magazines, though oddly Groia admits that it is "in part . . . fictionalized." He includes photographs and several group discographies. John Broven's *Walking to New Orleans: The Story of New Orleans Rhythm & Blues* is a history of performers and the recording business in the city,

1946-1973, illustrated and documented. Important figures covered include Roy Brown, Lloyd Price, Little Richard, Fats Domino, and Professor Longhair, but there is information about many other artists. Bill Millar's *The Drifers* is a history of the vocal group which began in postwar rhythm and blues and also had success and influence in rock 'n' roll through the 1950s, focusing in turn on the various singers making up the group. Lynn Ellis McCutcheon's *Rhythm and Blues: An Experience and Adventure in Its Origin and Development* describes the music and gives a detailed chronicle, divided into pioneer, rock 'n' roll, and soul eras. The accounts of major groups include discographies; two appendixes select singles and albums of special interest, the latter with brief commentary. Lawrence N. Redd's *Rock Is Rhythm and Blues* is a brief history from blues to rock in the first half, and the second half includes interviews with B. B. King, Brownie McGhee, Dave Clark, Arthur Crudup, Jerry Butler, and Jessie Whitaker: rhythm and blues is thus more a reference point than the subject of this book. *The Dave Given Rock 'n' Roll Stars Handbook: Rhythm and Blues Artists and Groups* is a biographical encyclopedia without pictures and with extensive discographies for about fifty acts, predominantly rhythm and blues but also rockabilly, rock, and soul. As with soul artists, there is some rhythm and blues coverage also in other rock histories and encyclopedias (see chapter 7). *Bim Bam Boom: The Magazine Devoted to the History of Rhythm and Blues,* begun in the early 1970s, published articles, discographies, and collector's advice.

V. SOUL

Black popular music in the 1960s and 1970s developed new stars and styles from the gospel, rhythm and blues, and urban blues backgrounds, and the name *soul* that was being applied affirmatively to the essence of black culture and black existence became attached as well to the Detroit, New York, Philadelphia, and other varieties of a new, smoother commercial black music.

The Tudors' *Black Music* has a section of soul discography. The words of current songs have been printed in *Rock and Soul Songs* magazine (see chapter 1), and A. X. Nicholas edited a collection called *The Poetry of Soul* in 1971, transcribing forty-three lyrics mostly from the late 1960s, with discography and brief polemical introduction.

Biographical materials appear in occasional magazine-format fan books of the kind that have also been published for various collections of rock or country stars. Two are *Black Music* (1974) and *The Stars and Superstars of Black Music* (1977), each selecting some two dozen stars of the time. Both of these were published in London. There are short entries in Stambler's *Encyclopedia of Pop, Rock, and Soul,* in Roxon's *Rock Encyclopedia,* and in Nite's *Rock On,* and somewhat fuller ones in Miller's *Rolling Stone Illustrated History of Rock and Roll:* see chapter 1, section B and chapter 7, section C. Donald Bogle's *Brown Sugar: Eighty Years of America's Black*

Female Superstars has quick journalistic chapters, heavily illustrated with publicity shots and film stills, on singers and stage personalities from Bessie Smith to Donna Summer.

Individual black pop stars have been treated in a few separate publications, but none yet has a serious or impressive study.

Aretha Franklin by James T. Olson is one of a large series of brief juvenile biographies with painted graphics, issued by a company called Creative Education in Mankato, Minnesota. The basic story of Franklin or other featured performers may be traced in such a book if nothing better is available. On Franklin, see also the chapter in Jones' *Big Star Fallin' Mama* (above, section IIC).

The Otis Redding Story by Jane Schiesel is likewise aimed at young readers, though slightly more substantial, with an album list at the end.

Stevie Wonder has two mid-career biographies. *The Stevie Wonder Scrapbook* by Jim Haskins is a large-format, illustrated biography; it has a bibliography of published sources. *Stevie Wonder,* assertedly by C. Dragonwagon, is a brief, illustrated paperback; the text is mostly taken up with a detailed, critical chronicle of his records.

Brother Ray: Ray Charles' Own Story, by Charles with collaborator David Ritz, is a casual autobiography for the general reader, reproducing talk. There are photographs and an informal discography.

Histories include *Right On: From Blues to Soul in Black America* by Michael Haralambos, tracing the development of urban electric black music with emphasis on its social environment. *The Soul Book,* edited by Ian Hoare and written by Hoare and three other British collaborators, gives the history from background through Motown and Memphis soul, an analysis of black lyrics, and a brief survey of soul in the early 1970s. The four authors each append a list of twenty favorite records. Phyl Garland's *The Sound of Soul* ventures into blues and jazz to treat B. B. King and John Coltrane as well as Nina Simone, Aretha Franklin, and others. The author is an editor and music critic for *Ebony* magazine, and her mode of writing is that of the magazine, journalism heralding black achievement. Rochelle Larkin's *Soul Music!* is an illustrated paperback survey of stars, music, and business, including chapters on James Brown, Aretha Franklin, Dionne Warwick, Ray Charles, and collective chapters touching many others.

Separate styles of music from Philadelphia and Detroit have separate chronicles. *The Sound of Philadelphia* by Tony Cummings traces strands of popular music in that city up into the soul sound produced there in the early 1970s, with many photographs. *The Story of Motown* by Peter Benjaminson is a corporate biography of Motown ("Motor Town," Detroit), its founder Berry Gordy, and Gordy's personal and corporate families, with many photographs. An appendix gives a Motown hit discography. David Morse's *Motown and the Arrival of Black Music* is a short, popular history with publicity shots of stars. A small chart gives an interesting code of conventions of orchestration and arrangement in the Holland,

Dozier, and Holland songs that have been a mainstay of the company. A British magazine called *Hot Buttered Soul* covers all kinds of black pop, with discographies, interviews, and news of the British music club scene.

BIBLIOGRAPHY

Albertson, Chris. *Bessie.* New York: Stein and Day, 1972.

_____. *Bessie Smith: Empress of the Blues.* New York: Walter Kane and Son, 1975.

Allen, William Francis; Ware, Charles Pickard; and Garrison, Lucy McKim, eds. *Slave Songs of the United States.* 1867. Reprint. Freeport, N.Y.: Books for Libraries Press, The Black Heritage Library Collection, 1971.

Bastin, Bruce. *Crying for the Carolines.* London: Studio Vista, 1971.

Benjaminson, Peter. *The Story of Motown.* New York: Grove Press, 1979.

Bim Bam Boom: The Magazine Devoted to the History of Rhythm and Blues. Bronx, N.Y., 1972- .

Black Music. London: Hamlyn, 1974.

Blues Unlimited: The Journal of the Blues Appreciation Society. London, 1963- .

Bogaert, Karel. *Blues Lexicon: Blues, Cajun, Boogie Woogie, Gospel.* Antwerp, Belgium: Standaard Uitgeverij, 1971.

Bogle, Donald. *Brown Sugar: Eighty Years of America's Black Female Superstars.* New York: Harmony Books, 1980.

Broven, John. *Walking to New Orleans: The Story of New Orleans Rhythm & Blues.* Bexhill-on-Sea, Sussex, England: Blues Unlimited, 1974.

Charles, Ray, and Ritz, David. *Brother Ray: Ray Charles' Own Story.* New York: Dial, 1978.

Charters, Samuel. *The Bluesmen: The Story and the Music of the Men Who Made the Blues.* New York: Oak Publications, 1967.

_____. *The Country Blues.* New York: Rinehart, 1959.

_____. *The Legacy of the Blues: A Glimpse into the Art and the Lives of Twelve Great Bluesmen. An Informal Study.* 1975. Reprint. New York: Da Capo, 1977.

_____. *The Poetry of the Blues.* New York: Oak Publications, 1963.

_____. *The Roots of the Blues: An African Search.* Boston: Marion Boyars, 1981.

_____. *Sweet as the Showers of Rain: The Bluesmen,* vol. 2. New York: Oak Publications, 1977.

Cone, James H. *The Spirituals and the Blues: An Interpretation.* New York: Seabury Press, 1972.

Cook, Bruce. *Listen to the Blues.* New York: Charles Scribner's Sons, 1973.

Courlander, Harold. *Negro Folk Music, U.S.A.* New York: Columbia University Press, 1963.

Cummings, Tony. *The Sound of Philadelphia.* London: Methuen, 1975.

De Korte, Juliann. *Ethel Waters: Finally Home.* Old Tappan, N.J.: Fleming H. Revell, 1978.

Dixon, Christa K. *Negro Spirituals: From Bible to Folk Song.* Philadelphia: Fortress Press, 1976.

Dragonwagon, C. *Stevie Wonder.* New York: Flash Books, 1977.

Epstein, Dena J. *Sinful Tunes and Spirituals: Black Folk Music to the Civil War.* Music in American Life. Urbana: University of Illinois Press, 1977.

Evans, David. *Big Road Blues: Tradition and Creativity in the Folk Blues.* Berkeley: University of California Press, 1982.

_____. *Tommy Johnson*. London: Studio Vista, 1971.

Fahey, John. *Charley Patton*. London: Studio Vista, 1970.

Ferlingere, Robert D., comp. *A Discography of Rhythm & Blues and Rock 'n' Roll Vocal Groups, 1945 to 1965*. Pittsburg, Calif.: Robert D. Ferlingere, 1976.

Ferris, William, Jr. *Blues from the Delta*. London: Studio Vista, 1970.

_____. *Blues from the Delta*. Garden City, N.Y.: Anchor/Doubleday, 1978.

Fisher, Miles Mark. *Negro Slave Songs in the United States*. 1953. Reprint. New York: Citadel Press, 1969.

Garland, Phyl. *The Sound of Soul*. Chicago: Henry Regnery, 1969.

Garon, Paul. *Blues and the Poetic Spirit*. London: Eddison Press, 1975.

_____. *The Devil's Son-in-Law: The Story of Peetie Wheatstraw and His Songs*. London: Studio Vista, 1971.

Given, Dave. *The Dave Given Rock 'n' Roll Stars Handbook: Rhythm and Blues Artists and Groups*. Smithtown, N.Y.: Exposition Press, 1980.

Godrich, John, and Dixon, Robert M. W., comps. *Blues and Gospel Records, 1902-1942*. London: Storyville Publications, 1969.

_____. *Recording the Blues*. London: Studio Vista, 1970.

Gonzalez, Fernando L., comp. *Disco-File: The Discographical Catalog of American Rock & Roll and Rhythm & Blues, Vocal Harmony Groups*. 2d ed. *1902 to 1976: Race, Rhythm & Blues, Rock & Roll, Soul*. Flushing, N.Y.: Fernando L. Gonzalez, 1977.

Goreau, Laurraine. *Just Mahalia, Baby*. Waco, Tex.: Word Books, 1975.

Groia, Philip. *They All Sang on the Corner: New York City's Rhythm & Blues Vocal Groups of the 1950s*. Branchport, N.Y.: Edmond Publishing, 1973.

Groom, Bob. *The Blues Revival*. London: Studio Vista, 1971.

Guralnick, Peter. *Feel Like Going Home: Portraits in Blues and Rock 'n' Roll*. New York: Sunrise Book/E. P. Dutton, 1971.

Handy, W. C. *Father of the Blues: An Autobiography*. Ed. Arna Bontemps. 1941. Reprint. New York: Collier Books, 1970.

Haralambos, Michael. *Right On: From Blues to Soul in Black America*. New York: Drake Publishers, 1975.

Harris, Sheldon. *Blues Who's Who: A Biographical Dictionary of Blues Singers*. New Rochelle, N.Y.: Arlington House, 1979.

Haskins, Jim, with Kathleen Benson. *The Stevie Wonder Scrapbook*. New York: Grosset and Dunlap, 1978.

Heilbut, Tony. *The Gospel Sound: Good News and Bad Times*. New York: Simon and Schuster, 1971.

Hoare, Ian, ed. *The Soul Book*. London: Eyre Methuen, 1975.

Holiday, Billie, with William Dufty. *Lady Sings the Blues*. 1956. Reprint. New York: Avon, 1976.

Hot Buttered Soul. Sheppey, Kent, England, 1975- .

Jackson, Irene V., comp. *Afro-American Religious Music: A Bibliography and a Catalogue of Gospel Music*. Westport, Conn.: Greenwood Press, 1979.

Jackson, Mahalia, with Evan McLeod Wylie. *Movin' on Up*. New York: Hawthorn Books, 1966.

Jones, Hettie. *Big Star Fallin' Mama: Five Women in Black Music*. New York: Viking Press, 1974.

Keil, Charles. *Urban Blues*. Chicago: University of Chicago Press, 1966.

Knaack, Twila. *Ethel Waters: I Touched a Sparrow.* Waco, Tex.: Word Books, 1978.

Krehbiel, Henry Edward. *Afro-American Folksongs: A Study in Racial and National Music.* 4th ed. 1941. Reprint. Portland, Maine: Longwood Press, 1976.

Larkin, Rochelle. *Soul Music!* New York: Lancer Books, 1970.

Leadbitter, Mike, ed. *Nothing but the Blues: An Illustrated Documentary.* London: Hanover Books, 1971.

————, and Slaven, Neil. *Blues Records: January, 1943 to December, 1966.* London: Hanover Books, 1968.

Leichter, Albert. *A Discography of Rhythm & Blues and Rock & Roll, circa 1946-1964: A Reference Manual.* Staunton, Va.: Albert Leichter, 1975.

————. *Supplement 1.* Staunton, Va.: Albert Leichter, 1978.

Living Blues: The Journal of the American Blues Tradition. Chicago, 1970- .

Lomax, John A. *Adventures of a Ballad Hunter.* 1947. Reprint. New York: Hafner Publishing, 1971.

Lovell, John, Jr. *Black Song: The Forge and the Flame. The Story of How the Afro-American Spiritual Was Hammered Out.* New York: Macmillan, 1972.

McCutcheon, Lynn Ellis. *Rhythm and Blues: An Experience and Adventure in Its Origin and Development.* Arlington, Va.: Beatty, 1971.

McKee, Margaret, and Chisenhall, Fred. *Beale Black and Blue: Life and Music on Black America's Main Street.* Baton Rouge: Louisiana State University Press, 1981.

Marsh, J.B.T. *The Story of the Jubilee Singers, with Their Songs.* 1881. Reprint. New York: Negro Universities Press, 1969.

Middleton, Richard. *Pop Music and the Blues: A Study of the Relationship and Its Significance.* London: Victor Gollancz, 1972.

Millar, Bill. *The Drifters: The Rise and Fall of the Black Vocal Group.* New York: Collier/Macmillan, 1971.

Morse, David. *Motown and the Arrival of Black Music.* New York: Macmillan, 1971.

Murray, Albert. *Stomping the Blues.* New York: McGraw-Hill, 1976.

Napier, Simon A. *Back Woods Blues: Selected Reprints from Blues Unlimited Magazine and Elsewhere.* Bexhill-on-Sea, Sussex, England: Blues Unlimited, 1968.

Neff, Robert, and Connor, Anthony. *Blues.* Boston: David R. Godine, 1975.

Nicholas, A. X., ed. *The Poetry of Soul.* New York: Bantam Books, 1971.

Oakley, Giles. *The Devil's Music: A History of the Blues.* New York: Taplinger, 1977.

Oliver, Paul. *Aspects of the Blues Tradition.* New York: Oak Publications, 1970.

————. *Bessie Smith.* Kings of Jazz Series. New York: A Perpetua Book/A. S. Barnes, 1961.

————. *Blues Fell This Morning: The Meaning of the Blues.* New York: Horizon, 1960.

————. *Conversation with the Blues.* New York: Horizon, 1965.

_____. *Savannah Syncopators: African Retentions in the Blues*. London: Studio Vista, 1970.

_____. *Screening the Blues*. London: Cassell, 1968.

_____. *The Story of the Blues*. Radnor, Pa.: Chilton Book, 1969.

Olson, James T. *Aretha Franklin*. Mankato, Minn.: Creative Education, 1975.

Olsson, Bengt. *Memphis Blues and Jug Bands*. London: Studio Vista, 1970.

Oster, Harry. *Living Country Blues*. Detroit: Folklore Associates, 1969.

Palmer, Robert. *Deep Blues*. New York: Viking Press, 1981.

Ramsey, Frederic, Jr. *Been Here and Gone*. New Brunswick, N.J.: Rutgers University Press, 1960.

Redd, Lawrence N. *Rock Is Rhythm and Blues (The Impact of Mass Media)*. East Lansing: Michigan State University Press, 1974.

Rock and Soul Songs. Derby, Conn., 1956- .

Rooney, James. *Bossmen: Bill Monroe and Muddy Waters*. New York: Dial Press, 1971.

Rowe, Mike. *Chicago Breakdown*. 1973. Reprint. New York: Da Capo, 1979.

Sackheim, Eric, comp. *The Blues Line: A Collection of Blues Lyrics*. New York: Grossman Publishers, 1969.

Sawyer, Charles. *The Arrival of B. B. King: The Authorized Biography*. Garden City, N.Y.: Doubleday, 1980.

Schiesel, Jane. *The Otis Redding Story*. Garden City, N.Y.: Doubleday, 1973.

Shaw, Arnold. *Honkers and Shouters: The Golden Years of Rhythm and Blues*. New York: Macmillan, 1978.

The Stars and Superstars of Black Music. London: Chartwell Books/Phoebus, 1977.

Stewart-Baxter, Derrick. *Ma Rainey and the Classic Blues Singers*. New York: Stein and Day, 1970.

Titon, Jeff Todd. *Early Downhome Blues: A Musical and Cultural Analysis*. Music in American Life. Urbana: University of Illinois Press, 1977.

_____, ed. *From Blues to Pop: The Autobiography of Leonard "Baby Doo" Caston*. JEMF Special Series, no. 4. Los Angeles: John Edwards Memorial Foundation, 1974.

Townley, Eric. *Tell Your Story: A Dictionary of Jazz and Blues Recordings, 1917-1950*. Chigwell, Essex, England: Storyville Publications, 1976.

Tudor, Dean, and Tudor, Nancy. *Black Music*. American Popular Music on Elpee. Littleton, Colo.: Libraries Unlimited, 1979.

Walker, Wyatt Tee. *"Somebody's Calling My Name": Black Sacred Music and Social Change*. Valley Forge, Pa.: Judson Press, 1979.

Warrick, Mancel; Hilsman, Joan R.; and Manno, Anthony. *The Progress of Gospel Music: From Spirituals to Contemporary Gospel*. New York: Vantage Press, 1977.

Waters, Ethel. *To Me It's Wonderful*. New York: Harper and Row, 1972.

_____, with Charles Samuels. *His Eye Is on the Sparrow: An Autobiography*. Garden City, N.Y.: Doubleday, 1951.

Whitburn, Joel. *Joel Whitburn's Top Rhythm and Blues Records 1949-1971: Facts about 4,000 Recordings Listed in Billboard's "Best Selling Rhythm and Blues (Soul) Singles" Charts. Grouped under the Names of the 1,200 Recording Artists*. Menomonee Falls, Wisc.: Record Research, 1973.

zur Heide, Karl Gert. *Deep South Piano: The Story of Little Brother Montgomery*. London: Studio Vista, 1970.

CHAPTER 5

Ragtime and Jazz

Besides the spirituals and the secular rural blues, there evolved from black culture in the south after the Civil War the elements that would make a secular urban music, an instrumental ensemble music with an improvisatory style of performance that early in the twentieth century came to be called *jazz*. From its early home in black New Orleans, jazz developed and expanded to other cities and other continents, to include brilliant artists who were white, gypsy, or Japanese along with its black stars, and to be the music of sophisticated dance floors, concert halls, and even cathedrals.

Is jazz part of American popular music? Jazz is deeply American, but it has not always been considered popular music. It has a long commercial recording history and it has sustained an industry of large touring bands and of clubs for smaller groups, so it is, at least sometimes, popular music in the sense of commercial music. Its great creative drive, however, has produced such sophisticated art and such serious audiences and critics that it sometimes seems to belong more nearly to chamber music than to commercial musical entertainment. But aside from the facts of its large audience, its interdependence with the entertainment business structure, and its sheer importance as an American music, it is placed among the popular arts by a long tradition of misunderstanding by some (never all) of the votaries of other serious kinds of music.

Jazz evoked respect from the conductor Ernest Ansermet in 1918, in Switzerland, and in the next two decades European enthusiasts began to give jazz serious attention, and then criticism and scholarship, before America was able to develop similar acknowledgment of the powerful and original music it had produced. American enthusiasm is still matched by that of jazz fans around the globe. The large size of the present chapter, which, nevertheless, will be perhaps less thorough in its coverage than other chapters in this book, reflects the devotion of the American and international jazz audience that has produced a great mass of comment and a considerable amount of serious explanation and judgment since the 1930s, more than has been produced for any other popular art.

PROLOGUE: RAGTIME

In the 1890s a peculiar new music became fashionable, a syncopated piano style that soon pervaded much of the production of the new Tin Pan

Alley industry. It had come from St. Louis and other cities and towns along the Mississippi, created by black piano players drawing on the rhythms of Afro-American folk tradition and accommodating those traditions to the compositional structures of western music. *Ragtime* boomed until about the time of World War I, about the time that America began to notice jazz. Some ragtime continued to be played after this time, and its influence in jazz and song continued to be felt. Around the time of World War II interest in ragtime began to revive, with a strong resurgence of the music itself and of studies devoted to it, through the 1970s.

A discography is David A. Jasen's *Recorded Ragtime, 1897-1958* which covers flat-disc 78 rpm ragtime recordings, but does not include the mildly imitative "ragtime songs." The list is by title, with an index by composer.

Biographies in the 1970s acknowledge the most creative ragtime composer and the most durable performer. Scott Joplin, his music revived as a new fashion in that decade, is the subject of Peter Gammond's *Scott Joplin and the Ragtime Era,* an illustrated popular history of Joplin and his contemporaries, with an annotated catalog of Joplin's works (pp.121-49 in the middle of the book, not to be confused with the reference list of the same works at the end), a bibliography, and a discography. Jim Haskins and Kathleen Benson's *Scott Joplin* is a modest-sized but thoroughly documented life story, with photographs. Eubie Blake, ninety-nine years old at this writing and still able to play on recent occasions in tribute to him, was writing songs in the nineteenth century. His composing, performing, and producing career with Noble Sissle, mostly between 1915 and 1933, is recalled in *Reminiscing with Sissle and Blake* by Robert Kimball and William Bolcom, a scrapbook of photographs, posters, reviews, stage patter, and miscellaneous souvenirs, with a thread of narrative. Songs, productions, collaborators, piano rolls, records, and films are listed at the end. Al Rose's *Eubie Blake* is a biography built on taped conversations with Blake at the age of ninety-six, with a section of photographs, program notes on the Broadway show *Eubie!,* and data lists. Lawrence T. Carter's *Eubie Blake: Keys of Memory* is a brief, undocumented biography concerned with affirming the place of ragtime in a black cultural heritage.

Histories of ragtime began with Rudi Blesh and Harriet Janis' *They All Played Ragtime* (1950, with later editions), a popular social history that later writers have sometimes called inaccurate but that has introduced the personalities of ragtime and given an enthusiastic account of the music to more readers than has any other book. Terry Waldo's *This Is Ragtime* is a history, especially of the various mid-century revivals of ragtime music, with many interviews with performers.

Critical analysis has filled two books and part of another. William J. Schafer and Johannes Riedel's *The Art of Ragtime: Form and Meaning of an Original Black American Art* is a musicological study of "classic ragtime" piano rag compositions, with brief chapters on what the authors see as peripheral or diluted forms. The introduction includes a bibliographic survey of history and criticism; appendixes have some sheet music covers, a comparison of ragtime and jazz piano styles with twenty-three pages of musical examples, an essay on Joplin's opera *Treemonisha,* and a bibliography. David A. Jasen and Trebor Jay Tichenor's *Rags and Ragtime: A Musical History* is partly a reference work cataloging some eight hundred published ragtime works, with biographical entries on forty-eight composers, and partly an exposition of their history and style. The music celebrated in Jasen and Tichenor is called "folk ragtime" by Edward A. Berlin in his *Ragtime: A Musical and Cultural History* (1980). Berlin proposes a revision and broadening of earlier definitions of ragtime. In part 1 of his book, he investigates the understandings of what ragtime was, which prevailed from about 1896 to 1920; part 2 analyzes the forms of ragtime as they evolved in that era; part 3 attempts a modern overview. Berlin stresses the importance of songs, as opposed to piano pieces. His third chapter, "The Ragtime Debate," has a valuable history of the reception and rejection of ragtime that is a microcosm of responses to popular music in general at various times in its history. Berlin also has a notable bibliography of about three hundred early articles on the music.

Ragtime magazines include *Rag Times* published bimonthly by the Maple Leaf Club in Los Angeles, *Ragtimer* by the Ragtime Society in Ontario, and *Mississippi Rag,* published in Minneapolis.

JAZZ

From ragtime, from blues, from brass band marches, and from various American currents that arose in Africa and in Europe, the black musicians of the south and midwest created jazz. Jazz has given rise to a large number of books.

A. JAZZ BIBLIOGRAPHY AND DISCOGRAPHY

Jazz Music in Print by John Voight is a current listing of available published jazz music, organized by name of the originating performer. But, whereas popular song music has many guides to its printed avatars, jazz music is profoundly a performed sound. Improvision is at its heart, and while printed arranged jazz is a respectable tradition, the great mass of jazz is either live or recorded sound, and the great reference projects of jazz scholarship are consequently discographies of jazz records (see below). The bibliography of jazz, on the other hand, except for the limited area addressed by Voight's book, is the discipline charged with keeping track of the flood of writing *about* the music.

A Bibliography of Jazz by Alan P. Merriam was the first major resource of its kind (1954, now reprinted). Merriam assembled 3,324 author entries through 1950 in an unselected, very full, though avowedly incomplete, listing of books and articles, with indexing by subject and periodical. The same year Robert George Reisner published *The Literature of Jazz* (slightly expanded in 1959), a brief, selective bibliography of jazz books, background books, jazz magazines, and some articles in general readership magazines. Donald Kennington's *The Literature of Jazz: A Critical Guide* (1971, revised in 1980 with Danny L. Read) has chapters of bibliographic survey of nine categories, including blues, followed by annotated listings of books only. Carl Gregor, sometimes cited by his aristocratic title Herzog zu Mecklenburg, has edited an *International Jazz Bibliography: Jazz Books from 1919 to 1968* (1969) and two volumes of continuation. The first version is a very full and very international list—thirty countries are represented—with indexes. There are no annotations, and the data are variable because they are taken by Gregor from varying sources and contributors. The *1970 Supplement,* bound together with a drum and percussion bibliography, monitors books for two more years, again relying a good deal on hearsay; there is no index. The *1971/72/73 Supplement . . . and Selective Bibliography of Some Jazz Background Literature and Bibliography of Two Subjects Previously Excluded* now includes dissertations and has a short section of "Beat, Rock, and Pop." Bernhard Hefele's *Jazz-Bibliographie* (1981) is a German and English list of sixty-six hundred items in twenty-eight subject areas, collected through 1979. *Jazz Index: Quarterly Bibliography of Jazz Literature in Periodicals and Collections* is a German-language world bibliography begun in 1977. Extensive jazz bibliographies are included in the black music bibliographies by De Lerma and by Skowronski cited in chapter 1, section C.

Libraries across the country house major collections of jazz recordings and literature. The premier collection is at the Rutgers University Institute of Jazz Studies in Newark, New Jersey. Other jazz collections include the following, alphabetically by state: the Arkansas Arts Center—Elizabeth Prewitt Taylor Memorial Library in Little Rock, which has its own published *Catalog of the John D. Reid Collection of Early American Jazz* compiled by Meredith McCoy and Barbara Parker; the Watkinson Library of Trinity College in Hartford, Connecticut; the Albert Pick Music Library of the University of Miami, Florida; the Archives of Traditional Music at Indiana University, Bloomington; a major collection of New Orleans materials at the Tulane University William Ransom Hogan Jazz Archives, New Orleans, and a smaller one at the Louisiana State Museum, also in New Orleans; the Berklee College of Music in Boston, a major jazz school; a New York Jazz Museum, presently inactive and relocating; the Free Library of Philadelphia Music Department; and North Texas State University in Denton, also a major school for musicians. Jazz is represented in the more general collections of the New York Public Library and the Library of Congress. Here might be mentioned a book by British library science professor Derek Langridge called *Your Jazz Collection,* a bibliographic, discographic, and collection-organizing guide more for professional librarians than for private collectors, but with useful groupings and criticisms of jazz writing.

Jazz discography, the primary discipline to keep track of the music and give access to it, has flourished to such a height that it is possible here to give a bibliography of bibliographies of such discographies! The latest and largest at the present writing is *Bibliography of Discographies: Jazz* (1981) by Daniel Allen, in a series on various kinds of recordings by various authors. Allen has 200 pages of references ranging from large books to short articles in special-interest magazines. David Edwin Cooper's *International Bibliography of Discographies: Classical Music and Jazz and Blues* has a part 2 (pp. 145-220) "Jazz and Blues," a listing of 665 discographies of various sizes. Volume 1 of De Lerma's *Bibliography of Black Music* (see chapter 1) lists 160 items as jazz discographies and another 602 "individual discographies" that are almost all jazz, besides other lists of discographic journals and of label discographies (which go beyond jazz). The Institute of Jazz Studies published two volumes of *Studies in Jazz Discography* in 1971-1972, then subsumed it into *Journal of Jazz Studies.*

The standard discography of earlier jazz is Brian Rust's *Jazz Records 1897-1942,* now in two volumes and two thousand pages, which traces record production from ragtime to the first jazz records in 1917 and up to the Petrillo recording ban of 1942. It excludes blues singers and the categories of records covered in Rust's other long works (*Dance Bands* and *Entertainment*—see chapter 3). Further history is cataloged in Jorgen Grunnet Jepsen's *Jazz Records, 1942-1965,* eight volumes, which were published in Denmark but printed in English.

Older discographies, dating back half a century, may still be useful. Charles Delaunay published one in Paris in 1936; an American printing of a revision in 1948 was called *New Hot Discography: The Standard Directory of Recorded Jazz:* "hot" jazz as distinguished from dance band music. More eclectic was Hilton R. Schleman's *Rhythm on Record: A Complete Survey and Register of All the Principal Recorded Dance Music from 1906 to 1936, and a Who's Who of the Artists Concerned in the Making* (1936, now reprinted) including jazz along with music of a lower temperature. In 1942, Charles Edward Smith and others published *The Jazz Record Book,* a brief history and an annotated survey of outstanding records available at the time—collaborator Frederic Ramsey, Jr., later pointed out that in the war year 1942 many records had just gone out of print. This book has also been reprinted, as has Orin Blackstone's *Index to Jazz: Jazz Recordings 1917-1944,* originally issued in parts between 1945 and 1948, which excluded the commercial in pursuit of "purer" jazz and blues. Its discographic information, derived from catalogs at the time, is sparse. Beginning in 1949, David Carey and various collaborators brought out alphabetical installments of *The Directory of Recorded Jazz and Swing Music.* Six volumes made it halfway through the letter L by 1957, when the project deferred to

Jepsen's work in progress (see above). A new era of recording was met by Frederic Ramsey, Jr.'s, *A Guide to Longplay Jazz Records* in 1954, which surveyed five years of these new records including the collected reissues of old sides that such records made possible.

Two record companies that specialized in jazz have separate discographies. Michael Ruppli with assistance from Bob Porter has compiled both *The Savoy Label* and *The Prestige Label.*

Currently available long-playing jazz records are critically evaluated in the Tudors' *Jazz* volume. An earlier similar project was *Jazz on Record: A Critical Guide* (1960) by Charles Fox and others, a critical encyclopedia of records in entries by artist. Len Lyons selects *The 101 Best Jazz Albums* as the core of a large book of critical commentary on many more records, organized in historical chapters. Peter Gammond and Peter Clayton in *Fourteen Miles on a Clear Night* give a liner-note-style page or two to each of forty-three favorite records; the mode is British whimsy, interspersed with cartoons.

B. JAZZ GENERAL REFERENCE

Reference works that are predominantly biographical, such as Feather's *Encyclopedias,* are listed under collective biography.

Guides to the jazz realm have included four versions of Joachim-Ernst Berendt's highly successful survey *The Jazz Book* between 1950 and 1973 (1975 in the United States), widely distributed around the world in eleven languages. Berendt first attempted to depict jazz as it had evolved to the age of bebop, and extended and rewrote with successive modern movements. His historical survey includes a helpful chart of jazz evolution. He has sections of biographies, of jazz elements, of instruments, singers, bands, and combos. Berendt then edited *The Story of Jazz: From New Orleans to Rock Jazz* (1978 in the United States), in which various German and American critics write chapters describing a style and characterizing the musicians who represent it: New Orleans; blues; Chicago; swing; Armstrong and Ellington; bebop, cool jazz, hard bop; free jazz; blues today; and rock jazz. Throughout, musicians' names are in boldface, with dates, so that even without an index this book has reference value. (See also Berendt's *Photo History* in section E, below.)

The beginning of such guides was a series of projects edited by Paul Eduard Miller. In 1939 he collected *Down Beat's Yearbook of Swing:* a chapter of history by cities, a list of hot jazz orchestras, biographical dictionary, discography, and other sorts of facts. In the mid-1940s he edited *Esquire's Jazz Book* (1943-1946) with reprinted articles, all-American band polls, biographies, photographs, and calendars of events. A later version, not by Miller, was *Esquire's World of Jazz* (1962 and 1975). Another early handbook, without the annual topicality, was *Guide to Jazz* by Hugues Panassié and Madeleine Gautier (Paris in 1954 and 1971, United States in

1956, now reprinted), a brief-entry encyclopedia of mostly traditional players, groups, terms, instruments, and musical pieces, with interwoven critical judgments by Panassié. The traditional emphasis is balanced by that of Leonard Feather's *The Book of Jazz from Then till Now: A Guide to the Entire Field* (1957) by an early advocate of bop and evolving modern jazz, exploring other-than-New-Orleans sources and stressing progressive development. Feather's book is organized in instrument-centered historical chapters; a separate section transcribes and analyzes seventeen great solos. In 1957, Barry Ulanov published *A Handbook of Jazz* collecting facts and essays. He includes a capsule history, a survey of instruments and one of schools, annotated record lists, a biographical dictionary in seventy pages, and chapters on such topics as jazz language and jazz as a profession. There is a helpful chronological table, through the mid-1950s. Martin T. Williams' *Where's the Melody? A Listener's Introduction to Jazz* (1966) is a series of practical essays in jazz appreciation, including analyses of particular recorded solos, an introductory discography, vignettes of jazz life and performance, and short critical essays on Horace Silver, Billie Holiday, Gene Krupa, four pianists, and Ornette Coleman.

Textbooks of jazz testify to the academic seriousness with which the music is addressed now, both as a subject of appreciative study and as a performer's craft. Some such books are essentially histories and are mentioned in section D. *The Anatomy of Jazz* by Leroy Ostransky is a musicological explanation and history of jazz for readers interested in classical music, and comparison of jazz and classical music for readers whose first interest is jazz. The point, made explicit in the final chapter, is to break down barriers and to discover mutual usefulness. Ostransky's later book *Understanding Jazz* is an introductory survey of the elements and major forms through the mid-1970s, less technical than *Anatomy*. Paul O. W. Tanner and Maurice Gerow's *A Study of Jazz* is a classroom text covering basic musicology and history to the early 1960s, with suggested student activities, musical examples in score, and a demonstration record. *The Jazz Text* by Charles Nanry with Edward Berger is a survey history and guide; it is largely general exposition, with only brief discussion of major performers. A concluding "Guide to Research" lists reference materials and discusses sociological methods of analysis: the approach of the book reflects Nanry's work as a teacher of jazz courses within a sociology department. Mark C. Gridley's *Jazz Styles* is a text for a jazz-appreciation course with emphasis on modern styles, two-thirds of it since 1940. There is a notably accessible layout, with tables, diagrams, photographs; and there is a long, annotated discography. Avril Dankworth's *Jazz: An Introduction to Its Musical Basis* is a brief British book of detailed musical description. Graham Collier's *Jazz: A Student's and Teacher's Guide* is also British, a school book that is half historical-and-biographical chapters on Armstrong, Ellington, Reinhardt, Parker, Davis, Brubeck, and Coleman, and half a series of chapters for student musicians. Jerry Coker's *The Jazz Idiom* is a short outline of practical jazz musicology, primarily for the student performer. Coker's *Listening to Jazz* addresses its explanations to the audience, in practical and nontechnical notes and listening suggestions keyed to the recorded Smithsonian Collection of Jazz. Detailed study is given to six great solos selected from that collection.

Specialized reference works include Robert Gold's *A Jazz Lexicon* (1964, updated in 1975 as *Jazz Talk*), a serious dictionary of jazz slang with most definitions substantiated by quotations from print. A bibliography lists many works, novels as well as histories and studies, that represent the language and the life it expresses. David Meeker's *Jazz in the Movies: A Guide to Jazz Musicians 1917-1977* is an international survey arranged alphabetically by title of film, listing composers or performers in 2,239 films of varying lengths. There is an index. Eric Townley's *Tell Your Story,* mentioned in chapter 4, explains the titles of jazz and blues recordings.

C. JAZZ BIOGRAPHY AND MATERIALS RELEVANT TO PARTICULAR FIGURES

COLLECTIVE BIOGRAPHY. The most comprehensive biographical reference is a series of three volumes by Leonard Feather. *The Encyclopedia of Jazz* came out in 1955 with about a thousand biographies, and a new edition in 1960 included twice as many. Both had introductory chapters of history and analysis. *The Encyclopedia of Jazz in the Sixties* (1966) covers a thousand musicians active early in that decade; supporting apparatus includes sample results of Feather's famous "blindfold test" judgments of artists by other artists, tables of poll winners, and other data. With Ira Gitler, Feather produced in 1976 *The Encyclopedia of Jazz in the Seventies,* fourteen hundred biographies covering the years 1966-1975. Smaller compilations include John Jörgensen and Erik Wiedemann's *Mosaik Jazzlexikon* (1966), a German-language encyclopedia of mostly American jazz and blues performers. A bibliography includes many European titles. Brian Case and Stan Britt's *The Illustrated Encyclopedia of Jazz* is a large, colorful paperback, uniform with other volumes on rock and on country. Four hundred entries, with album discographies, cover present and some past performers (no blues artists), illustrated with color reproductions of 275 record jackets and other photographs. *Jazz* by Morley Jones is a pocket-sized book in the format of pocket travel guides. Brief chapters and subject essays introduce groups of critical biographical notes, each with small photographs and recommended record list, for about fifty artists.

Smaller selections of longer biographical chapters make up several books that trace successions of greatest stars. A volume called *Kings of Jazz* edited by Stanley Green collects eleven studies that are also published separately as brief books, mostly by British critics, on Armstrong, Beiderbecke, Davis, Dodds, Ellington, Gillespie, Morton, Oliver, Parker, Bessie Smith, and

Waller. Green is credited with some small revision of the separate booklets for the collected publication. Benny Green in *The Reluctant Art: The Growth of Jazz* chooses only five figures making crucial contributions: Beiderbecke, Goodman, Young, Holiday, Parker. Rudi Blesh's *Combo: USA* shows the author's traditional preferences in his selection of eight: Armstrong, Bechet, Teagarden, Young, Holiday, Krupa, Christian, and Blake. Leonard Feather's progressive sympathies show in his dozen in *From Satchmo to Miles:* Armstrong, Ellington, Holiday, Fitzgerald, Basie, Young, Parker, Gillespie, Peterson, Charles, Don Ellis, and Davis, along with a profile of promoter Norman Granz. Nat Shapiro and Nat Hentoff's *The Jazz Makers* compiles critical biographies of twenty-one figures from Morton to Gillespie, by the editors and seven other jazz writers. Robert George Reisner's *The Jazz Titans* has briefer notes on thirty-three major figures; Reisner includes in the volume his "Parlance of Hip," a short lexicon of jazz talk (see also Robert Gold's book in section B, above).

Less ambitious introductions to key figures are Studs Terkel's *Giants of Jazz,* with brief lives of twelve artists, and James Lincoln Collier's *The Great Jazz Artists,* from Joplin to Coltrane, for young readers.

Artists of particular eras and styles are gathered in some books. For the old New Orleans tradition, Samuel Charters compiled *Jazz: New Orleans, 1885-1963—An Index to the Negro Musicians of New Orleans.* Originally published in 1958, this biographical directory covers musical activity through 1931. Charters wrote in 1962 that his work on the history of jazz in New York had changed his views somewhat of the central importance of New Orleans, but his revision of this book the following year is relatively minor. Al Rose and Edmond Souchon's *New Orleans Jazz: A Family Album,* prefaced by their conservative definition of jazz, provides a biographical directory of about a thousand players in an album of over six hundred photographs. Noel Rockmore's *Preservation Hall Portraits* is a book of black and white prints of Rockmore's paintings done at the Preservation Hall jazz gallery in the 1960s; sixty-six musicians are shown with short biographical notes, along with a few group portraits. Martin T. Williams' *Jazz Masters of New Orleans* collects his judicious and nonsectarian essays on Bolden, Morton, Oliver, the New Orleans Rhythm Kings, Bechet, Singleton, Ory, Bunk Johnson, and Red Allen.

Later styles are more sparely acknowledged in collective biographical books particular to their eras. Richard Hadlock's *Jazz Masters of the Twenties,* another volume of the Macmillan series with Williams' book just mentioned (of which Williams is the general editor), treats Armstrong, Hines, Beiderbecke, the Chicagoans, Waller, James P. Johnson, Teagarden, Henderson, Redman, Smith, and Eddie Lang. Gene Fernett's *Swing Out: Great Negro Dance Bands* matches his book on less jazz-oriented bands cited in chapter 3. This volume is a picture-and-text survey, a couple of pages devoted to each of twenty-five bands, with a brief catalog and a large photograph section of lesser known aggregations. *Strike Up the Band! Bandleaders of Today* (1949), by Alberta Powell Graham, introduced thirty-five jazz bandleaders of that day to younger readers. A large musical population from about the first half of jazz history is John Chilton's *Who's Who of Jazz: Storyville to Swing Street,* with career biographies of between a thousand and fifteen hundred jazz musicians born in this country before 1920. Leaders, and the prominent sidemen each worked with, are given in capitals, but there is no index for tracing these references through the book. Joe Goldberg's *Jazz Masters of the Fifties* has chapters on Mulligan, Monk, Blakey, Davis, Rollins, the Modern Jazz Quartet, Mingus, Desmond, Charles, Coltrane, Taylor, and Coleman. A. B. Spellman's *Black Music: Four Lives* (originally *Four Lives in the Bebop Business*) is devoted to Taylor, Coleman, Herbie Nichols, and Jackie McLean. The stories are treated as variations of the life struggle of the black jazz musician at the intersection of show business and serious modern jazz. Pauline Rivelli and Robert Levin's *Giants of Black Music,* a set of reprinted articles from *Jazz and Pop* magazine (which Rivelli edited), treats the "new jazz" of the 1960s, including interviews with Coltrane, Sanders, and other artists, along with essays in advocacy. *Jazz Guitarists: Collected Interviews from Guitar Player Magazine* profiles forty mostly recent figures, but includes an article on Reinhardt.

INDIVIDUAL FIGURES. *Louis: The Louis Armstrong Story, 1900-1971* by Max Jones and John Chilton is an illustrated biography (250 photographs) written with Armstrong's cooperation and includes materials and extended statements supplied by him, though the book was published after his death. There is a chronology and a film list. Two earlier books cover Armstrong's brilliant and influential early years: Robert Goffin's *Horn of Plenty,* translated from the French by James F. Bezou in 1947 and now reprinted, recreates Armstrong's life and career up to 1933. Armstrong's own *Satchmo* reports his career only up through his arrival in Chicago in 1922, though some of the photographs are of a later date.

Count Basie and His Orchestra: Its Music and Its Musicians by Raymond Horricks is a British critic's survey of Basie's bands from 1936 to the 1950s. Two chapters of history lead to four sets of biographies of the bandsmen: "Principal" and "Additional," 1936-1950, and the same two categories after 1950; the biographies are often substantial short chapters, covering fifty-five musicians in all. There is a forty-page tabular discography. Stanley Dance's *The World of Count Basie* is also about many musicians (compare his books on Ellington and on Hines, below, and his *The World of Swing* in section D). In what Dance calls an "oral history" project of interviews with thirty-four musicians, he presents first a section centering on Basie and then one similarly built around bandleader Jay McShann as a second force in Kansas City and southwest jazz.

Sidney Bechet's *Treat It Gentle* is the transcription of a talking autobiography by the New Orleans clarinet and soprano sax artist, mostly about his American career before he settled in Europe in 1949. The beginning is a long novelistic evocation of his grandfather's violent death on a Louisiana plantation.

Bix Beiderbecke was the first great white soloist, a Chicago and New York cornetist and pianist, whose life and early death were romanticized and novelized but whose achievement is now established by solid analysis in several books. *Bix: Man and Legend* by Richard M. Sudhalter and Philip R. Evans is an extended biography attempting to redocument Beiderbecke's life and career, with sixty pages of detailed chronology and seventy pages of discography, transcribed solos, and an afterword note on his unorthodox cornet fingering. Ralph Berton's *Remembering Bix* is a large memoir from personal recollection. *Bugles for Beiderbecke* by Charles H. Wareing and George Garlick is half biography and half critical study of Beiderbecke's place in jazz history. The biography is more than half devoted to his time with the Goldkette and Whiteman orchestras at the end of his brief career. There is a long discographic chapter. Burnett James' *Bix Beiderbecke* is one of the short Kings of Jazz series paperbacks, with a discography of album reissues of his sides from the 1920s.

Bunny: A Bio-Discography of Jazz Trumpeter Bunny Berigan, by Vince Danca, is a booklet that is half casual biography and half detailed discography.

In Search of Buddy Bolden: First Man of Jazz, by Donald M. Marquis, is a documentary history that often falls back on conjecture in portraying the first known significant jazz musician, a New Orleans cornetist. Marquis emphasizes the man rather than the music, and his account challenges other histories, especially Bunk Johnson's statements recorded in Ramsey and Smith's *Jazzmen* (section E, below).

Cab Calloway tells about his life as bandleader, song composer, and radio and stage personality in *Of Minnie the Moocher and Me;* his co-author Bryant Rollins intersperses short memoirs by Calloway's wife, children, and associates. There are photographs, rosters of his bands, reprints of two old pamphlets by Calloway ("Hepsters Dictionary" from 1944, "Prof. Cab Calloway's Swingformation Bureau" from 1939), and a list of compositions.

Hoagy Carmichael's songs, most notably "Stardust," became monuments of Tin Pan Alley, but his early career was in Chicago jazz. His 1946 book *The Stardust Road* is a lyrically reminiscent account of his youth, with vignettes of Bix Beiderbecke. An autobiography in 1965, *Sometimes I Wonder,* includes his early memories in a more connected but still popularly recreative style, recalling mostly the 1920s and 1930s.

Lee Collins was a trumpeter in New Orleans in the 1920s and in Chicago in the 1930s and 1940s, and he made European tours in 1951 and 1954. His story makes one of the University of Illinois Music in American Life volumes, *Oh, Didn't He Ramble: The Life Story of Lee Collins as Told to Mary Collins,* edited by Frank J. Gillis and John W. Miner.

John Coltrane expanded the domain of tenor and soprano saxophone jazz in the 1950s and 1960s as he moved from hard bop to new sounds in collaboration with Miles Davis, and then on to influential experiments in "free jazz," which he understood as spiritual expression. He died in 1967. He is represented in three books from the mid-1970s. J. C. Thomas' *Chasin' the Trane: The Music and Mystique of John Coltrane,* more popular in style than the two next to be mentioned, interlaces biographical narrative with paragraphs of recollection from friends, colleagues, and critics. Thomas includes many photographs and a full discography. Bill Cole's *John Coltrane,* derived from Cole's doctoral dissertation, is a critical biography with stress on Coltrane's religious sensibility, interpreted especially in terms provided by the Nigerian writer Fela Sowande. Cole gives detailed examination of over fifty transcribed passages of Coltrane's playing. Documentation includes a long chart of recording data. *Coltrane: A Biography,* by Cuthbert Ormond Simpkins, is a lyrical and ideological account of Coltrane's life and music, printing many reviews, letters, interviews, and some of Coltrane's manuscript workbook pages.

Eddie Condon played banjo and guitar rhythm in Chicago and New York from the 1920s to the 1940s and played, as well, a social, managerial, and entrepreneurial jazz role. With Thomas Sugrue he wrote *We Called It Music: A Generation of Jazz* in 1947; interrupted by historical briefings by Sugrue, Condon writes witty memoirs of his life in jazz up to the time of opening his New York club. Appendixes give a catalog of Chicago bands and a Condon discography. In 1973 he produced *The Eddie Condon Scrapbook of Jazz* with Hank O'Neal, a book of photographs and clippings, with minimal commentary, from his whole career. His *Treasury of Jazz,* edited with Richard Gehman, is not specifically about his own history or brand of jazz, and is listed separately in section D.

Miles Davis has been one of the most influential trumpet players of the modern era, influential in the beginnings of cool jazz, of hard bop, and of jazz-rock fusion, returning to activity in 1981 after several years of self-imposed silence. Bill Cole's *Miles Davis: A Musical Biography* is not a personal life story but an account of Davis' musical evolution and an analysis of his playing. Appendixes give a long table of recording sessions, a long book and article bibliography, and thirteen performance transcriptions.

Eric Dolphy: A Musical Biography and Discography, by Vladimir Simosko and Barry Tepperman (published by the Smithsonian Institution, in an unusual public-establishment tribute to so recent a figure), includes an essay on Dolphy's place in jazz as one of the hard bop innovators with Coltrane, Coleman, and Cecil Taylor from the late 1950s to his early death in 1964, and an account of his career, followed by a full formal and annotated discography. There are also a bibliography and photographs.

Duke Ellington's preeminent place as bandleader and composer is acknowledged in the largest book list for any figure in jazz. One biography, Barry Ulanov's *Duke Ellington,* came out as a mid-career tribute in 1946 (now reprinted). Ulanov draws on interviews and materials provided by Ellington and members of his band, dramatizing them with much reconstructed dialogue. There are photographs, and a discography is included from 1925 to 1945. *Duke Ellington: His Life and Music,* edited by Peter Gammond in 1958, collects essays and reviews by fourteen writers; there are survey reviews of records by decades, a catalog of major sidemen, and a record guide by year. Photographs render public images. Stanley Dance's *The World of Duke Ellington* (1970) is an anthology of interview accounts of Ellington by his contemporaries and co-musicians and of articles by Dance, many previously published in jazz magazines. Ellington's own *Music Is My Mistress* (1973) is a large gathering of reminiscences, anecdotes of others, and photographs. Appended are lists of singers, arrangers, symphonic orchestras Ellington teamed with, "band boys and barbers," honors and awards, a select discography, a composition list, and a bibliography. Derek Jewell's *Duke: A Portrait of Duke Ellington* (1977) is a popular biography, the first full treatment after Ellington's death, by the popular music critic of the London *Sunday Times.* In Mercer Ellington and Stanley Dance's *Duke Ellington in Person* (1978), Duke's son, who played, arranged, did business for his father's band, and took it over at Duke's death, extends the biographers' public accounts with intimate recollections, which he declares are shaped by both love and hate. A list of compositions is annotated from the listing in his father's book, and there is a note on recordings available at the time of writing. Don R. George's *Sweet Man: The Real Duke Ellington* (1981) is an anecdotal memoir by a songwriting collaborator of Ellington's.

Pops Foster—The Autobiography of a New Orleans Jazzman edited by Tom Stoddard presents the memoirs of an astonishing seventy-year career beginning in 1899 and including many significant groups and orchestras in New Orleans, Los Angeles, and New York. The book includes an introduction on bass technique by Bertram Turetzky, interchapter comments by Ross Russell, and a discography by Brian Rust.

Pete Fountain, Dixieland-revival and pop clarinetist, has written a popular autobiography *A Closer Walk.* A record list is included.

Dizzy Gillespie, both an influential bop-era trumpet player and an eccentric showman whose personal mannerisms and dress still shape the popular caricature of the hipster and the beatnik, collaborated with Al Fraser in writing *To Be, or Not . . . to Bop: Memoirs.* A sprawling book, it alternates Gillespie's narrative with two hundred interview statements by people who figure in his life and career, ranging from a paragraph to pages.

Benny Goodman's clarinet and orchestra symbolized *swing,* big-band danceable jazz from the 1930s on. Goodman wrote an early-career book *The Kingdom of Swing* in 1939—Goodman was only thirty years old; his collaborator Irving Kolodin contributed two chapters of commentary. In 1969, D. Russell Connor and Warren H. Hicks compiled *B. G. on the Record: A Bio-Discography of Benny Goodman,* based on Connor's earlier *BG—Off the Record,* a very large book of facts. The later edition covers forty-two career years, with annotations of record entries and with photographs. *Benny: King of Swing. A Pictorial Biography Based on Benny Goodman's Personal Archives, with 212 Illustrations,* introduced by Stanley Baron, is a large photo album.

Hampton Hawes tells his story of early success as a jazz pianist in the 1940s and the 1950s, of army service, drug addiction, prison, a pardon from President Kennedy, and a second career in *Raise Up Off Me.*

Fletcher Henderson's orchestra, first organized in 1923, was one of the pioneer and best black jazz orchestras. Walter C. Allen's *Hendersonia: The Music of Fletcher Henderson and His Musicians* is a 650-page discography including career-story facts.

The World of Earl Hines by Stanley Dance, volume 2 of Dance's *The World of Swing,* is, like Dance's companion volumes, an "oral history" collection; in this one Hines tells his own story in taped reminiscences that take up half the book while the other half gathers statements from twenty musicians associated with Hines from the Chicago scene.

Bunk Johnson, a trumpet player in the 1920s in towns around New Orleans, is featured in *Willie Geary "Bunk" Johnson: The New Iberia Years* by Austin M. Sonnier, Jr. A few pages of biography introduce a discography from the time of his rediscovery in the 1940s, a section of remarkable photographs, and a catalog of other players from the same time and places.

Max Kaminsky grew up in Boston and played trumpet with the white Chicago groups, then played in big bands and in postwar clubs in New York. His autobiography *My Life in Jazz* presents him as a "traditional" jazzman unreconciled to bop.

Stan Kenton's twelve west-coast bands have occasioned large claims and controversy for innovative arranging. A popular story of Kenton's life and career, sometimes critical of both, is Carol Easton's *Straight Ahead: The Story of Stan Kenton.*

George Lewis, New Orleans clarinetist, has a popular biography *Call Him George* by Ann Fairbairn, with photographs and sentiment. Tom Bethell's *George Lewis: A Jazzman from New Orleans* is a more serious book about a career that stretched from 1919 to 1968. Bethell tells the story in the light of Henry Kmen's thesis on the origin of jazz, which minimizes surviving African elements in the music. Photographs include several taken in 1950 by Stanley Kubrick, later a famous filmmaker, in his days as a *Look* magazine photographer. There is an elaborate discography.

Milton "Mezz" Mezzrow's *Really the Blues* is a slangy account of his street, prison, and jazz life: he was a white Chicago reedman. Two polemical appendixes deal with his style of play, and there is a glossary of the jive language exemplified in the book.

Charles Mingus, bass player and composer, wrote *Beneath the Underdog,* a personal monologue woven around his life story. The book is a serious and artful interior exploration, with little direct narrative of the external facts of his career or the jazz world at large.

Ferdinand "Jelly Roll" Morton, rag and jazz pianist and composer, died in 1941. *Mr. Jelly Roll: The Fortunes of Jelly Roll Morton, New Orleans Creole and "Inventor of Jazz"* by Alan Lomax (1950, with a second edition in 1973) tells jazz history according to the flamboyant Morton from records he made for Lomax at the Library of Congress in 1938. Other people's comments are interspersed by Lomax, and appendixes give transcriptions and sheet music, a list of compositions, and a discography. Martin T. Williams' *Jelly Roll Morton* is a brief, critical biography in the Kings of Jazz series.

King Joe Oliver, trumpeter, bandleader, and early mentor of Louis Armstrong, has a biography and discography, *King Oliver,* by Walter C. Allen.

The Story of the Original Dixieland Jazz Band by H. O. Brunn is a history and an essay in advocacy. Basing his work in part on interviews and documents from members of the band, Brunn claims central importance for this white group as making the first jazz record and popularizing jazz in New York and on their European tour. Despite defensive overstatement— "more than entitled to the phrase . . . 'The Creators of Jazz' "—the book is a thoroughly documented account of their career from 1915 to 1938.

Drew Page, clarinet and sax man throughout a long career, has written a personal narrative, *Drew's Blues: A Sideman's Life with the Big Bands.*

Charlie "Bird" Parker began playing alto sax with Jay McShann's big band in Kansas City, but his ensemble playing in New York in the 1940s made him, with Dizzy Gillespie, the center of the new bebop or bop style. By the time of his death in 1955, he was one of the greatest jazz soloists. In Robert George Reisner's *Bird: The Legend of Charlie Parker,* collected in 1962, eighty-one friends and associates remember Parker; there are many photographs, a chronology of his life, and a discography. Ross Russell's *Bird Lives! The High Life and Hard Times of Charlie (Yardbird) Parker* is a large-scale, intimate biography. Max Harrison's *Charlie Parker* is a short, critical biography in the Kings of Jazz series.

Art Pepper, a west-coast alto sax player, has written an autobiography called *Straight Life.*

Artie Shaw led highly successful big bands in the swing era that vied with those of another clarinetist, Benny Goodman. His book *The Trouble with*

Cinderella: An Outline of Identity is a ruminative and personal autobiography explaining his eventual decision to abandon his career.

Willie "the Lion" Smith was one of the Harlem "stride" style pianists of the 1920s. In 1964 he published a book of recollections, *Music on My Mind: The Memoirs of an American Pianist,* with four interludes of exposition by his collaborator, George Hoefer.

Jack Teagarden played trombone and sang throughout a career of forty years, including teamwork with Louis Armstrong. A popular-style biography, *Jack Teagarden: The Story of a Jazz Maverick,* by Jay D. Smith and Lenn Guttridge was published four years before his death in 1964.

Fats Waller was a "stride" pianist, organist, songwriter, and radio and movie entertainer. Ed Kirkeby's *Ain't Misbehavin': The Story of Fats Waller* is a popular, undocumented biography concluding with a narrative of Kirkeby's years as Waller's manager and includes a selective but large discography and photographs of Waller and his contemporaries. Joel Vance's *Fats Waller: His Life and Times* is a short, documented life story. In the same year that Vance's book appeared, 1977, Maurice Waller published *Fats Waller,* telling his father's story. He gives a twenty-four-page table of recording dates and personnel, tables of published and unpublished songs, and the manuscripts of three songs, one of which was unpublished.

Dicky Wells played trombone with the big bands; Stanley Dance collaborated with him to write *The Night People: Reminiscences of a Jazzman.*

D. JAZZ HISTORY AND COMMENTARY

The fullest history of all jazz is Frank Tirro's *Jazz: A History* (1977), a broad-ranging book that undertakes to place jazz in social and musical history and to present many detailed examinations of musical (and for blues, verbal) examples, many photographs and other illustrations, and many separate characterizations of the work of individual musicians. Appendixes give musical transcriptions of some full pieces (in addition to passages printed in the text); a synoptic chronology of jazz, culture, and society; a large annotated bibliography; a hundred-album discography; and a glossary. James Lincoln Collier's *The Making of Jazz: A Comprehensive History* (1978) is a large reading history, descriptive although without detailed musical analysis, detailed in its narrative although without documentation. Martin T. Williams' *The Jazz Tradition* (1970) collects and extends essays he wrote for *Evergreen Review* and other magazines in the 1960s, to suggest a dialectical history of all jazz, in which improvising innovators alternate with synthesizing composers. Chapters center on Morton, Armstrong, Beiderbecke, Hawkins, Holiday, Ellington, Basie and Young, Parker, Monk, Lewis and the Modern Jazz Quartet, Rollins, Silver, Davis, Coltrane, and Coleman. His concluding discography is organized as discursive chapter notes. Edward Lee's *Jazz: An Introduction* (1972) is a British musician's concise survey history with many musical examples, up to an approving notice of jazz-rock fusion. Albert Murray's *Stomping the Blues,* mentioned in chapter 4, is strong on illustrations, as is Joachim-Ernst Berendt's *Photo History* (in section E, below).

Older general histories include Dave Dexter, Jr.'s, *Jazz Cavalcade: The Inside Story of Jazz* (1946). Dexter has a survey of jazz periodicals at the time, a guide to records, and chapters on radio jazz programs, jazz in movies, jazz overseas, singers and their records, and a poll of the favorite dozen jazz records of various musicians. Iain Lang's *Jazz in Perspective: The Background of the Blues* (1947) aimed to educate the British public to the background and the earthier side of jazz in distinction from dance band "industrial jazz." Lang gives the New Orleans-Chicago-Harlem-Kansas City history with emphasis on social conditions but also with a large place given to white musicians. A last chapter prints somewhat formalized lyrics of sixty blues songs. Barry Ulanov's *A History of Jazz in America* (1952) is a popular narrative history, its final chapters on bop and cool, including a glossary but not listing records or source notes. Marshall W. Stearn's *The Story of Jazz* (1956) is a scholarly but fairly short survey of jazz history: African and American backgrounds, New Orleans, bands, "Bop and After," and some analytic chapters on the musical elements and social context. A long bibliography by Robert George Reisner is included (expanded in the 1970 paperback), along with a "Syllabus of Fifteen Lectures on the History of Jazz," with recommended readings and records. Dave Dexter, Jr., whose earlier book begins this paragraph, also wrote *The Jazz Story: From the '90s to the '60s* (1964), a brief overview with some chapters divided into short, titled sections and some devoted to paragraph-per-artist surveys; he also gives a short, annotated bibliography of modern jazz and record suggestions by chapter.

Three elementary histories have been written to introduce jazz to young readers. The poet Langston Hughes wrote *The First Book of Jazz* (1955, updated in 1976). James Lincoln Collier's *Inside Jazz* (1973) has a useful last thirty pages giving a paragraph of introductory notes to each of thirty-seven representative albums. Charles Boeckman's *Cool, Hot and Blue: A History of Jazz for Young People* (1968) lays stress on early phases of jazz and gives very little history after the 1940s.

Serious historical books about the evolution of jazz date back half a century. Hugues Panassié's *Hot Jazz: The Guide to Swing Music* (translated from the original *Le Jazz Hot* in 1936) was a pioneering descriptive study of the New Orleans and Chicago styles and of early swing orchestras, critically evaluating performers and records. The book gave considerable prominence, more than have subsequent studies, to the contribution of the white Chicago players—Nichols, Trumbauer, Beiderbecke, Pollack. In 1942, Panassié's *The Real Jazz* undertook to rebalance that emphasis. A revision

(1960) extends this book through the 1950s but with disapproval of bop and later movements. In 1938 Winthrop Sargeant published *Jazz: Hot and Hybrid,* a good descriptive musicological study of jazz as it had evolved up through the swing era. Later expansions of the book, in 1946 and 1975, treat later developments somewhat impatiently. Sargeant gives special attention to rhythm, along with melody, scalar structure, and harmony. Wilder Hobson's *American Jazz Music* (1939) was an effort to characterize the natural jazz music behind commercial adaptations, focusing on thirty recorded examples. Hobson moves from basic stylistic elements to a historical survey, from New Orleans to Basie swing. Sidney Finkelstein's *Jazz: A People's Music* (1948) is a brief history, up to the bebop movement, that places jazz in a long tradition of unwritten music outside the classical canon, but that denies that it is "primitive"—rather, it asserts that jazz is part of the whole of western music. Finkelstein's is a social history, not in recounting social context but in stressing the human appeal and meaning of the music along with technical discussion. André Hodeir's *Jazz, Its Evolution and Essence* (translated in 1956 from the 1954 *Hommes et Problèmes du Jazz*) is a widely acknowledged major study of jazz development from the perspective of the early 1950s, with both detailed analysis and theoretical generalizations in a historical argument for the legitmacy of the then controversial bop movement. A revision in 1979 drops a chapter and changes the discography slightly. Gunther Schuller's *Early Jazz: Its Roots and Musical Development* (1968) is volume 1 in a promised larger history, this volume breaking off in the early 1930s. Schuller has a notably careful study of African musical practices as described by current ethnomusicology, and he gives subtle study to key musical moments. Armstrong and Morton receive long attention; there is a chapter on leading performers of the 1920s, one on big bands in New York and the southwest, and one on early Ellington. An appendix prints an interview with George Morrison, a most unusual jazz pioneer who started as a black classical violinist in Colorado around 1911. Schuller also has a glossary and a brief discography.

Of period and movement histories, the largest collection concerns New Orleans, in a succession of books beginning to be published about the time of a fervent revival of the early music itself in the 1940s. The first fanfare was Rudi Blesh's *Shining Trumpets: A History of Jazz,* a large-scale history, study, and defense of the New Orleans tradition. Blesh finds in that school the true African-derived folk heart of jazz, what critics of other persuasions have labelled the primitivist understanding of jazz. The book grounds its argument in close analysis of performances, of which forty-seven are transcribed. A 1952 postscript makes some uneasy accommodation to bop, which is further than some of Blesh's co-partisans have been willing to go. Stephen Longstreet has written two books in this tradition. *The Real Jazz Old and New* (1956) quotes anonymously from numerous musicians to make a mosaic history. (A scornful review by Whitney Balliett alleges errors.) *Sportin' House: A History of the New Orleans Sinners and the Birth of Jazz* prints the author's sketches, paintings, and undocumented oral history of the Storyville red-light district. Prostitution is given more attention than the music. It is odd to find among the New Orleans enthusiasts both this book and a surprisingly moralistic defense in William L. Grossman and Jack K. Farrell's *The Heart of Jazz,* which finds the original and revival New Orleans music to embody beneficial and valid *content*—"a synthesis of Christian feeling and robust vitality"—in comparison to other forms, which the authors approve less. Rex Harris' *Jazz,* and an abridgement of that book called *The Story of Jazz,* is a British critic's history where jazz is defined as New Orleans-Chicago ensemble playing to the exclusion of blues, bands, and everything modern (though the later version has a modern jazz chapter by Sheldon Meyer). Two more solid studies appeared in the 1970s. Jack V. Buerkle and Danny Barker's *Bourbon Street Black: The New Orleans Black Jazzman* is the collaboration of a sociologist and a veteran banjoist studying the living community of black New Orleans jazz musicians as a society and as individuals, based on interviews and statistical analysis, with photographs of the people and the locale. *Brass Bands and New Orleans Jazz*, by William J. Schafer and Richard B. Allen, works out of the oral history Hogan Jazz Archive at Tulane University, tracing the tradition of brass street bands in the city as a major source for jazz but also as a distinct musical entity from 1890 to 1970. A short, evocative social history is Frederick Turner's *Remembering Song: Encounters with the New Orleans Jazz Tradition.* For further treatment of New Orleans jazz see also Williams' *Jazz Masters of New Orleans* in section C, above.

Other styles and periods of jazz are less centered on particular places, but two other books are place histories. Samuel B. Charters and Leonard Kunstadt's *Jazz: A History of the New York Scene* includes much primary documentation on the first decades of the century, where they place the emphasis of the book. The account bridges many jazz styles from dance music at the turn of the century to the Modern Jazz Quartet and hard bop in the late 1950s. Ross Russell's *Jazz Style in Kansas City and the Southwest* is a scholarly history of the city in the 1920s and 1930s as a center apart from the New Orleans and Chicago circles, the early stage for Benny Moten, Count Basie, Lester Young, Jack Teagarden, and Charlie Parker, among others. Russell includes an extensive photograph section.

Jazz in the 1920s, in retrospect, is traced in *Best of Jazz: Basin Street to Harlem* by Humphrey Lyttelton, a trumpeter and BBC program host. Lyttelton takes up fourteen landmark recordings from 1917 to 1930 and provides for each a background essay and commentary. Richard Hadlock's *Jazz Masters of the Twenties* is mentioned in section C, above. Two books with "jazz" in the title actually appeared in 1926. Paul Whiteman and Mary Margaret McBride wrote *Jazz* out of career anecdotes and lighthearted boosting of the new popular music of the period, Whiteman's "symphonic jazz." The book begins with an evocation of the slaves arriving in the new world bearing their African heritage, but Whiteman's jazz was far from those origins. A fascinating sentence for the history of blacks and whites in jazz occurs near the end where Whiteman says, "My men are of every kind of ancestry—Italian, German, French, English, Scandinavian." Henry O. Osgood had the same music in mind in *So This Is Jazz.* From a later point of view, it wasn't, but Osgood's book is a document of the version of jazz that was visible to the smart journalism of the mid-1920s—Whiteman, Gershwin, Grofé, and Irving Berlin—though with some mention of spirituals and blues.

Jazz in the 1930s was most prominently big band jazz, though as has been noted in chapter 3 not all big bands played jazz. Albert McCarthy, who wrote a large work on the nonjazz dance bands, has also written *Big Band Jazz,* a similarly large-format history with many photographs, including in chapter groups many aggregations that played outside the major city jazz centers. Personnel are listed in the text for many bands. There is an album discography by chapters. See also Fernett's book in section C, above. Stanley Dance's *The World of Swing,* later joined by a volume centered on Earl Hines (in section C, above), consists of chapter-interviews with forty men and women, concentrating on players rather than leaders, and on the idea of "swing." Dance includes photographs, a table of opinions of jazz-men on miscellaneous topics, and a list of bands in Harlem theaters. A volume in the Macmillan Jazz Masters series, *Jazz Masters of the Thirties* by Rex Stewart, is actually a posthumous collection of articles on big-band jazz in the 1920s and 1930s by Stewart, a cornetist for Fletcher Henderson and Duke Ellington. A short piece on Count Basie by Hsio Wen Shih and a profile of Stewart himself by Francis Thorne are appended; as in others of this series, there are a few photographs and no index. John S. Wilson's *The Collector's Jazz: Traditional and Swing* (1958) is a discursive guide to prewar jazz available on album reissues in the 1950s. The short last section of "Backgrounds" is only a list, but the main catalog by artists has useful brief characterizations of perhaps three hundred musicians and groups.

Jazz in the 1940s was stirred by the movement called bebop or bop. Ira Gitler's *Jazz Masters of the Forties* is a history of the bop revolution. Nine chapters each take up a principal artist and other co-instrumentalists, beginning with "Charlie Parker and the Alto and Baritone Saxophonists," with a record list for each chapter. Leonard Feather's *Inside Bebop* (on the cover, *Inside Jazz*) was an early (1949) up-to-the-moment history featuring Parker and Gillespie, with a section of musical analysis and a section of profiles of ninety-two musicians. (Compare Feather's later *Encyclopedias* in section C, above.) Arnold Shaw's *The Street That Never Slept: New York's Fabled 52d St.* bridges the 1930s and 1940s in a large history of a jazz night-spot neighborhood from reminiscences of its citizens, both musicians and others.

Jazz in the 1950s and 1960s saw the rise of cool, hard bop, free jazz, and various revivals, and generalizations such as those in the paragraphs above become even less safe. Several books attempt to provide an overview. Goldberg's *Jazz Masters of the Fifties* has been cited in section C, above. In 1956 Alun Morgan and Raymond Horricks, two young British critics, wrote *Modern Jazz: A Survey of Developments since 1939,* from the last years of prewar swing when Henry Minton established a club where bop was born, through the succeeding west coast cool movement and the rival movement of younger black artists in New York, closing with the continuing work of Ellington and Basie and a glance at some Europeans. John S. Wilson's *Jazz: The Transition Years, 1940-1960* is another narrative from the big band soloists (Lester Young) who led the way for bop (Parker, Gillespie) to the cool jazz reaction (early Miles Davis, west coast players), blues resurgence, hard bop (Rollins, Coltrane), free jazz (Coleman), third stream, and the New Orleans revival. It also includes a look at jazz overseas and a consideration of the audience. *Jazz Masters in Transition, 1957-69,* by Martin T. Williams, is a collection of eighty-seven short reviews and essays he wrote for periodicals in that period. Max Harrison and four other British critics compiled *Modern Jazz: The Essential Records,* a catalog with about a page of critical comment for each of two hundred LP records from 1945 to 1970. *Jazz in the Sixties: The Expansion of Musical Resources and Techniques,* by Michael J. Budds, is a short analytic study ("Color and Instrumentation," "Texture and Volume," and other chapters), with citations of seventy-seven records.

Free Jazz by Ekkehard Jost is a careful study of the work of the musicians in one sixties movement, with chapters on Coltrane and modal playing, Mingus, Coleman, Taylor, Coltrane from 1965 to 1967, Shepp, Ayler, Cherry, the Chicagoans, and Sun Ra. Jost gives musical examples and diagrams. The book is published in Austria, which curiously has become the other world center of this style of jazz. Four other books treat the jazz of this phase with the strong social and political commitment their authors find expressed in the music. The prominent poet, critic, and political leader LeRoi Jones, later named Imamu Amiri Baraka, collected in *Black Music* his reviews and liner notes from the mid-1960s, prefaced and generally toned with his passionate argument that jazz must be understood in terms of the life experience of black Americans. He closes with "A Brief Discography of the New Music"—Coleman, Coltrane, Rollins, Taylor, Dolphy, Ayler, Shepp, Sun Ra, and a few others. Frank Kofsky's *Black Nationalism and the Revolution in Music* is a set of angrily polemical essays arguing that jazz, and specifically the work of Coltrane, is the voice of black revolutionary nationalism. *Fire Music: A Political History of Jazz,* by Rob Backus, is a manifesto-as-history "presented as a patchwork of quotations" to show oppression leading to revolutionary anger in the jazz of the 1960s and 1970s. Valerie Wilmer's *As Serious as Your Life: The Story of the New Jazz* is a study and defense of the "new music" following Coltrane, sharply distinguished from the commercially successful jazz-rock fusion music of the 1970s. She includes her own photographs and a biographical dictionary of the musicians of the movement.

Jazz-rock fusion also has had its defense. In Julie Coryell and Laura Friedman's *Jazz-Rock Fusion: The People, the Music,* the authors interview and profile fifty-eight musicians. Select discographies at the end run to more than thirty pages and include records in which the player figured as a sideman.

Two books may be noted that deal exclusively with jazz as export, influence, and transplanted stock. Chris Goddard's *Jazz Away from Home* traces jazz in Europe, especially Paris and London, from the arrival of musicians in the American army in World War I through the 1920s. An appendix is a section of recollections about Django Reinhardt, the great gypsy jazz guitarist, although his career came after the span covered by the book. More exotic is a German history, *Jazz in Deutschland: Die deutsche Jazz-Chronik 1900-1960* by Horst H. Lange, which includes a remarkable chapter on jazz in the Third Reich.

Between history and criticism may be placed some studies of jazz at large that emphasize its social history. LeRoi Jones' *Blues People* tells the story of blues and jazz as an index to the evolution of black American culture. Neil Leonard's *Jazz and the White Americans: The Acceptance of a New Art Form* is a scholarly, sociological study of white attitudes toward jazz in the 1920s and 1930s. Leroy Ostransky's *Jazz City: The Impact of Our Cities on the Development of Jazz* studies the urban settings that became jazz centers, including a good deal of nonjazz history as a matrix for the rise of the music. Francis Newton (Eric J. Hobsbawm), a prominent British economic and social historian, published *The Jazz Scene* in 1959, a study of jazz in its business and social context, with particular reference to England. Ronald L. Morris' *Wait Until Dark: Jazz and the Underworld, 1880-1940* combines documented history of gangster power in the world of jazz clubs with the unpersuasive thesis that these patrons made jazz what it became. *American Music from Storyville to Woodstock,* edited by Charles Nanry, is an anthology of papers, mostly from a jazz and sociology conference at the Rutgers Institute of Jazz Studies in 1970, on jazz in society from the 1920s to the 1950s, and on rock in the 1950s and 1960s.

Critical essays about jazz have been collected into a number of books, usually after having appeared in the numerous jazz periodicals that are the primary forum for jazz discussion. In 1956 Eddie Condon and Richard Gehman edited *Eddie Condon's Treasury of Jazz,* a large anthology of profiles and essays, most of them by prominent critics and jazzmen. There is a general section, one on Condon's Chicago contemporaries, one on bop, one on swing, and one of jazz-related fiction. Martin T. Williams has edited two collections. *The Art of Jazz: Essays on the Nature and Development of Jazz* ranges from Ansermet's pioneering remarks in 1918 to an early notice of

Coltrane. "Record notes" are appended to each item in the anthology, and a basic album library is listed at the end. *Jazz Panorama: From the Pages of the Jazz Review* gathers reviews, essays, and interviews published in that magazine from 1958 to 1961, on subjects ranging from the 1920s to the 1960s. Williams supplies brief headnotes on contributors, subjects, and occasions, and a few photographs. Ralph J. Gleason edited *Jam Session: An Anthology of Jazz* selecting writings from 1939 to the mid-1950s, including eight pieces of his own. *The Jazz Word* by Dom Cerulli, Burt Korall, and Mort Nasatir collects forty-two short pieces from the late 1950s, some original in this book but most reprinted, tending to the light, occasional, and belletristic.

Single critics who have published volumes of their jazz essays and journalism will be listed within this paragraph alphabetically. Whitney Balliett has written on jazz for *The New Yorker* for a quarter of a century, and his pieces have reappeared in seven collections: in 1961, *The Sound of Surprise,* articles from 1954 to 1959; in 1962, *Dinosaurs in the Morning,* articles from 1957 to 1961; in 1968, *Such Sweet Thunder,* articles from 1962 to 1966; in 1971, *Ecstasy at the Onion,* articles from 1966 to 1971; in 1976, *New York Notes,* articles from 1972 to 1975; in 1977, *Improvising,* in part overlapping three other books; and in 1981, *Night Creature,* articles from 1975 to 1980. Ralph de Toledano published a collection, perhaps the first of this category, in 1947 called *Frontiers of Jazz* (a slightly revised version appeared in 1962) on mainstream music and artists—"The Blues," "Duke Ellington"—so that, despite the word "frontiers" in the title, there was nothing avant-garde, marginal, or neglected about the material. Leonard Feather's *The Passion for Jazz* reprints his articles from the *Los Angeles Times* and various jazz periodicals from 1975 to 1980. Gary Giddins, in *Riding on a Blue Note,* collects his pieces from *The Village Voice* in the 1970s. Ralph Gleason's *Celebrating the Duke: & Louis, Bessie, Billie, Bird, Carmen, Miles, Dizzy & Other Heroes* is his essays and liner notes written in the decade before his death in 1975, the year of publication. The last third of the book is devoted to Ellington. Benny Green's *Drums in My Ears* is his pieces published in Britain from 1956 to 1971. Max Harrison, another British critic, collects works from the same period in *A Jazz Retrospect.* André Hodeir's *Toward Jazz,* translated from his pieces in French periodicals in the 1950s, includes detailed commentaries, more general critical evaluations, and yet more general essays on the nature of jazz and of jazz criticism. The same author's *The Worlds of Jazz* is a collection of literary diversions for in-group fans of jazz and jazz writing—skit, interior monologue, and put-on—tricky going for the uninitiated reader. Burnett James' *Essays on Jazz* are taken or adapted from his contributions to the British *Jazz Monthly* magazine, serious and tending to the academic. Derek Jewell's *The Popular Voice: A Musical Record of the 60s and 70s* is rock and jazz journalism from 1963 to 1978, mostly from the London *Sunday*

Times. John Sinclair and Robert Levin's *Music and Politics* reprints their essays from *Jazz and Pop* magazine, reviewing jazz and some rock from a radical political angle.

Journals of many species, often with short publication life, publish jazz criticism and news. The international scattering of jazz magazines is breathtaking: three that happen to share the simple title *Jazz* are published in New York State; in Warsaw, Poland; and in Mutteux, Switzerland. Other jazz periodicals appear in virtually every European and some Asian and Latin American nations, and several appear in Canada and Australia. For the American student or fan of jazz, the principal resources aside from local newsletters will be mentioned here, including a few from outside the United States. There is one excellent academic review devoted to jazz, the *Journal of Jazz Studies* published twice yearly by the Institute of Jazz Studies at Rutgers University in New Jersey. An excellent critical review, *The Jazz Review,* was published in New York from 1958 to 1961 and was edited by Nat Hentoff and Martin Williams; Williams' selections published as *Jazz Panorama* have been noted above, and the entire run has been reproduced by Kraus Reprint Company. As the Whitney Balliett collections testify, jazz has been consistently noticed in *The New Yorker,* and jazz coverage also appears regularly in *Saturday Review. Down Beat,* a prestigious slick-paper monthly published since 1934 and now with a circulation over 100,000, features jazz in articles and reviews, along with some rock and pop coverage. A *Down Beat Yearbook* began to be published in 1956. *High Fidelity* covers jazz and pop in its "Backbeat" section. *Cadence Magazine* is a jazz and blues monthly begun in 1976. *Jazz Report: The Record Collector's Magazine,* a bimonthly, has some book and record reviews along with data for collectors. Some of the major jazz periodicals have specialities within jazz. *Jazz Journal International* from England is broad in scope but excludes the free-form avant-garde. *Jazz Times* and *Storyville,* both British, feature New Orleans. *Coda,* an impressive monthly published in Toronto, supports modern jazz. *Jazz and Pop* (monthly from 1962, apparently ceasing in 1971) emphasized the politics of the music.

E. STUDIES OF THE JAZZ LIFE

The fans of many different musics show great interest in the personal lives of their favorite performers, but jazz and blues have elicited something further. Rising from deep sources in a black American culture little known to surrounding white society, jazz presented to its black and white audience testimony of vitality and creative genius rising above oppression and poverty. The mystery of artistic creation has been strongly presented by the spectacle of the art of jazz emerging from lowly obscurity and continuing its unpredictable creative evolution in one decade after another. The mystery and mystique of jazz, and its give and take with the communities that bore it or adopted it, are reflected in a variety of books about the jazz life. They may be divided into, first, collections of profiles and interviews and, second, photograph albums.

The first and a very important compilation of interviews of what has come to be called oral history was *Jazzmen* edited by Frederic Ramsey, Jr., and Charles Edward Smith in 1939. Based on talk with seventy-six players, nine authors constructed the history, with some interposed explanatory chapters on the music. The range was New Orleans, Chicago, and New York in the 1920s and 1930s, and the material gathered became the source for facts and legends in many later books. In 1955, Nat Shapiro and Nat Hentoff edited *Hear Me Talkin' to Ya: The Story of Jazz as Told by the Men Who Made It*. The editors weave together bits of narrative and comment from some 150 musicians and a few observers about various topics of discussion, rather than letting any voice speak at length, though many are quoted repeatedly. Both interviews and previously published accounts are used, and the overall movement is from New Orleans to Chicago, Harlem, Kansas City, and a bit of San Francisco. Fortunately, there is a good index. Hentoff compiled two other volumes of his own writings with similar intent. *The Jazz Life* (1961) collects his hip journalism on the jazz-club ambience of the 1940s and 1950s, about drugs, jazz festivals, and recording sessions, with profiles of Basie, Mingus, Lewis, Davis, Monk, and Coleman. *Jazz Is* (1976) has essays on Ellington, Holiday, Armstrong, Teddy Wilson, Mulligan, Davis, Mingus, Parker, Coltrane, Taylor, Gato Barbieri, and jazz economics, interspersed with collages of quotations from jazz artists. There are photographs of each figure featured, and of some others, by Bob Parent. Also in 1976, Leonard Feather collected *The Pleasures of Jazz: Leading Performers on Their Lives, Their Music, Their Contemporaries,* brief interviews with forty-three jazz figures of the 1950s and 1960s, mostly reprinted from the *Los Angeles Times* and elsewhere, including some interviews with survivors of earlier eras such as Eubie Blake, Hoagy Carmichael, and Red Norvo. One recent book compiles older material: Art Hodes and Chadwick Hansen put together *Selections from the Gutter: Jazz Portraits from "The Jazz Record,"* reprints from Hodes' magazine that ran from 1943 to 1947. The "selections" are portraits of jazzmen by critics and by themselves, particularly New Orleans and Chicago musicians. Michael Ullman's *Jazz Lives: Portraits in Words and Pictures* is interview profiles, some previously published in *The New Republic* and other magazines, of nineteen musicians and four music business people. Valerie Wilmer's *Jazz People* profiles fourteen black artists. An odd book is *Conversations with Jazz Musicians,* apparently part of a series of books of haphazardly chosen interviews; anonymous corporate editing digests interviews taped by Zane Knauss with eleven miscellaneous more and less significant musicians he was able to meet.

Photograph albums begin with Orrin Keepnews and Bill Grauer, Jr.'s, *A Pictorial History of Jazz* (1955, revised 1966), a full display of jazz artists from Buddy Bolden to Ornette Coleman, with captions and brief chapter introductions. *Jazz Street. Photographs by Dennis Stock, with an Introduction and Commentary by Nat Hentoff* is a lateral rather than historical survey in pictures annotated but not dated of jazz people around the country performing and at leisure. Valerie Wilmer's *The Face of Black Music* collects her photographs of jazz and blues artists from 1963 to 1976. *Jazz People,* with photographs by Ole Brask and text by Dan Morgenstern, is a survey history in a large Abrams-artbook format (but black and white). After some vintage pictures of early players, the book is Brask's work interspersed with anecdotes. Joachim-Ernst Berendt's *Jazz: A Photo History* is that very successful German jazz commentator's ample collection of 370 photographs with biographical captions, including a final section on Europe and Japan. More specialized studies include William P. Gottlieb's *The Golden Age of Jazz: On-Location Portraits, in Words and Pictures, of More Than 200 Outstanding Musicians from the Late '30s through the '40s,* with candid pictures and slight text. Rose and Souchon's *New Orleans Jazz: A Family Album* has been mentioned in section C, above. *The Cotton Club* by Jim Haskins is a chronicle of the Harlem night spot for white audiences that was a showcase for jazz and other entertainment from 1923 to 1936, moving to Broadway for a last four years. Burt Goldblatt's *Newport Jazz Festival: The Illustrated History* covers those occasions from 1954 to 1976.

BIBLIOGRAPHY

Allen, Daniel. *Bibliography of Discographies: Jazz,* vol. 2. New York: R. R. Bowker, 1981.

Allen, Walter C. *Hendersonia: The Music of Fletcher Henderson and His Musicians.* Highland Park, N.J.: Walter C. Allen, 1973.

————, and Rust, Brian. *King Joe Oliver.* Belleville, N.J.: Walter C. Allen, 1955.

Armstrong, Louis. *Satchmo: My Life in New Orleans.* New York: Prentice-Hall, 1954.

Backus, Rob. *Fire Music: A Political History of Jazz.* Chicago: Vanguard Books/ Emancipation/Black Graphics International, 1976.

Balliett, Whitney. *Dinosaurs in the Morning: 41 Pieces on Jazz.* 1962. Reprint. Westport, Conn.: Greenwood Press, 1978.

————. *Ecstasy at the Onion: Thirty-one Pieces on Jazz.* Indianapolis: Bobbs-Merrill, 1971.

————. *Improvising: Sixteen Jazz Musicians and Their Art.* New York: Oxford University Press, 1977.

————. *New York Notes: A Journal of Jazz, 1972-1975.* Boston: Houghton Mifflin, 1976.

————. *Night Creature: A Journal of Jazz, 1975-1980.* New York: Oxford University Press, 1981.

————. *The Sound of Surprise: 46 Pieces on Jazz.* London: William Kimber, 1961.

————. *Such Sweet Thunder.* London: Macdonald, 1968.

Bechet, Sidney. *Treat It Gentle.* 1960. Reprint. New York: Da Capo, 1975.

Benny: King of Swing. A Pictorial Biography Based on Benny Goodman's Personal Archives, with 212 Illustrations. New York: William Morrow, 1979.

Berendt, Joachim-Ernst. *Jazz: A Photo History.* Trans. William Odom. New York: Schirmer Books, 1979.

_____. *The Jazz Book. From New Orleans to Rock and Free Jazz.* Trans. Dan Morgenstern and Helmut and Barbara Bredigkeit. New York: Lawrence Hill, 1975.

_____, ed. *The Story of Jazz: From New Orleans to Rock Jazz.* Englewood Cliffs, N.J.: Prentice-Hall, 1978.

Berlin, Edward A. *Ragtime: A Musical and Cultural History.* Berkeley: University of California Press, 1980.

Berton, Ralph. *Remembering Bix: A Memoir of the Jazz Age.* New York: Harper and Row, 1974.

Bethell, Tom. *George Lewis: A Jazzman from New Orleans.* Berkeley: University of California Press, 1977.

Blackstone, Orin. *Index to Jazz: Jazz Recordings 1917-1944. 1945-1948.* Reprint. Westport, Conn.: Greenwood Press, 1978.

Blesh, Rudi. *Combo: USA. Eight Lives in Jazz.* Philadelphia: Chilton Book, 1971.

_____. *Shining Trumpets: A History of Jazz.* 1946, 1958. Reprint. New York: Da Capo, 1975.

_____, and Janis, Harriet. *They All Played Ragtime: The True Story of an American Music.* New York: Knopf, 1950.

_____. *They All Played Ragtime.* 4th ed. New York: Oak, 1971.

Boeckman, Charles. *Cool, Hot and Blue: A History of Jazz for Young People.* Washington, D.C.: Robert B. Luce, 1968.

Brunn, H. O. *The Story of the Original Dixieland Jazz Band.* Baton Rouge: Louisiana State University Press, 1960.

Budds, Michael J. *Jazz in the Sixties: The Expansion of Musical Resources and Techniques.* Iowa City: University of Iowa Press, 1978.

Buerkle, Jack V., and Barker, Danny. *Bourbon Street Black: The New Orleans Black Jazzman.* New York: Oxford University Press, 1973.

Cadence Magazine: The American Review of Jazz and Blues. Redwood, N.Y., 1976- .

Calloway, Cab, and Rollins, Bryant. *Of Minnie the Moocher and Me.* New York: Thomas Y. Crowell, 1976.

Carey, David A., et al. *The Directory of Recorded Jazz and Swing Music,* vols. 1-4. Fordingbridge, Hampshire, England: Delphic Press, 1949-1952.

_____, vols. 5-6. London: Cassell, 1954-1957.

Carmichael, Hoagy. *The Stardust Road.* 1946. Reprint. Westport, Conn.: Greenwood Press, 1969.

_____, with Stephen Longstreet. *Sometimes I Wonder: The Story of Hoagy Carmichael.* 1965. Reprint. New York: Da Capo, 1976.

Carter, Lawrence T. *Eubie Blake: Keys of Memory.* Detroit: Balamp Publishing, 1979.

Case, Brian, and Britt, Stan. *The Illustrated Encyclopedia of Jazz.* New York: Harmony Books, 1978.

Cerulli, Dom; Korall, Burt; and Nasatir, Mort. *The Jazz Word.* New York: Ballantine Books, 1960.

Charters, Samuel Barclay IV, comp. *Jazz: New Orleans, 1885-1963—An Index to the Negro Musicians of New Orleans.* Rev. ed. New York: Oak, 1963.

_____, and Kunstadt, Leonard. *Jazz: A History of the New York Scene.* Garden City, N.Y.: Doubleday, 1962.

Chilton, John. *Who's Who of Jazz: Storyville to Swing Street.* Philadelphia: Chilton Book, 1972.

Coda: The Jazz Magazine. Toronto, Ontario, Canada, 1958- .

Coker, Jerry. *The Jazz Idiom.* Englewood Cliffs, N.J.: Prentice-Hall, 1975.

_____. *Listening to Jazz.* Englewood Cliffs, N.J.: Prentice-Hall, 1978.

Cole, Bill. *John Coltrane.* New York: Schirmer Books, 1976.

_____. *Miles Davis: A Musical Biography.* New York: William Morrow, 1974.

Collier, Graham. *Jazz: A Student's and Teacher's Guide.* Cambridge, England: Cambridge University Press, 1977.

Collier, James Lincoln. *The Great Jazz Artists.* New York: Four Winds Press, 1977.

_____. *Inside Jazz.* New York: Four Winds Press, 1973.

_____. *The Making of Jazz: A Comprehensive History.* Boston: Houghton Mifflin, 1978.

Condon, Eddie, and Gehman, Richard, eds. *Eddie Condon's Treasury of Jazz.* 1956. Reprint. Westport, Conn.: Greenwood Press, 1975.

_____, and O'Neal, Hank. *The Eddie Condon Scrapbook of Jazz.* New York: St. Martin's Press, 1973.

_____, and Sugrue, Thomas. *We Called It Music: A Generation of Jazz.* New York: Henry Holt, 1947.

Connor, D. Russell. *BG—Off the Record: A Bio-Discography of Benny Goodman.* Fairless Hill, Pa.: Gaildonna Publishing, 1958.

_____, and Hicks, Warren W. *B.G. on the Record: A Bio-Discography of Benny Goodman.* New Rochelle, N.Y.: Arlington House, 1969.

Conversations with Jazz Musicians, vol. 2. Detroit: Gale Research Co., 1977.

Cooper, David Edwin. *International Bibliography of Discographies: Classical Music and Jazz and Blues.* Littleton, Colo.: Libraries Unlimited, 1975.

Coryell, Julie, and Friedman, Laura. *Jazz-Rock Fusion: The People, the Music.* New York: Delacorte Press, 1978.

Danca, Vince. *Bunny: A Bio-Discography of Jazz Trumpeter Bunny Berigan.* Rockford, Ill.: Vince Danca, 1978.

Dance, Stanley. *The World of Count Basie.* New York: Charles Scribner's Sons, 1980.

_____. *The World of Duke Ellington.* New York: Charles Scribner's Sons, 1970.

_____. *The World of Swing,* vol. 1. New York: Charles Scribner's Sons, 1974.

_____. *The World of Earl Hines,* vol. 2. The World of Swing. New York: Charles Scribner's Sons, 1977.

Dankworth, Avril. *Jazz: An Introduction to Its Musical Basis.* New York: Oxford University Press, 1968.

Delaunay, Charles. *New Hot Discography: The Standard Directory of Recorded Jazz.* Ed. Walter E. Schaap and George Avakian. New York: Criterion, 1948.

De Toledano, Ralph. *Frontiers of Jazz.* 2d ed. New York: Frederick Ungar, 1962.

Dexter, Dave, Jr. *Jazz Cavalcade: The Inside Story of Jazz.* New York: Criterion Music Corp., 1946.

_____. *The Jazz Story: From the '90s to the '60s.* Englewood Cliffs, N.J.: Prentice-Hall, 1964.

Down Beat. Chicago, 1934- .

Down Beat Yearbook. Chicago, 1956- .

Easton, Carol. *Straight Ahead: The Story of Stan Kenton.* New York: William Morrow, 1973.

Ellington, Edward Kennedy. *Music Is My Mistress.* Garden City, N.Y.: Doubleday, 1973.

Ellington, Mercer, with Stanley Dance. *Duke Ellington in Person.* Boston: Houghton Mifflin, 1978.

Esquire's World of Jazz. New York: Esquire/Grosset and Dunlap, 1962.

_____. New York: Thomas Y. Crowell, 1975.

Fairbairn, Ann. *Call Him George.* New York: Crown Publishers, 1969.

Feather, Leonard. *The Book of Jazz from Then till Now: A Guide to the Entire Field.* New York: Horizon Press, 1957.

_____. *The Encyclopedia of Jazz.* New York: Horizon Press, 1955.

_____. *The Encyclopedia of Jazz in the Sixties.* New York: Horizon Press, 1966.

_____. *From Satchmo to Miles.* New York: Stein and Day, 1972.

_____. *Inside Bebop.* New York: J. J. Robbins and Sons, 1949.

_____. *The New Edition of the Encyclopedia of Jazz. Completely Revised, Enlarged and Brought Up to Date.* New York: Horizon Press, 1960.

_____. *The Passion for Jazz.* New York: Horizon Press, 1980.

_____. *The Pleasures of Jazz: Leading Performers on Their Lives, Their Music, Their Contemporaries.* New York: Horizon Press, 1976.

_____, and Gitler, Ira, eds. *The Encyclopedia of Jazz in the Seventies.* New York: Horizon Press, 1976.

Fernett, Gene. *Swing Out: Great Negro Dance Bands.* Midland, Mich.: Pendell, 1970.

Finkelstein, Sidney. *Jazz: A People's Music.* 1948. Reprint. New York: Da Capo, 1975.

Fountain, Pete, with Bill Nealy. *A Closer Walk: The Pete Fountain Story.* Chicago: Henry Regnery, 1972.

Fox, Charles; Gammond, Peter; Morgan, Alun; and Korner, Alexis, eds. *Jazz on Record: A Critical Guide.* London: Hutchinson, 1960.

Gammond, Peter, ed. *Duke Ellington: His Life and Music.* 1958. Reprint. New York: Da Capo, 1977.

_____. *Scott Joplin and the Ragtime Era.* New York: St. Martin's Press, 1975.

_____, and Clayton, Peter. *Fourteen Miles on a Clear Night: An Irreverent, Skeptical, and Affectionate Book about Jazz Records.* 1966. Reprint. Westport, Conn.: Greenwood Press, 1978.

George, Don R. *Sweet Man: The Real Duke Ellington.* New York: G. P. Putnam's Sons, 1981.

Giddins, Gary. *Riding on a Blue Note: Jazz and American Pop.* New York: Oxford University Press, 1981.

Gillespie, Dizzy, with Al Fraser. *To Be, or Not . . . to Bop: Memoirs.* Garden City, N.Y.: Doubleday, 1979.

Gillis, Frank J., and Miner, John W., eds. *Oh, Didn't He Ramble: The Life Story of Lee Collins as Told to Mary Collins.* Music in American Life. Urbana: University of Illinois Press, 1974.

Gitler, Ira. *Jazz Masters of the Forties.* New York: Collier/Macmillan, 1966.

Gleason, Ralph J. *Celebrating the Duke: & Louis, Bessie, Billie, Bird, Carmen, Miles, Dizzy & Other Heroes.* Boston: Atlantic Monthly Press Book/Little, Brown, 1975.

———, ed. *Jam Session: An Anthology of Jazz.* New York: G. P. Putnam's Sons, 1958.

Goddard, Chris. *Jazz Away from Home.* New York: Paddington Press, 1979.

Goffin, Robert. *Horn of Plenty: The Story of Louis Armstrong.* Trans. James F. Bezou. 1947. Reprint. New York: Da Capo, 1977.

Gold, Robert S. *A Jazz Lexicon.* New York: Knopf, 1964.

———. *Jazz Talk.* Indianapolis: Bobbs-Merrill, 1975.

Goldberg, Joe. *Jazz Masters of the Fifties.* New York: Macmillan, 1965.

Goldblatt, Burt. *Newport Jazz Festival: The Illustrated History.* New York: Dial Press, 1977.

Goodman, Benny, and Kolodin, Irving. *The Kingdom of Swing.* New York: Stackpole Sons, 1939.

Gottlieb, William P. *The Golden Age of Jazz: On-Location Portraits, in Words and Pictures, of More Than 200 Outstanding Musicians from the Late '30s through the '40s.* New York: Simon and Schuster, 1979.

Graham, Alberta Powell. *Strike Up the Band! Bandleaders of Today.* New York: Thomas Nelson and Sons, 1949.

Green, Benny. *Drums in My Ears: Jazz in Our Time.* New York: Horizon Press, 1973.

———. *The Reluctant Art: The Growth of Jazz.* 1963. Reprint. Plainview, N.J.: Books for Libraries Press, 1975.

Green, Stanley, ed. *Kings of Jazz.* South Brunswick, N.J.: A. S. Barnes, 1978.

Gregor, Carl, ed. *International Jazz Bibliography: Jazz Books from 1919 to 1968.* Strasbourg: P. H. Heitz, 1969.

———. *1970 Supplement to International Jazz Bibliography and International Drum and Percussion Bibliography.* Graz, Austria: Universal Edition, 1971.

———. *1971/72/73 Supplement to International Jazz Bibliography (ijb) and Selective Bibliography of Some Jazz Background Literature and Bibliography of Two Subjects Previously Excluded.* Graz, Austria: Universal Edition, 1975.

Gridley, Mark C. *Jazz Styles.* Englewood Cliffs, N.J.: Prentice-Hall, 1978.

Grossman, William L., and Farrell, Jack W. *The Heart of Jazz.* New York: New York University Press, 1956.

Hadlock, Richard. *Jazz Masters of the Twenties.* New York: Macmillan, 1965.

Harris, Rex. *Jazz.* London: Penguin Books, 1952.

———. *The Story of Jazz.* 1955. Reprint. Westport, Conn.: Greenwood Press, 1980.

Harrison, Max. *Charlie Parker.* Kings of Jazz. New York: A. S. Barnes, 1961.

———. *A Jazz Retrospect.* Boston: Crescendo Publishing, 1976.

———, et al., comps. *Modern Jazz: The Essential Records: A Critical Selection.* London: Aquarius Books, 1975.

Haskins, Jim. *The Cotton Club.* New York: Random House, 1977.

———, with Kathleen Benson. *Scott Joplin.* Garden City, N.Y.: Doubleday and Co., 1978.

Hawes, Hampton, and Asher, Don. *Raise Up Off Me.* New York: Coward, McCann and Geoghegan, 1974.

Hefele, Bernhard. *Jazz-Bibliographie*. Munich: K. G. Saur, 1981.

Hentoff, Nat. *Jazz Is*. New York: Ridge Press/Random House, 1976.

_____. *The Jazz Life*. 1961. Reprint. New York: Da Capo, 1975.

High Fidelity. New York, 1951- .

Hobson, Wilder. *American Jazz Music*. 1939. Reprint. New York: Da Capo, 1976.

Hodeir, André. *Jazz, Its Evolution and Essence*. Rev. ed. Trans. David Noakes. New York: Da Capo, 1979.

_____. *Toward Jazz*. Trans. Noël Burch. 1962. New York: Da Capo, 1976.

_____. *The Worlds of Jazz*. Trans. Noël Burch. New York: Grove Press, 1972.

Hodes, Art, and Hansen, Chadwick. *Selections from the Gutter: Jazz Portraits from "The Jazz Record."* Berkeley: University of California Press, 1977.

Horricks, Raymond. *Count Basie and His Orchestra: Its Music and Its Musicians*. 1957. Reprint. Westport, Conn.: Negro Universities Press, 1971.

Hughes, Langston. *The First Book of Jazz*. New York: Franklin Watts, 1955.

_____. *The First Book of Jazz, updated ed. 1976*.

James, Burnett. Bix Beiderbecke. Kings of Jazz. New York: A. S. Barnes, 1961.

_____. *Essays on Jazz*. London: Jazz Book Club/Sidgwick and Jackson, 1962.

Jasen, David A. *Recorded Ragtime, 1897-1958*. Hamden, Conn.: Archon Books/ Shoestring Press, 1973.

_____, and Tichenor, Trebor Jay. *Rags and Ragtime: A Musical History*. New York: Seabury Press, 1978.

Jazz. Warsaw, Poland, 1956- .

Jazz. Mutteux, Switzerland, 1968- .

Jazz. Northport, N.Y., 1977- .

Jazz and Pop: The Magazine about Music. New York, 1962-1971.

Jazz Guitarists: Collected Interviews from Guitar Player Magazine. Saratoga, Calif.: Guitar Player Books, 1978.

Jazz Index: Quarterly Bibliography of Jazz Literature in Periodicals and Collections. Frankfurt, 1977- .

Jazz Journal International. London, 1948- .

Jazz People. New York: Harry N. Abrams, 1976.

Jazz Report: The Record Collector's Magazine. Ventura, Calif., 1958- .

The Jazz Review. New York, 1958-1961.

Jazz Times. Twickenham, Middlesex, England, 1964- .

Jepsen, Jorgen Grunnet. *Jazz Records, 1942-1965. A Discography*. 8 vols. Holte, Denmark: Karl Emil Knudsen, 1964-1965.

Jewell, Derek. *Duke: A Portrait of Duke Ellington*. New York: W. W. Norton, 1977.

_____. *The Popular Voice: A Musical Record of the 60s and 70s*. London: Andre Deutsch, 1980.

Jones, LeRoi. *Black Music*. New York: William Morrow, 1967.

_____. *Blues People: Negro Music in White America*. New York: William Morrow, 1963.

Jones, Max, and Chilton, John. *Louis: The Louis Armstrong Story, 1900-1971*. Boston: Little, Brown, 1971.

Jones, Morley. *Jazz*. Ed. Alan Rich. New York: Simon and Schuster, 1980.

Jörgensen, John, and Wiedemann, Erik. *Mosaik Jazzlexikon*. Hamburg: Mosaik Verlag, 1966.

Jost, Ekkehard. *Free Jazz.* Studies in Jazz Research. Graz, Austria: Universal Edition, 1974.

Journal of Jazz Studies, Incorporating Studies in Jazz Discography. New Brunswick, N.J., 1973- .

Kaminsky, Max, with V. E. Hughes. *My Life in Jazz.* London: Jazz Book Club, 1965.

Keepnews, Orrin, and Grauer, Bill, Jr. *A Pictorial History of Jazz: People and Places from New Orleans to Modern Jazz.* New York: Crown Publishers, 1955.

Kennington, Donald. *The Literature of Jazz: A Critical Guide.* Chicago: American Library Association, 1970.

―――, and Read, Danny L. *The Literature of Jazz: A Critical Guide.* 2d ed. rev. Chicago: American Library Association, 1980.

Kimball, Robert, and Bolcom, William. *Reminiscing with Sissle and Blake.* New York: Viking Press, 1973.

Kirkeby, Ed, with Duncan P. Scheidt and Sinclair Traill. *Ain't Misbehavin': The Story of Fats Waller.* New York: Dodd, Mead, 1966.

Kofsky, Frank. *Black Nationalism and the Revolution in Music.* New York: Pathfinder Press, 1970.

Lang, Iain. *Jazz in Perspective: The Background of the Blues.* 1947. Reprint. New York: Da Capo, 1976.

Lange, Horst H. *Jazz in Deutschland: Die deustche Jazz-Chronik 1900-1960.* Berlin: Colloquium Verlag Otto H. Hess, 1966.

Langridge, Derek. *Your Jazz Collection.* Hamden, Conn.: Archon Books/Shoestring Press, 1970.

Lee, Edward. *Jazz: An Introduction.* 1972. Reprint. New York: Crescendo Publishing, 1977.

Leonard, Neil. *Jazz and the White Americans: The Acceptance of a New Art Form.* Chicago: University of Chicago Press, 1962.

Lomax, Alan. *Mr. Jelly Roll: The Fortunes of Jelly Roll Morton, New Orleans Creole and "Inventor of Jazz."* New York: Duell, Sloan and Pearce, 1950.

―――. 2d ed. Berkeley: University of California Press, 1973.

Longstreet, Stephen. *The Real Jazz Old and New.* 1956. Reprint. Westport, Conn.: Greenwood Press, 1969.

―――. *Sportin' House: A History of the New Orleans Sinners and the Birth of Jazz.* Los Angeles: Sherbourne Press, 1965.

Lyons, Len. *The 101 Best Jazz Albums: A History of Jazz on Records.* New York: William Morrow, 1980.

Lyttelton, Humphrey. *Best of Jazz: Basin Street to Harlem.* New York: Crescendo/ Taplinger, 1978.

McCarthy, Albert. *Big Band Jazz.* New York: G. P. Putnam's Sons, 1974.

McCoy, Meredith, and Parker, Barbara, comps. *Catalog of the John D. Reid Collection of Early American Jazz.* Little Rock: Arkansas Arts Center, 1975.

Marquis, Donald M. *In Search of Buddy Bolden: First Man of Jazz.* Baton Rouge: Louisiana State University Press, 1978.

Meeker, David. *Jazz in the Movies: A Guide to Jazz Musicians 1917-1977.* New Rochelle, N.Y.: Arlington House, 1977.

Merriam, Alan P., with Robert J. Benford. *A Bibliography of Jazz.* 1954. Reprint. New York: Da Capo, 1970.

Mezzrow, Milton, and Wolfe, Bernard. *Really the Blues.* New York: Random House, 1946.

Miller, Paul Eduard, ed. *Down Beat's Yearbook of Swing.* 1939. Reprint. Westport, Conn.: Greenwood Press, 1978.

_____. *Esquire's Jazz Book.* Chicago: Books, 1943-1944.

_____. *Esquire's 1946 Jazz Book.* New York: Smith and Durrell, 1946.

Mingus, Charles. *Beneath the Underdog.* Ed. Nel King. 1971. Reprint. New York: Penguin, 1975.

Mississippi Rag: The Voice of Traditional Jazz and Ragtime. Minneapolis, Minn.: 1974- .

Morgan, Alun, and Horricks, Raymond. *Modern Jazz: A Survey of Developments since 1939.* 1956. Reprint. Westport, Conn.: Greenwood Press, 1977.

Morris, Ronald L. *Wait Until Dark: Jazz and the Underworld, 1880-1940.* Bowling Green, Ohio: Bowling Green University Popular Press, 1980.

Murray, Albert. *Stomping the Blues.* New York: McGraw-Hill, 1976.

Nanry, Charles, ed. *American Music from Storyville to Woodstock.* New Brunswick, N.J.: Transaction Books, 1972.

_____, with Edward Berger. *The Jazz Text.* New York: Van Nostrand Reinhold, 1979.

Newton, Francis [Eric J. Hobsbawm]. *The Jazz Scene.* 1959. Reprint. New York: Da Capo, 1975.

The New Yorker. New York, 1925- .

Osgood, Henry O. *So This Is Jazz.* 1926. Reprint. New York: Da Capo, 1978.

Ostransky, Leroy. *The Anatomy of Jazz.* 1960. Reprint. Westport, Conn.: Greenwood Press, 1973.

_____. *Jazz City: The Impact of Our Cities on the Development of Jazz.* Englewood Cliffs, N.J.: Prentice-Hall, 1978.

_____. *Understanding Jazz.* Englewood Cliffs, N.J.: Prentice-Hall, 1977.

Page, Drew. *Drew's Blues: A Sideman's Life with the Big Bands.* Baton Rouge: Louisiana State University Press, 1980.

Panassié, Hugues. *Hot Jazz: The Guide to Swing Music.* Trans. Lyle and Eleanor Dowling. 1936. Reprint. Westport, Conn.: Negro Universities Press/Greenwood Press, 1970.

_____. *The Real Jazz.* 1960. Rev. ed. Reprint. Westport, Conn.: Greenwood Press, 1973.

_____, and Gautier, Madeleine. *Guide to Jazz.* Trans. Desmond Flower; ed. A. A. Gurwitch. 1956. Reprint. Westport, Conn.: Greenwood Press, 1973.

Pepper, Art, and Pepper, Laurie. *Straight Life: The Story of Art Pepper.* New York: Schirmer Books, 1979.

Ragtimer. Weston, Ontario, Canada, 1962- .

Rag Times. Los Angeles, 1968- .

Ramsey, Frederic, Jr. *A Guide to Longplay Jazz Records.* New York: Long Player Publications, 1954.

_____, and Smith, Charles Edward, eds. *Jazzmen.* New York: Harcourt Brace, 1939.

Reisner, Robert George, ed. *Bird: The Legend of Charlie Parker.* 1962. Reprint. New York: Da Capo, 1975.

_____. *The Jazz Titans: Including "The Parlance of Hip."* 1960. Reprint. New York: Da Capo, 1977.

———. *The Literature of Jazz: A Preliminary Bibliography*. New York: New York Public Library, 1954.

———. *The Literature of Jazz: A Selective Bibliography*. 2d ed. Rev. and enlarged. New York: New York Public Library, 1959.

Rivelli, Pauline, and Levin, Robert. *Giants of Black Music*. 1970. Reprint. New York: Da Capo, 1979.

Rockmore, Noel. *Preservation Hall Portraits*. Baton Rouge: Louisiana State University Press, 1968.

Rose, Al. *Eubie Blake*. New York: Schirmer Books, 1979.

———, and Souchon, Edmond. *New Orleans Jazz: A Family Album*. Rev. ed. Baton Rouge: Louisiana State University Press, 1978.

Ruppli, Michael, comp., with Bob Porter. *The Prestige Label: A Discography*. Discographies, no. 3. Westport, Conn.: Greenwood Press, 1980.

———. *The Savoy Label: A Discography*. Discographies, no. 2. Westport, Conn.: Greenwood Press, 1980.

Russell, Ross. *Bird Lives! The High Life and Hard Times of Charlie (Yardbird) Parker*. New York: Charterhouse, 1973.

———. *Jazz Style in Kansas City and the Southwest*. Berkeley: University of California Press, 1971.

Rust, Brian. *Jazz Records 1897-1942*. 4th rev. and enlarged ed. 2 vols. New Rochelle, N.Y.: Arlington House, 1978.

Sargeant, Winthrop. *Jazz: Hot and Hybrid*. 1938. 3d ed., enlarged. New York: Da Capo, 1975.

Saturday Review. New York, 1924- .

Schafer, William J., with Richard B. Allen. *Brass Bands and New Orleans Jazz*. Baton Rouge: Louisiana State University Press, 1977.

———, and Riedel, Johannes, with Michael Polad and Richard Thompson. *The Art of Ragtime: Form and Meaning of an Original Black American Art*. Baton Rouge: Louisiana State University Press, 1973.

Schleman, Hilton R. *Rhythm on Record: A Complete Survey and Register of All the Principal Recorded Dance Music from 1906 to 1936, and a Who's Who of the Artists Concerned in the Making*. 1936. Reprint. Westport, Conn.: Greenwood Press, 1978.

Schuller, Gunther. *Early Jazz: Its Roots and Musical Development*. New York: Oxford University Press, 1968.

Shapiro, Nat, and Hentoff, Nat, eds. *Hear Me Talkin' to Ya: The Story of Jazz as Told by the Men Who Made It*. 1955. Reprint. New York: Dover Publications, 1966.

———. *The Jazz Makers*. 1957. Reprint. Westport, Conn.: Greenwood Press, 1975.

Shaw, Arnold. *The Street That Never Slept: New York's Fabled 52d St*. New York: Coward, McCann and Geoghegan, 1971.

Shaw, Artie. *The Trouble with Cinderella: An Outline of Identity*. 1952. Reprint. New York: Da Capo, 1979.

Simosko, Vladimir, and Tepperman, Barry. *Eric Dolphy: A Musical Biography and Discography*. Washington, D.C.: Smithsonian Institution Press, 1974.

Simpkins, Cuthbert Ormond. *Coltrane: A Biography*. New York: Herndon House, Publishers, 1975.

Sinclair, John, and Levin, Robert. *Music and Politics*. New York: World Publishing, 1971.

Smith, Charles Edward, with Frederic Ramsey, Jr., Charles Payne Rogers, and William Russell. *The Jazz Record Book*. 1942. Reprint. Westport, Conn.: Greenwood Press, 1978.

Smith, Jay D., and Guttridge, Len. *Jack Teagarden: The Story of a Jazz Maverick*. 1960. Reprint. New York: Da Capo, 1976.

Smith, Willie, with George Hoefer. *Music on My Mind: The Memoirs of an American Pianist*. 1964. Reprint. New York: Da Capo, 1975.

Sonnier, Austin M., Jr. *Willie Geary "Bunk" Johnson: The New Iberia Years*. New York: Crescendo Publishing, 1977.

Spellman, A. B. *Four Lives in the Bebop Business*. New York: Pantheon Books, 1966.

———. *Black Music: Four Lives*. New York: Schocken, 1970.

Stearns, Marshall W. *The Story of Jazz*. 1956. Reprint. New York: Oxford University Press, 1970.

Stewart, Rex. *Jazz Masters of the Thirties*. 1972. Reprint. New York: Da Capo, 1980.

Stock, Dennis. *Jazz Street*. Garden City, N.Y.: Doubleday, 1960.

Stoddard, Tom, ed. *Pops Foster—The Autobiography of a New Orleans Jazzman*. Berkeley: University of California Press, 1971.

Storyville. Chigwell, Essex, England, 1965- .

Studies in Jazz Discography. New Brunswick, N.J., 1971-1972.

Sudhalter, Richard M., and Evans, Philip R., with W. Dean-Myatt. *Bix: Man and Legend*. New Rochelle, N.Y.: Arlington House, 1974.

Tanner, Paul O. W., and Gerow, Maurice. *A Study of Jazz*. 2d ed. Dubuque, Iowa: Wm. C. Brown, 1973.

Terkel, Studs. *Giants of Jazz*. New York: Thomas Y. Crowell, 1957.

Thomas, J. C. *Chasin' the Trane: The Music and Mystique of John Coltrane*. Garden City, N.Y.: Doubleday, 1975.

Tirro, Frank. *Jazz: A History*. New York: W. W. Norton, 1977.

Townley, Eric. *Tell Your Story: A Dictionary of Jazz and Blues Recordings, 1917-1950*. Chigwell, Essex, England: Storyville Publications, 1976.

Tudor, Dean, and Tudor, Nancy. *Jazz*. American Popular Music on Elpee. Littleton, Colo.: Libraries Unlimited, 1979.

Turner, Frederick. *Remembering Song: Encounters with the New Orleans Jazz Tradition*. New York: Viking Press, 1982.

Ulanov, Barry. *Duke Ellington*. 1946. Reprint. New York: Da Capo, 1975.

———. *A Handbook of Jazz*. 1957. Reprint. Westport, Conn.: Greenwood Press, 1975.

———. *A History of Jazz in America*. 1952. Reprint. New York: Da Capo, 1972.

Ullman, Michael. *Jazz Lives: Portraits in Words and Pictures*. Washington, D.C.: New Republic Books, 1980.

Vance, Joel. *Fats Waller: His Life and Times*. Chicago: Contemporary Books, 1977.

Voight, John. *Jazz Music in Print*. 2d ed. Boston: Hornpipe Music Publishing, 1978.

Waldo, Terry. *This Is Ragtime*. New York: Hawthorn Books, 1976.

Waller, Maurice, and Calabrese, Anthony. *Fats Waller*. New York: Schirmer Books, 1977.

Wareing, Charles H., and Garlick, George. *Bugles for Beiderbecke*. London: Sidgwick and Jackson, 1958.

Wells, Dicky, as told to Stanley Dance. *The Night People: Reminiscences of a Jazz-man.* Boston: Crescendo Publishing, 1971.

Whiteman, Paul, and McBride, Mary Margaret. *Jazz.* 1926. Reprint. New York: Arno Press, 1974.

Williams, Martin T. *Jazz Masters in Transition, 1957-69.* 1970. Reprint. New York: Da Capo, 1980.

———. *Jazz Masters of New Orleans.* 1967. Reprint. New York: Da Capo, 1979.

———. *The Jazz Tradition.* New York: Oxford University Press, 1970.

———. *Jelly Roll Morton.* Kings of Jazz. New York: A. S. Barnes, 1963.

———. *Where's the Melody? A Listener's Introduction to Jazz.* New York: Pantheon Books, 1966.

———, ed. *The Art of Jazz: Essays on the Nature and Development of Jazz.* New York: Oxford University Press, 1959.

———. *Jazz Panorama: From the Pages of the Jazz Review.* 1962. Reprint. New York: Da Capo, 1979.

Wilmer, Valerie. *As Serious as Your Life: The Story of the New Jazz.* London: Allison and Busby, 1977.

———. *The Face of Black Music.* New York: Da Capo, 1976.

———. *Jazz People.* London: Allison and Busby, 1970.

Wilson, John S. *The Collector's Jazz: Traditional and Swing.* Philadelphia: J. B. Lippincott, 1958.

———. *Jazz: The Transition Years, 1940-1960.* New York: Appleton-Century-Crofts, 1966.

CHAPTER 6

Country and Folk Music

Commercial broadcasting and recording of what was then called hillbilly music began in the early 1920s, and today a tenth or more of the sales of the American record industry is musical entertainment calling itself *country:* about three times the volume of jazz sales, close to the level of sales for "pop," and about a quarter those of rock. This "country" music is now largely urban in its audience, its business and technical sophistication, and in the interests addressed in its songs. Yet it traces descent from, and still sometimes clearly displays, the styles and values of southern and midwestern rural white folk culture.

This chapter will include such country-derived and related forms as white gospel and bluegrass and also the commercial music called *folk.* Adaptation for modern performance of various kinds of American, English, and other ballads and lyric folk songs became an important phenomenon in the popular culture of the 1960s, together with the writing of new, often topical, songs in similar styles. Long before that decade and since, however, other artists whom some critics have described as "troubadours" have worked in this same vein. Their ancestors include the Hutchinson family in the last century (see chapter 2), and their influence is clear in contemporary rock. "Folk" and "country" performers usually place themselves in separate categories, but they often share musical sources, forms, instrumentation, and a critical attitude toward modern urban society.

I. COUNTRY MUSIC
IA. COUNTRY MUSIC BIBLIOGRAPHY AND DISCOGRAPHY

The Tudor's *Grass Roots Music,* like its three companion volumes (*Black Music, Jazz, Contemporary Popular*), is an extensively annotated buying guide, this one to seventeen hundred long-playing records in the categories of British and American traditional and folk revival, bluegrass, southwestern, country, sacred, and troubadour. The authors condense published reviews and give short introductions to each style, a briefly annotated bibliography, and label and store directories. *Joel Whitburn's Top Country and Western Records 1949-1971* tabulates country hits for those years, forty-one hundred records under the names of 650 recording artists, from

Billboard's Top Fifteen Country and Western lists that began in 1949 (the previous designation for such records there had been "folk"). Jerry Osborne's *55 Years of Recorded Country/Western Music* is a record collector's discography and price guide, with a dealers' directory. Fred J. Karlin's *Edison Diamond Discs* (cited in section IA of chapter 3) covers some early country recordings. Neil V. Rosenberg has compiled *Bill Monroe and His Blue Grass Boys: An Illustrated Discography,* a full formal listing.

Research materials on country music are available at the Country Music Foundation Library and Media Center in Nashville and at the John Edwards Memorial Foundation at the University of California, Los Angeles.

IB. COUNTRY MUSIC GENERAL REFERENCE

The first country music reference book was Linnell Gentry's *A History and Encyclopedia of Country, Western, and Gospel Music* first published in 1961 and still useful though it has many successors. Gentry begins with an anthology of thirty-seven magazine articles from 1904 to 1958, gives a list of country music radio shows from 1924 with rosters of performers, and has a section of detailed biographical entries, another list of names without data, and a short list of gospel singers. Other encyclopedia-format books are principally biographical references and are placed below under "Collective Biography."

Among the modern popular song traditions, country music places relatively strong emphasis on the lyrics of its songs, in particular on the content of the lyrics. The Tin Pan Alley, Broadway, and Hollywood traditions, and vocal jazz, which derives much of its material from those sources, tend toward wit, novelty, and froth. The song styles that are closer to folk songs —blues and country—tend toward testimony about life and feelings. Of course there is great diversity in any style and great overlap among the styles, and this distinction is only of general tendencies. (Both tendencies appear in rock, according to whether it is closer to country and troubadour or closer to the pop love-song mainstream.) Country fans and fans of "country" rock set enough store by their songs' words that several books print many such song lyrics. Mentioned below (section D) are two learned studies of particular folk-country genres.

Lyrics of some of the classic country songs, with anecdotes of their composition, are compiled by Dorothy Horstman in *Sing Your Heart Out, Country Boy.* Carol Offon's *Country Music: The Poetry* is a paperback anthology, with casual historical headnotes, of seventy-three old and newer country hits. The present guide omits songbooks, but notice should be taken of the *Old-Time String Band Songbook* by John Cohen and Mike Seeger. Prefatory material gives both scholarly and practical information about the original performers and their playing styles, followed by words and music of representative hillbilly songs recorded between 1925 and 1935. Many current country lyrics have appeared in the Charleton Company's *Country Song Roundup* magazine since 1947.

Business data on the country music world can be sought in *Country Music Sourcebook* or in the *Country Music Who's Who,* edited by Thurston Moore. Both are trade books of directory listings, advertisements, and miscellaneous data; the latter book includes a historical section and has been published from time to time since 1960. *The Bluegrass Directory 1981-82* is a smaller directory of businesses attached to bluegrass music.

IC. COUNTRY MUSIC BIOGRAPHY AND MATERIALS RELEVANT TO PARTICULAR FIGURES

COLLECTIVE BIOGRAPHY. Collected biographical facts about country music artists are found in one serious anthology of historical reference-guide essays, in a series of "encyclopedias," and in a spate of fan books. The anthology is *Stars of Country Music* edited by Bill C. Malone and Judith McCulloh, containing biographical essays by several of the best writers on country music history. The folklorist D. K. Wilgus provides a brief foreword tracing the history of scholarly interest in the subject, and the essays that follow give life and career stories and source surveys for Uncle Dave Macon, Vernon Dalhart, Bradley Kincaid, the Carter Family, Jimmie Rodgers, Gene Autry, Bob Wills, Roy Acuff, Bill Monroe, Ernest Tubb, Hank Williams, Lester Flatt and Earl Scruggs, Chet Atkins, Johnny Cash, Loretta Lynn, Merle Haggard, Charley Pride, Tom T. Hall, and Johnny Rodriguez. Opening and closing chapters give briefer treatments to a collection of pioneers and a collection of recent stars (1975).

The biographical encyclopedias begin with Linnell Gentry's *History and Encyclopedia,* cited in section IB, above. Irwin Stambler and Grelun Landon wrote an *Encyclopedia of Folk, Country and Western Music* similar to their *Pop, Rock, and Soul* volume (chapter 1, section B): biographical and some subject entries make modest use of photographs (distinguishing their project from more promotional works of the collective souvenir program variety). Many records are mentioned in the biographies, but there are no individual discographies. Songwriters, music company figures, and other nonperformers are represented. *The Encyclopedia of Country and Western Music,* by Len Brown and Gary Friedrich (who also produced a rock volume), is a short, "pocketbook" work with brief entries that give recording affiliations and mention principal hits but tell little else. Melvin Shestack's *The Country Music Encyclopedia* has some three hundred performers' biographies, many with promotional photographs, and some short, topical entries. A selected but long album discography is appended, with a list of country music radio stations in 1974 and sheet music for eight representative songs. Jeannie Sakol's *The Wonderful World of Country Music* is a large-page paperback encyclopedia of people and topics (song sharks, *Songwriter Magazine*). Notices of some performers are tucked into group entries, like "Austin City Limits" for artists who have been featured in that television concert series: consult Sakol's index as well as the alphabetical order of entries. Perhaps the most attractive of these volumes is Fred Dellar and Roy Thompson's *The Illustrated Encyclopedia of Country Music*. Biographical entries by two British writers of about 450 performers are illustrated with several hundred color reproductions of record jackets and other color and black-and-white photographs. Songs mentioned are printed in boldface, and some entries have selective discographies. Robert Anderson and Gail North have compiled the *Gospel Music Encyclopedia,* a volume for the performers of this religious cousin of country, not to be confused with black gospel (see chapter 4).

The lighter collections of profiles, all emphasizing pictures, catch the stars of a given year in company with a few past or established performers. *Honkytonk Heroes* (1975) by Raeanne Rubenstein is an album of candid black-and-white shots of Nashville personalities. Andy Gray's *Great Country Music Stars* (1975) is a large-format chronicle and album of promotional shots, some in color, with more historical coverage than most, and ending with some performers from England, where the book was published. Bryan Chalker's *Country Music* (1976), also British, is a collection of illustrated articles on country-pop stars. It includes a short biographical directory of another hundred. *Just Country* (1976) by Robert Cornfield and Marshall Fallwell, Jr., is essentially a photograph album but does include extensive text retelling the stories of past and present stars. *Meet the Stars of Country Music* (1977) by Carolyn Rada Hollaran gives illustrated promotional sketches of forty-two stars. A few oldtimers are included (Jimmie Rodgers but not Hank Williams) and several lesser known or mostly pop figures (John Denver, but not Johnny Cash). The paperback cover calls this book "volume 1." Andrew David's *Country Music Stars* (1980) has photographs, a page of biography, and a record list for each of forty stars and groups at the end of the 1970s. Two of these biographical-promotional albums present only women. Joan Dew's *Singers and Sweethearts: The Women of Country Music* (1977) has illustrated biographies of Loretta Lynn, Tammy Wynette, June Carter, Dolly Parton, and Tanya Tucker, at greater length than the treatments in the books with more stars. A remarkable assertion from Dew's introduction is that 80 percent of country records are bought by women. *Those Bold and Beautiful Country Girls* (1979), by Michael Kosser, has photographs and admiring biographical sketches of modern women country stars in several collective chapters and in separate treatments of Dolly Parton, Barbara Mandrell, Crystal Gayle, and Minnie Pearl. One loosely defined modern party of country personalities is separately treated in *The Outlaws: Revolution in Country Music* by Michael Bane. The Nashville and Texas performers claiming this name and image and treated by Bane are Waylon Jennings, Willie Nelson, Tompall Glaser,

"Cowboy" Jack Clement, and David Allen Coe. (See also the book on Jennings and Nelson below).

Gospel Song Writers Biography compiled by Mrs. J. R. (Ma) Baxter and Videt Polk has 102 biographical sketches, with photographs, of the writers of country gospel standards.

INDIVIDUAL FIGURES. *Roy Acuff: The Smoky Mountain Boy* by Elizabeth Schlappi is a devoted biography of an elder statesman of the Grand Ole Opry and of country generally. Schlappi gives a chronology of Acuff's government-sponsored tours abroad, a discography, a bibliography, and private as well as performance photographs.

Chet Atkins, with Bill Neely, has written his own *Country Gentleman,* telling the story of his career as virtuoso country guitarist and as executive for RCA records.

The Carter Family—A. P. Carter, his wife Sara, and his sister-in-law Maybelle—have been the subject of pamphlets and articles and of a juvenile biography, *The Carter Family,* by Robert M. Krishof and Stacey Harris. They are best introduced in the histories (section ID, below) and in the chapter by John Atkins in Malone and McCulloh's book (above in "Collective Biography").

Johnny Cash has published an inspirational autobiography (the phrase here and elsewhere in the present survey characterizes the author's tone and intent) called *Man in Black,* which prints several lyrics by Cash and others. Christopher S. Wren's *Winners Got Scars Too: The Life and Legends of Johnny Cash* is a thorough popular biography through the 1960s.

Tennessee Ernie Ford wrote *This Is My Story, This Is My Song,* a folksy and inspirational story of his life as a recording and televison star singing popular and gospel material.

Merle Haggard, with Peggy Russell, wrote *Sing Me Back Home: My Story,* a popular account with an intermezzo of photographs, documents, and interview statements by acquaintances. It reflects Haggard's prominence as a singer of some controversial songs of patriotism and social comment that this book is published by the New York Times Book Company.

Tom T. Hall's *The Storyteller's Nashville* presents his career as songwriter, performer, and raconteur. His intention to tell the reader his story, rather than to accommodate the drop-in reference user, apparently precludes chapter titles as well as index.

Waylon Jennings shares *Waylon and Willie: The Full Story in Words and Pictures of Waylon Jennings and Willie Nelson* by Bob Allen, which has brief chapters of biography and recording history.

Kris Kristofferson by Beth Kalet is a brief fan book. Many of the illustrations are stills from his movies. Appendixes give an awards list and discography.

Loretta Lynn: Coal Miner's Daughter is an autobiography with collaborator George Vecsey that has been widely popular and that has been adapted into a movie of the same name as the subtitle. The book reproduces Lynn's blunt eastern Kentucky talk in telling her life story from poverty and marriage at the age of fourteen to stardom as a singer and songwriter.

Bill Monroe is the father of bluegrass—more than a style, it is a whole genre of popular music that is perhaps returning to folk status as a hobby of private singing and instrumental playing. Neil V. Rosenberg's *Bill Monroe and His Blue Grass Boys: An Illustrated Discography* has already been mentioned; it may be added here that the book includes a biographical sketch with photographs. James Rooney's *Bossmen: Bill Monroe and Muddy Waters* is a pair of illustrated biographies joined to assert the primacy of each within his respective music. The stories are largely told in interview statements.

Willie Nelson has half of Bob Allen's book listed above under Waylon Jennings, and is featured in Lana Nelson Fowler's *Willie Nelson Family Album,* a scrapbook of photographs, album covers, and blurbs interspersed with lyrics of Nelson's songs. See also Michael Bane's *The Outlaws,* above.

Dolly Parton by Otis James is a brief, illustrated paperback career story. Alanna Nash's *Dolly* is a large journalistic book with many photographs, some in color. Both books have discographies. There is also *The Official Dolly Parton Scrapbook* by Connie Berman, an illustrated paperback biography.

Carl Perkins, with Ron Rendleman, wrote *Disciple in Blue Suede Shoes,* a brief autobiography of Perkin's rockabilly career interpreted from the religious perspective of a later conversion. There are photographs and some lyrics of his more serious songs.

The Tex Ritter Story by Johnny Bond is a large, documented biography of Ritter's singing, stage, and film careers. Appendixes detail each and print several songs he made famous.

Jimmie Rodgers: The Life and Times of America's Blue Yodeler by Nolan Porterfield is a full and fully scholarly book, like others in the Music in American Life series, built on interviews and primary print sources. There is an elaborate discography, a table of Rodgers' famous "blue yodels," and a catalog of his performing appearances. In 1935, Rodgers' widow Carrie Cecil Williamson Rodgers published *My Husband Jimmie Rodgers* (the title page calls her only "Mrs. Jimmie Rodgers"), a sentimental memoir; a 1975 reprint has an introduction and a five-page chronology contributed by Porterfield.

J. D. Sumner: Gospel Music Is My Life is an assisted autobiography, credited to Bob Terrell, with many photographs of this country gospel singer with the Blackwood Brothers and other groups.

Hank Williams' story of celebrity, dissipation, and early death has been told several times. *Sing a Sad Song* by Roger M. Williams is a journalistic biography from public sources and interviews but without cooperation of

Hank Williams' family. A full discography is supplied by the editors of *Country Music Magazine. Hank Williams: Country Music's Tragic King* by Jay Caress is a popular biography, also with a large discography, this one by Caress and Jerry Rivers. Most recently, Chet Flippo's *Your Cheatin' Heart* is also a storytelling as opposed to a critical biography, undocumented but claiming research, drawing especially on the papers of Williams' first wife. All three books supply photographs.

Hank Williams, Jr., has had an independent singing career. With Michael Bane he wrote *Living Proof: An Autobiography,* built around the story of his serious mountain-climbing injury and his recovery from it. The book has little direct recollection of Hank Williams, Sr.

Bob Wills, the star bandleader of western swing, is the subject of another of the Illinois series of volumes, *San Antonio Rose: The Life and Music of Bob Wills* by Charles A. Townsend. There is some musical analysis, but most of the book is a detailed history derived from interviews and scrapbooks; the author calls his book "basically oral history." There is a discography and a "filmusicography" by Bob Pinson. Al Stricklin, who played piano with Wills and the Texas Playboys from 1935, has co-authored *My Years with Bob Wills* with Jon McConal. The book has some early band photographs.

Tammy Wynette, helped by Joan Dew, has written an autobiography named for her most popular song, *Stand by Your Man,* a long book for a mid-career and mid-thirties life story, with photographs and a large index.

ID. COUNTRY MUSIC HISTORY AND COMMENTARY

The standard history is Bill C. Malone's *Country Music USA: A Fifty-Year History* (1968), the first thorough and rigorous study of the subject. Malone draws on a remarkable range of sources, including many interviews, correspondence, and obscure periodicals. His discussions have frequent references to representative recordings available at the time of the writing. A decade later, Malone published another book that may be mentioned here though it also bears on several other topics in American popular music. In that study, called *Southern Music/American Music,* Malone surveys southern folk music and the popular forms deriving from it, including minstrelsy, spirituals, ragtime, blues, jazz, hillbilly, Cajun, black and white gospel, rock, soul, and modern country. Selected individual performers, including contemporary performers, are given careful attention despite the small size and wide scope of the book. Documentation includes extended bibliographic notes.

The fullest history before Malone's was Robert Shelton's *The Country Music Story: A Picture History of Country and Western Music,* a reasonably full narrative with a photograph collection. Four later useful books appeared almost together in the late 1970s. Douglas B. Green's *Country Roots: The Origins of Country Music* disclaims any rivalry with Malone's scholarship and seeks rather to be interpretive, but nevertheless provides an excellent survey and commentary for early country, with good and unusual photographs. A chronological chart shows events and top records from 1923. *The Illustrated History of Country Music, by the Editors of Country Music Magazine,* edited by Patrick Carr, has twelve chapters by seven writers. Some chapters are better than others; among the best are those by Charles K. Wolfe on origins and on modern country. The book is a popular reading history without notes. Frye Gaillard's *Watermelon Wine: The Spirit of Country Music* uses human-interest reporting on people and scenes in current country music to open pathways back into the past of the country music business and its culture. Gaillard has a good collection of pictures and many quotations from song lyrics reflecting southern country and city life. An appendix gives whole lyrics of fifty-five songs. *Country: The Biggest Music in America* by Nick Tosches is an entertaining and somewhat mischievous foray into history and the current scene, tending to the comic and the scandalous. Much miscellaneous erudition surfaces despite the throw-away style; the early rock as well as country lore is fascinating. Presentation is unsystematic, but there is an index. Less ambitious are three brief survey histories. *Take Me Home* by Steven D. Price is a rudimentary survey, quoting copiously from public-domain blues and folk songs. A "Biographies" section gives a descriptive sentence each to forty personalities. Irwin Stambler and Grelun Landon, compilers of one of the country encyclopedias, have written *Golden Guitars: The Story of Country Music* for younger readers. *Country Is My Music!* by Lois Lazarus (1980) is the latest popular account at this writing. Each edition of the *Country Music Who's Who* includes a historical section that is also separately published as *Pictorial History of Country Music*—volume 1 from the 1965 edition and volume 2 from the 1966 edition were brought out as reprints in 1969, and volumes 3 and 4 came out in 1970 and 1971. All are scrapbooks of illustrated historical articles, documents, and discography.

Histories of segments of country music mostly focus on Tennessee. An exception is *The Improbable Rise of Redneck Rock* by Jan Reid, a rambling, affectionate account of the Austin, Texas, country-rock style and scene in the early 1970s. For the rest, two books trace the Tennessee folk-to-country connections and a number evoke Nashville and its proud comedy, the Opry. Charles K. Wolfe's *Tennessee Strings: The Story of Country Music in Tennessee* is one of a series of books on the state's history and culture sponsored by the Tennessee Historical Commission and published by the University of Tennessee. Wolfe traces hill folk music into the towns and through its commerical evolution. There is a coordinated record, issued by the Rounder Company (catalog number 1030). *Tom Ashley, Sam McGee, and Bukka White,* edited by Thomas G. Burton and also published by the University of Tennessee, consists of three essays on singers representing three folk traditions in the state: Anglo-American folk song, country, and blues.

There are photographs, song transcriptions, chronologies, and discographies.

The Nashville Sound: Bright Lights and Country Music, by Paul Hemphill, is a pop journalism account of the city's country music culture, including a quick history of the music at large. Teddy Bart's *Inside Music City, USA* focuses on the writing of country songs. There are interview articles on Nashville songwriters Boudeleaux Bryant, Jack Clement, Harlan Howard, Billy Edd Wheeler, Hank Cochran, John D. Loudermilk, Willie Nelson, Bobby Russell, and Marijohn Wilkin, and chapters on the business of publishing songs, including an interview with Chet Atkins as Artists and Repertory executive. Song lists for the writers and a directory of publishers are furnished.

The Grand Ole Opry: The Early Years, 1925-35, oddly enough published in London, is a scrapbook history assembled by the knowledgable historian Charles K. Wolfe, with old photographs, advertisements, clippings, and a record list. Myron Tassin and Jerry Henderson's *Fifty Years at the Grand Ole Opry* is a fan's album of photographs, a few in color, with brief historical text. Jack Hurst's *Nashville's Grand Ole Opry* is a lavish Abrams picture book. It includes a section of songs.

Bluegrass, by Bob Artis, is a chronicle with chapters on the Stanley Brothers, Don Reno and Red Smiley, Jimmy Martin, Jim and Jesse, the Osborne Brothers, and later acts at lesser length. Appendixes give records, bluegrass magazines and radio stations, and organizations. Steven D. Price's *Old as the Hills: The Story of Bluegrass Music* is a less detailed survey; short chapters give history and treat Monroe, Flatt and Scruggs, and assortments of others.

Gospel music is the subject of Lois S. Blackwell's *The Wings of the Dove: The Story of Gospel Music in America,* an insider's and believer's account of the history, culture, and songs of white country gospel; many hymns are quoted and there are photographs of performers. The scholarship on southern hymnody of George Pullen Jackson and others is relevant to the background of this music but is not properly a part of the literature of gospel as a popular music.

Two unusual critical books have appeared in the Music in American Life series. Archie Green's *Only a Miner: Studies in Recorded Coal-Mining Songs* is a large, rigorous study of the history and the social and industrial context of a series of such songs. Norm Cohen's *Long Steel Rail: The Railroad in American Folksong* is a large scholarly history and anthology. Cohen works as far as possible with commercial recordings as his primary sources, supplemented by archives of field-collected folksong, so that his book, like other projects associated with the John Edwards Memorial Foundation at UCLA, is properly an investigation of hillbilly and "race" popular music at the borders of folksong, rather than what is often regarded as folksong—the oral tradition as clear as possible of commercial influence. A small critical study of one song is Martha Anne Turner's *The Yellow Rose of Texas,* tracing the folk lyric background of that popular song.

Scholarly journals, fan magazines, and business bulletins all monitor country music. The kinship of country music to American folk culture has led to considerable academic interest, and articles on country music appear in the major folklore journals, *Journal of American Folklore, Southern Folklore Quarterly,* and *Western Folklore.* (The *Journal of American Folklore* published a "Hillbilly Issue" in 1965—volume 78, no. 309.) The *JEMF Quarterly* at UCLA is devoted to country and related musics. The *Journal of Country Music* is published by the Country Music Foundation in Nashville. Scholarly books and articles on country music are noted in the Modern Language Association's annual *MLA International Bibliography,* volume 1, under folklore, section 5 (folk poetry), subsection "Songs," subheading "North America."

Magazines for followers of country music are scattered over the world, only slightly less widely than those for jazz, blues, and rock. England and Australia seem especially fond of country, and magazines on it are also published in France, Germany, Sweden, and New Zealand. An American fan might sometimes consult the British *Country Music People*—it can be found, at least, in the Library of Congress. In the United States there are *Country Music* publishing news, features, and reviews from New York, and the tabloid *Music City News* from Nashville. *CMA Closeup,* published in Nashville by the Country Music Association, is a newsletter of that association and the industry.

Bluegrass Unlimited is a bluegrass monthly published since 1966. *Music Country,* formerly *Muleskinner News,* also covers bluegrass.

II. FOLK

Commercially recorded folk, folk-revival, and folk-style music is surveyed in the Tudors' *Grass Roots Music* volume (in section IA, above), and some such records can be found listed and evaluated in the rock consumer guides (see chapter 7). *Songs of Protest, War and Peace: A Bibliography and Discography,* by R. Serge Denisoff, lists songs of both the left and the right, most of them in folk style, which have addressed these particular political issues, and also surveys journalistic and scholarly comment and polemics on such songs.

The best general reference is *The Folk Music Sourcebook* by Larry Sandberg and Dick Weissman, a wide-ranging reference book covering among other areas folk, blues, gospel, ragtime, bluegrass, and commercial revivals of these musics. There are many lists: directories, annotated bibliographies, discographies; and also survey histories and explanatory discussions for the listener and the amateur musician. *Folksingers and Folksongs in America:*

A Handbook of Biography, Bibliography and Discography, by Ray M. Lawless, was published in 1960 and again with an updating supplement in 1965; much of its information is now out of date. Lawless covers both traditional and commercial folksong in a biographical directory, chapters on instruments and festivals, a fully annotated bibliography of folksong collections, a survey of archives, a list of song titles, and an album discography. Kristin Baggelaar and Donald Minton's *Folk Music: More Than a Song* (1976) is an encyclopedia like Stambler and Landon's but with less country and more folk: career biographies of folk and folk-pop singers are supplemented with a few topical entries. Some records are characterized in the text, but no discographies are given and no references are noted. *The Face of Folk Music,* with photographs by David Gahr and text by Robert Shelton (1968), is an album of performing and candid photographs of blues, gospel, folk, and principally folk-pop singers and groups of the 1960s.

Few individual singers can be pursued in books.

Joan Baez wrote *Daybreak* in 1968, a short book of reminiscences and reveries at the time of her involvement in antiwar and antidraft protests.

Judy Collins by Vivian Claire is a short, illustrated paperback biography, with a chapter of critical annotations of songs by albums and a separate discography, for a singer whose first fame was in the folksong revival of the 1960s; her later work has included a highly successful recording of Stephen Sondheim's Broadway song "Send in the Clowns."

John Denver by Leonore Fleischer is a short paperback of text and publicity photographs of the hundred-million-selling pop troubadour. For a book of this kind, Fleischer gives a balanced account, quoting a surprising amount of the critics' negative remarks. A discography through the mid-1970s is appended.

Woody Guthrie: A Life by Joe Klein (1980) is a full-scale biography by a political journalist based on interviews and newly available personal papers, with many photographs. Edward Robbin's *Woody Guthrie and Me: An Intimate Reminiscence* is a memoir, by a political activist, of his friendship with Guthrie in California in the 1930s, including some photographs and printing some song lyrics. Guthrie himself published a book, and two more were edited from his writing. *Bound for Glory,* in 1943, was a recreated story of his life that he wrote at the age of thirty. *Born to Win* (1965) is an anthology of his songs, other verse, drawings, and miscellaneous writings, mainly from the late 1940s. *Seeds of Man: An Experience Lived and Dreamed* is a literary narrative built of embroidered recollections of events in Guthrie's young manhood; it was compiled in 1976 from manuscripts he wrote in 1947-1948 and in 1953.

Burl Ives wrote *Wayfaring Stranger* in 1948, an informal, mid-career memoir of his life as a wandering singer of folksongs and as a Broadway actor.

Gordon Lightfoot by Alfrieda Gabiou is a short, illustrated paperback about the Canadian country-folk singer and songwriter, including a discography.

Phil Ochs is the subject of *Death of a Rebel* by Marc Eliot, telling of Ochs' rise as a protest singer of the 1960s and his painful decline and eventual suicide. There are many photographs and a discography; passages from songs are interspersed.

Pete Seeger, a durable and influential singer, songwriter, and political minstrel from the 1940s to the 1980s, is given a large, documented biography in *How Can I Keep from Singing: Pete Seeger,* by David King Dunaway. In 1972 Seeger collected and rewrote his short articles for folkmusic magazines as *The Incompleat Folksinger,* on songs, people, movements, and how to make Seeger's kind of music.

Folk revival history and criticism begins with a book by singer Oscar Brand in 1962, *The Ballad Mongers: Rise of Modern Folk Song*, tracing a legacy from American folksong proper to its beneficiaries, the twentieth-century troubadours, up through the 1950s. Brand stresses the social and economic context—as did the performers themselves—with anecdotal backgrounds of many songs. Josh Dunson's *Freedom in the Air: Song Movements of the '60s* (1965) is a more partisan popular account of the morally and politically activist songwriters of the early 1960s and their predecessors: Guthrie, Earl Robinson, Pete Seeger, Dylan, Ochs, Tom Paxton, Malvina Reynolds, and others are treated briefly. Donald Myrus' *Ballads, Blues, and the Big Beat* (1966) introduces the subject to school-age readers, with record recommendations. Jacques Vassal wrote *Folksong: Une Histoire de la Musique Populaire aux États-Unis* in 1971, translated in 1976 under the title *Electric Children: Roots and Branches of Modern Folkrock,* a celebration of American and English folk-pop and folk-rock performers of the 1960s with background chapters on black and white folksong and on Woody Guthrie. There is a title-only record list. Two books by R. Serge Denisoff in the early 1970s approached this music by way of academic social analysis. *Great Day Coming: Folk Music and the American Left* is a political history of the use of folk and folk-like songs for political and social causes, and the reaction against it, from the 1930s through the 1960s. *Sing a Song of Social Significance* collects his articles on several genres of protest songs; many lyrics are quoted. Dave Laing and three others wrote *The Electric Muse: The Story of Folk into Rock* in 1975. Sections cover the American folk revival (Laing and Robert Shelton); attempt to place the phenomenon in the perspective of folk music (Karl Dallas); and report the British skiffle, folk, and folk-rock fashions (Robin Denselow). Many performers and events are mentioned, but the prevailing mode is journalistic generalization. Jerome Rodnitzky's *Minstrels of the Dawn: The Folk-Protest Singer as a Cultural Hero* focuses on Guthrie, Ochs, Baez, and Dylan, with background and epilogues, giving an account somewhere between sympathetic and objective. Eric von Schmidt and Jim Rooney's *Baby Let Me Follow You Down: The Illustrated Story of the Cambridge Folk Years* tells about the folk club ambience in Boston and Cambridge from 1958 to the mid-1960s, principally in interviews and photographs.

The leading magazine of the folk revival has been *Sing Out: The Folk Song Magazine,* which has printed old and new songs, profiles, interviews, essays, and news.

BIBLIOGRAPHY

Allen, Bob. *Waylon and Willie: The Full Story in Words and Pictures of Waylon Jennings and Willie Nelson.* New York: Quick Fox, 1979.

Anderson, Robert, and North, Gail, comps. *Gospel Music Encyclopedia.* New York: Sterling Publishing, 1979.

Artis, Bob. *Bluegrass: From the Lonesome Wail of a Mountain Love Song to the Hammering Drive of the Scruggs-Style Banjo—The Story of an American Musical Tradition.* New York: Hawthorn Books, 1975.

Atkins, Chet, with Bill Neely. *Country Gentleman.* Chicago: Henry Regnery, 1974.

Baez, Joan. *Daybreak.* New York: Dial Press, 1968.

Baggelaar, Kristin, and Minton, Donald. *Folk Music: More Than a Song.* New York: Thomas Y. Crowell, 1976.

Bane, Michael. *The Outlaws: Revolution in Country Music.* N. p.: Country Music Magazine Press/Doubleday/Dolphin, 1978.

Bart, Teddy. *Inside Music City, USA.* Nashville: Aurora Publishers, 1970.

Baxter, Mrs. J. R., and Polk, Videt, comps. *Gospel Song Writers Biography.* Dallas, Chattanooga, and Pangburn, Ark.: Stamps-Baxter Music and Printing, 1971.

Berman, Connie. *The Official Dolly Parton Scrapbook.* New York: Grosset and Dunlap, 1978.

Blackwell, Lois S. *The Wings of the Dove: The Story of Gospel Music in America.* Norfolk, Va.: Donning, 1978.

The Bluegrass Directory 1981-82. Murphys, Calif.: BD Products, 1981.

Bluegrass Unlimited. Broad Run, Va., 1966- .

Bond, Johnny. *The Tex Ritter Story.* New York: Chappell Music, 1976.

Brand, Oscar. *The Ballad Mongers: Rise of Modern Folk Song.* New York: Funk and Wagnalls, 1962.

Brown, Len, and Friedrich, Gary. *The Encyclopedia of Country and Western Music.* New York: A Tower Book, 1971.

Burton, Thomas G., ed. *Tom Ashley, Sam McGee, and Bukka White: Tennessee Traditional Singers.* Knoxville: University of Tennessee Press, 1981.

Caress, Jay. *Hank Williams: Country Music's Tragic King.* New York: Stein and Day, 1979.

Carr, Patrick, ed. *The Illustrated History of Country Music, by the Editors of Country Music Magazine.* Garden City, N.Y.: *Country Music* Magazine Press Book/Doubleday, 1979.

Cash, Johnny. *Man in Black.* Grand Rapids, Mich.: Zondervan Publishing House, 1975.

Chalker, Bryan. *Country Music*. London: Phoebus Publishing, 1976.

Claire, Vivian. *Judy Collins*. New York: Flash Books, 1977.

CMA Closeup. Nashville, 1959- .

Cohen, John, and Seeger, Mike. *Old-Time String Band Songbook*. New York: Oak, 1976.

Cohen, Norm. *Long Steel Rail: The Railroad in American Folksong*. Music in American Life. Urbana: University of Illinois Press, 1981.

Cornfield, Robert, with Marshall Fallwell, Jr. *Just Country: Country People, Stories, Music*. New York: McGraw-Hill, 1976.

Country Music. New York, 1972- .

Country Music People. Footscray, Sidcup, Kent, England, 1969- .

Country Music Sourcebook. Los Angeles, annually.

Country Music Who's Who. Nashville, 1965, 1966, 1970, 1972. (See also Moore, Thurston.)

Country Song Roundup. Derby, Conn., 1947- .

David, Andrew. *Country Music Stars: People at the Top of the Charts*. Chicago: Domus Books, 1980.

Dellar, Fred, and Thompson, Roy. *The Illustrated Encyclopedia of Country Music*. New York: Harmony Books, 1977.

Denisoff, R. Serge. *Great Day Coming: Folk Music and the American Left*. Music in American Life. Urbana: University of Illinois Press, 1971.

_____. *Sing a Song of Social Significance*. Bowling Green, Ohio: Bowling Green University Popular Press, 1972.

_____. *Songs of Protest, War and Peace: A Bibliography and Discography*. Santa Barbara, Calif.: American Bibliographic Center—Clio Press, 1973.

Dew, Joan. *Singers and Sweethearts: The Women of Country Music*. Garden City, N.Y.: *Country Music* Magazine Press Book/Dolphin Books, 1977.

Dunaway, David King. *How Can I Keep from Singing: Pete Seeger*. New York: McGraw-Hill, 1981.

Dunson, Josh. *Freedom in the Air: Song Movements of the '60s*. New York: International Publishers, 1965.

Eliot, Marc. *Death of a Rebel*. Garden City, N.Y.: Doubleday, 1979.

Fleischer, Leonore. *John Denver*. New York: Flash Books, 1976.

Flippo, Chet. *Your Cheatin' Heart: A Biography of Hank Williams*. New York: Simon and Schuster, 1981.

Ford, Tennessee Ernie. *This Is My Story, This Is My Song*. Englewood Cliffs, N.J.: Prentice-Hall, 1963.

Fowler, Lana Nelson, comp. *Willie Nelson Family Album*. Amarillo, Tex.: H. M. Poirot, 1980.

Gabiou, Alfrieda. *Gordon Lightfoot*. New York: Quick Fox, 1979.

Gahr, David, and Shelton, Robert. *The Face of Folk Music*. New York: Citadel Press, 1968.

Gaillard, Frye. *Watermelon Wine: The Spirit of Country Music*. New York: St. Martin's Press, 1978.

Gentry, Linnell. *A History and Encyclopedia of Country, Western, and Gospel Music*. 1961. Reprint. St. Clair Shores, Mich.: Scholarly Press, 1972.

Gray, Andy. *Great Country Music Stars*. London: Hamlyn, 1975.

Green, Archie. *Only a Miner: Studies in Recorded Coal-Mining Songs.* Music in American Life. Urbana: University of Illinois Press, 1972.

Green, Douglas B. *Country Roots: The Origins of Country Music.* New York: Hawthorn Books, 1978.

Guthrie, Woody. *Born to Win.* New York: Macmillan, 1965.

_____. *Bound for Glory.* 1943. Reprint. New York: E. P. Dutton, 1976.

_____. *Seeds of Man: An Experience Lived and Dreamed.* New York: E. P. Dutton, 1976.

Haggard, Merle, with Peggy Russell. *Sing Me Back Home: My Story.* New York: New York Times Book, 1981.

Hall, Tom T. *The Storyteller's Nashville.* Garden City, N.Y.: Doubleday, 1979.

Hemphill, Paul. *The Nashville Sound: Bright Lights and Country Music.* New York: Simon and Schuster, 1970.

Hollaran, Carolyn Rada. *Meet the Stars of Country Music.* Nashville: Aurora Publishers, 1977.

Horstman, Dorothy. *Sing Your Heart Out, Country Boy.* New York: E. P. Dutton, 1975.

Hurst, Jack. *Nashville's Grand Ole Opry.* New York: Abrams, 1975.

Ives, Burl. *Wayfaring Stranger.* New York: Whittlesey House/McGraw-Hill, 1948.

James, Otis. *Dolly Parton.* New York: Quick Fox, 1978.

JEMF Quarterly. Los Angeles, 1965- .

Journal of American Folklore. Washington, D.C., 1888- .

Journal of Country Music. Nashville, 1970- .

Kalet, Beth. *Kris Kristofferson.* New York: Quick Fox, 1979.

Karlin, Fred J. *Edison Diamond Discs 50001-52651, 1912-1929,* vol. 1. Santa Monica, Calif.: Bona Fide Publishing, 1972.

Klein, Joe. *Woody Guthrie: A Life.* New York: Alfred A. Knopf, 1980.

Kosser, Michael. *Those Bold and Beautiful Country Girls.* New York: Delilah Book/Mayflower Books, 1979.

Krishof, Robert K., and Harris, Stacy. *The Carter Family: Country Music's First Family.* Minneapolis: Lerner Publications, 1978.

Laing, Dave; Dallas, Karl; Denselow, Robin; and Shelton, Robert. *The Electric Muse: The Story of Folk into Rock.* London: Methuen, 1975.

Lawless, Ray M. *Folksingers and Folksongs in America: A Handbook of Biography, Bibliography and Discography.* New ed. New York: Duell, Sloan and Pearce, 1965.

Lazarus, Lois. *Country Is My Music!* New York: Julian Messner, 1980.

Lynn, Loretta, with George Vecsey. *Loretta Lynn: Coal Miner's Daughter.* Chicago: Bernard Geis Associates/Henry Regnery, 1976.

Malone, Bill C. *Country Music USA: A Fifty-Year History.* Austin: American Folklore Society/University of Texas Press, 1968.

_____. *Southern Music/American Music.* Lexington: University Press of Kentucky, 1979.

_____, and McCulloh, Judith, eds. *Stars of Country Music: Uncle Dave Macon to Johnny Rodriguez.* Music in American Life. Urbana: University of Illinois Press, 1975.

Modern Language Association. *MLA International Bibliography of Books and Articles on the Modern Languages and Literatures: General, English, Ameri-*

can, Medieval and Neo-Latin, Celtic Literatures; and Folklore, vol. 1. New York: MLA, annually.

Moore, Thurston, ed. *The Country Music Who's Who.* Cincinnati: Ohio: Cardinal Enterprises, 1959. (See also *Country Music Who's Who*).

———. *Pictorial History of Country Music: From the 1965 Edition of the Country Music Who's Who,* vol. 1. Denver: Heather Enterprises, 1969.

———. *From the 1966 Edition of the Country Music Who's Who.* Denver: Heather Enterprises, 1969.

———. *From the 1970 Edition of Country Music Who's Who,* vol. 3. Denver: Heather Enterprises, 1970.

———. *One of the Many Features of the 1972 Country Music Who's Who,* vol. 4, Denver: Heather Enterprises, 1971.

Muleskinner News. Elon College, N.C., 1969- ; *Music Country,* 1978- .

Music City News. Nashville, 1963- .

Myrus, Donald. *Ballads, Blues, and the Big Beat.* New York: Macmillan, 1966.

Nash, Alanna. *Dolly.* Los Angeles: A Country Music Magazine Book/Reed Books, 1978.

Offon, Carol. *Country Music: The Poetry.* New York: Ballantine Books, 1977.

Osborne, Jerry. *55 Years of Recorded Country/Western Music.* Ed. Bruce Hamilton. Phoenix: Osborne and Hamilton, 1976.

Perkins, Carl, with Ron Rendleman. *Disciple in Blue Suede Shoes.* Grand Rapids, Mich.: Zondervan Publishing House, 1978.

Porterfield, Nolan. *Jimmie Rodgers: The Life and Times of America's Blue Yodeler.* Music in American Life. Urbana: University of Illinois Press, 1979.

Price, Steven D. *Old as the Hills: The Story of Bluegrass Music.* New York: Viking Press, 1975.

———. *Take Me Home: The Rise of Country and Western Music.* New York: Praeger Publishers, 1974.

Reid, Jan. *The Improbable Rise of Redneck Rock.* 1974. Reprint. New York: Da Capo, 1977.

Robbin, Edward. *Woody Guthrie and Me: An Intimate Reminiscence.* Berkeley, Calif.: Lancaster-Miller Publishers, 1979.

Rodgers, Mrs. Jimmie. *My Husband Jimmie Rodgers.* 1935. Reprint. Nashville: Country Music Foundation Press, 1975.

Rodnitzky, Jerome. *Minstrels of the Dawn: The Folk-Protest Singer as a Cultural Hero.* Chicago: Nelson-Hall, 1976.

Rooney, James. *Bossmen: Bill Monroe and Muddy Waters.* New York: Dial Press, 1971.

Rosenberg, Neil V., comp. *Bill Monroe and His Blue Grass Boys: An Illustrated Discography.* Nashville: Country Music Foundation Press, 1974.

Rubenstein. Raeanne. *Honkytonk Heroes: A Photo Album of Country Music.* New York: Harper and Row, 1975.

Sakol, Jeannie. *The Wonderful World of Country Music.* New York: Grosset and Dunlap, 1979.

Sandberg, Larry, and Weissman, Dick. *The Folk Music Sourcebook.* New York: Alfred A. Knopf, 1976.

Schlappi, Elizabeth. *Roy Acuff: The Smoky Mountain Boy.* Gretna, La.: Pelican Publishing, 1978.

Seeger, Pete. *The Incompleat Folksinger.* Ed. Jo Metcalf Schwartz. New York: Simon and Schuster, 1972.

Shelton, Robert. *The Country Music Story: A Picture History of Country and Western Music.* Indianapolis: Bobbs-Merrill, 1966.

Shestack, Melvin. *The Country Music Encyclopedia.* New York: Thomas Y. Crowell, 1974.

Sing Out: The Folk Song Magazine. New York: 1950- .

Southern Folklore Quarterly. Gainesville, Fla., 1937- .

Stambler, Irwin, and Landon, Grelun. *Encyclopedia of Folk, Country and Western Music.* New York: St. Martin's Press, 1969.

———. *Golden Guitars: The Story of Country Music.* New York: Four Winds Press, 1971.

Stricklin, Al, with Jon McConal. *My Years with Bob Wills.* San Antonio, Tex.: Naylor, 1976.

Tassin, Myron, and Henderson, Jerry. *Fifty Years at the Grand Ole Opry.* Gretna, La.: Pelican Publishing Co., 1975.

Terrell, Bob. *J. D. Sumner: Gospel Music Is My Life.* Nashville: Impact Books, 1971.

Tosches, Nick. *Country: The Biggest Music in America.* New York: Stein and Day, 1977.

Townsend, Charles R. *San Antonio Rose: The Life and Music of Bob Wills.* Music in American Life. Urbana: University of Illinois Press, 1976.

Tudor, Dean, and Tudor, Nancy. *Grass Roots Music.* American Popular Music on Elpee. Littleton, Colo.: Libraries Unlimited, 1979.

Turner, Martha Anne. *The Yellow Rose of Texas: The Story of a Song.* Southwestern Studies Monograph no. 31. El Paso: Texas Western Press, 1971.

Vassal, Jacques. *Electric Children: Roots and Branches of Modern Folkrock.* Trans. Paul Barnett. New York: Taplinger Publishing, 1976.

———. *Folksong: Une Historie de la Musique Populaire aux États-Unis.* New ed. Paris: Éditions Du Jour, 1971.

Von Schmidt, Eric, and Rooney, Jim. *Baby, Let Me Follow You Down: The Illustrated Story of the Cambridge Folk Years.* Garden City, N.Y.: Anchor Books, 1979.

Western Folklore. Los Angeles, 1942- .

Whitburn, Joel. *Joel Whitburn's Top Country and Western Records 1949-1971.* Menomonee Falls, Wisc.: Record Research, 1972.

Williams, Hank, Jr., with Michael Bane. *Living Proof: An Autobiography.* New York: G. P. Putnam's Sons, 1979.

Williams, Roger M. *Sing a Sad Song: The Life of Hank Williams.* Garden City, N.Y.: Doubleday, 1970.

Wolfe, Charles K. *The Grand Ole Opry: The Early Years, 1925-35.* Old Time Music, booklet 2. London: Old Time Music, 1975.

———. *Tennessee Strings: The Story of Country Music in Tennessee.* Knoxville: University of Tennessee Press, 1977.

Wren, Christopher S. *Winners Got Scars Too: The Life and Legends of Johnny Cash.* New York: Dial Press, 1971.

Wynette, Tammy, with Joan Dew. *Stand by Your Man.* New York: Simon and Schuster, 1979.

CHAPTER 7

Rock

The dominant popular music of America and much of the rest of the world for more than a generation now has been *rock*. In about 1953, records began to be heard on pop radio stations displaying a heavy backbeat and other stylistic features that formerly belonged to the rhythm and blues music played and sold to the black public. That new music came to be called *rock 'n' roll*. The dominance of Tin Pan Alley styles faded quickly as a younger buying public voted with its unprecedented abundance of spending money in favor of the new records, in a new, handy 45 rpm packaging. A flood of new groups of musicians recorded the music and it was sold by new, small record companies—it crowded the airwaves on the new disc-jockey radio programming. After a decade of explosive growth in both sales and style, the music was generally called *rock*. Especially in the heavy sales and growing sophistication of its 33 rpm long-playing albums, it was paradoxically both the center of a huge industry and the symbol of countercultural values. As the center of so much business, appeal, and perhaps influence in a time of American cultural and political upheaval, rock music began to receive serious study. Writing about rock began as objective and even suspicious examination by outsiders. Time brought up a generation inside the music which then produced a growing body of more sympathetic explanation, history, and criticism.

A. ROCK BIBLIOGRAPHY AND DISCOGRAPHY

The Literature of Rock, 1954-1978 by Frank Hoffman is the only book-length effort to keep track of writings about rock, with annotated entries for books, chapters of books, and periodical articles on rock subjects. Hoffman's book does have extensive coverage, but it is made to seem bigger than it is by separate listings for each entry from the various pop and rock encyclopedias. Listing of books is spotty, but the bibliography of articles is strong in the number of musicians and groups represented and in the categorization by styles.

Rock libraries, beyond the scope of a standard reference collection, have not yet been gathered, but there is an intriguing listing in the Ash *Subject Collections* library directory under "Music, Rock" of the Fitz Hugh Ludlow Memorial Library in San Francisco, which specializes in materials relating to "psychoactive drug-using musicians and their art."

Discography of rock has not reached the level of rigor displayed, for example, in the various compilations by Brian Rust. It has been pursued by independent enthusiasts who have now published their own large compilations (three have been mentioned under "Rhythm and Blues" in chapter 4). All four are worth listing here together for their collective testimony of rock zeal and because any one may be quite difficult to find. Fernando L. Gonzalez first published in 1974, and expanded in 1977, *Disco-File: The Discographical Catalog of American Rock & Roll and Rhythm & Blues, Vocal Harmony Groups;* Robert D. Ferlingere compiled *A Discography of Rhythm & Blues and Rock 'n' Roll Vocal Groups, 1945 to 1965;* Albert Leichter did *A Discography of Rhythm & Blues and Rock & Roll, circa 1946-1964;* and Brock Helander did *Rock 'n' Roll to Rock: A Discography*— this one, not described in chapter 4, lists records, identification numbers, and approximate release dates for about five hundred artists and groups, taking its data mostly from other published reference sources. More specialized is John Blair's *The Illustrated Discography of Surf Music, 1959-1965,* in a magazine format; a brief historical preface is followed by listings according to artists, including a large number who produced only one or two songs.

Collectors' price guides are a related species of book offering some of the same data as the discographies. Steve Propes has published *Those Oldies but Goodies: A Guide to 50s Record Collecting* cataloging 45 rpm records, mostly rhythm and blues along with a short chapter of rock 'n' roll and rockabilly. He gives brief characterization of the artist or group and then scarcity and value notes for the records. Propes also compiled *Golden Oldies: A Guide to 60s Record Collecting* and a combined *Golden Goodies: A Guide to 50s & 60s Popular Rock & Roll Record Collecting.* Jerry Osborne has published similar works. *Popular and Rock Records 1948-1978,* expanded from an earlier version, *The Record Collector's Price Guide,* suggests sale value of thirty thousand pop singles, some 78s, and some paper record sleeves. His *Record Albums 1948-1978* is similar for albums. Both include directories of dealers and collectors. Another such book is Randal C. Hill's *The Official Price Guide to Collectible Rock Records,* which prefaces a photograph and a biographical sketch to many of its entries; Hill also has directories.

Tabulations of hits from the weekly *Billboard* sales rankings are surprisingly numerous. The most widely distributed are probably Joel Whitburn's in the series described in chapter 1. The three volumes relevant to rock are *Top Pop Records, 1955-1970: Facts about 9,800 Recordings Listed in Billboard's "Hot 100" Charts, Grouped under the Names of the 2,500 Recording Artists; Joel Whitburn's Pop Annual, 1955-1977;* and, in part, *Joel Whitburn's Top LPs, 1945-1972.* The most distinctive presentation of hits is *The Miles Chart Display: Top 100, 1955-1970* (volume 1) and *1971-1975* (volume 2) edited by various members of the Miles family, displaying sales in individual graphs—nearly ten thousand in the first volume alone—of chart ranking over time. The ranking data also fill several other books. Joseph Edwards' *Top 10's and Trivia of Rock & Roll and Rhythm &*

Blues 1950-1973 has annual supplements from 1974 to 1979 (without the trivia). Stephen Nugent and Charlie Gillett's *Rock Almanac: Top Twenty American and British Singles and Albums of the '50s, '60s, and '70s* covers the years 1953 to 1973, though not published until 1978. Introductory essays discuss radio and records in the United States and Britain, and, curiously, reggae music. Charles Miron's *Rock Gold: All the Hit Charts from 1955 to 1976* gives monthly top-ten lists taken from *Record World* magazine. Stewart Goldstein and Alan Jacobson's *Oldies but Goodies: The Rock 'n' Roll Years* gives all top-forty songs by month from 1955 to 1963, some earlier songs, and some later ones not "contaminated" by the "British sound." Separate lists give songs from the period that the authors regard as not true oldies and group together hits and performers in various other ways. Peter E. Berry's *And the Hits Just Keep on Comin',* a strange choice for publication by a university press, lists top fifty and weekly top hits by year from 1955 to 1976, with a disc jockey's anecdotal introduction to each year. *Twenty Years of Pop* by Ken Barnes is a skimpier set of annotated lists of selected hits by year from 1950 to 1970, and title/artist lists of top ten hits for 1971, 1972, and 1973: the charts are British, the artists predominantly American.

Three evaluative guides to rock have appeared since 1979. The Tudors' *Contemporary Popular Music,* like its companion volumes on jazz, black music, and grass roots music, is a consensus-annotated buying guide, this one to about 750 LP records, perhaps 300 of them various kinds of rock, with section introductions that include bibliographical references. Thirty times as many records are given brief, opinionated descriptions in Dave Marsh and John Swenson's *The Rolling Stone Record Guide: Reviews and Ratings of Almost 10,000 Currently Available Rock, Pop, Soul, Country, Blues, Jazz, and Gospel Albums,* the latter six categories represented insofar as they show ties to rock. Robert Christgau in *Christgau's Record Guide: Rock Albums of the Seventies* gathers, with some revision, his review notes from the "Consumer Guide" column he wrote for various periodicals from 1969 to 1979, assigning and justifying A, B, C, D, or E grades for around three thousand albums. An appendix gives a basic record library by years through the decade. Between this category of critical guides and the previous category of bare lists may be placed *Rock Critics' Choice: The Top 200 Albums* by Paul Gambaccini and Susan Ready, tabulating the nominations of forty-seven American and British rock writers and disc jockeys; for each of the two hundred albums there are black-and-white picture of the album cover and a list of songs on the album. The second half of the book gives each judge's top ten choices.

B. ROCK GENERAL REFERENCE

Rock "encyclopedias" that are primarily biographical in content are listed in section C, below.

Two current reference books appeared in 1980 promising an up-to-date overview of the world of rock and looking toward annual renewal. Ronald Zalkind's *Contemporary Music Almanac 1980/81* is a very large collection of miscellaneous data about pop music. Its pulp almanac format deemphasizes the visual (though there are some black-and-white photographs) and stresses the compilation of facts: a calendar of events and hits of 1979, brief survey essays on the music and its history, facts on studios, disc jockeys, technology, and biographies. A large section, about half the book, covers the business of the music (compare Zalkind's *Getting Ahead in the Music Business,* cited in chapter 1). There is a section of book reviews, a bibliography, a film chart, an awards section including gold records list, and a trivia section of puzzles and quizzes. Michael Gross and Maxim Jakubowski's *The Rock Year Book 1981,* on the other hand, is heavily illustrated, with reports on styles, new performers, British and U.S. charts by week, a critical catalog of major albums, another of films, a section of album covers and one on technology, and corporate, venue, magazine, and broadcasting directories.

Pete Frame's Rock Family Trees is a book of thirty heavily annotated fold-out charts tracing the evolving and shifting personnel of major rock groups, with emphasis on British musicians.

Rock Hardware: The Instruments, Equipment and Technology of Rock, by Tony Bacon, is a lavish catalog with many photographs and diagrams, some in color, and with a manufacturers' directory.

The lyrics of rock songs are collected in several books. Besides the editions of the lyrics of the Beatles, Bob Dylan, and Bernie Taupin for Elton John (noted in section C, below), there has been a succession of general anthologies since Richard Goldstein's *The Poetry of Rock* in 1969, a collection notable for good, brief, critical headnotes. Bob Atkinson's *Songs of the Open Road: The Poetry of Folk Rock and the Journey of the Hero* is a brief collection of 1960s lyrics by such singer-songwriters as Bob Dylan, George Harrison, and Paul Simon. Bruce Chipman's *Hardening Rock: An Organic Anthology of the Adolescence of Rock 'n' Roll* combines lyrics of the 1950s and early 1960s with photographs of performers and of the daily life of their young audience. *Lyric Voices: Approaches to the Poetry of Contemporary Song* (1972), by Barbara Farris Graves and Donald J. McBain, is an anthology of 1960s rock and troubadour lyrics, with the apparatus of a secondary school or college freshman poetry textbook, reflecting the effort made by some teachers and students to study rock lyrics as poetry. A similar interest generated David Morse's *Grandfather Rock: The New Poetry and the Old,* which pairs lyrics of rock and minstrel songwriters of the 1960s with roughly comparable lyric poems from the historical canon of English and American literature. Matt Damsker's *Rock Voices: The Best Lyrics of an Era* collects forty-nine songs from between 1965 and 1979, with introductory notes on the songs and their thirty writers. An interesting project, which again looks to possible classroom use, is *The*

Rock Music Source Book by Bob Macken, Peter Fornatale, and Bill Ayres, a large catalog of rock song titles grouped according to fifty personal, social, and political topics addressed in the lyrics of those songs. The editors conceived the project to be useful to teachers planning classroom discussions of such topics: compare the *Stecheson Classified Song Directory,* noted in chapter 1, intended for broadcasters; either book might serve the purpose of the other.

Album Cover Album, edited by Storm Thorgerson and Roger Dean, traces the progress of the illustrations that have decorated the protective paper jackets of records. The introduction by Dominy Hamilton gives a brief but informative history of record jackets from Edison cylinders onward, and the book itself presents color reproductions in various sizes of nearly seven hundred albums with notes of their titles, designers, dates, companies, and the recording artists they presented. Another similar collection is *The Face of Rock & Roll: Images of a Generation* by Bruce Pollock and John Wagman. A curious special study is Karl-Georg Waldinger's *Semiotische Analyse eines Popmusik-Covers,* a sixty-page scholarly "semiotic" or sign-interpretive explication of the meaning conveyed by the illustration on an Eric Clapton record jacket.

C. ROCK BIOGRAPHY AND MATERIALS RELEVANT TO PARTICULAR FIGURES

COLLECTIVE BIOGRAPHY

Biographical encyclopedias of rock musicians have appeared in almost every year since the first, Lillian Roxon's *Rock Encyclopedia,* in 1969. Roxon's has been revised (1978) by Ed Naha; it gives pop-journalism biographical entries with albums and single records lists and has a small photograph section. Len Brown and Gary Friedrich's *Encyclopedia of Rock & Roll* (1970) is a short pocketbook of brief biographical notes, most unillustrated; as in the authors' country-and-western volume, the main information provided is recording affiliations. Similarly small is Graham Wood's *An A-Z of Rock and Roll* (1971) which covers American and British stars from 1955 to 1961. *Rock-Lexikon* (1973) by Siegfried Schmidt-Joos and Barry Graves is a German-language encyclopedia of American and European pop in the 1960s and 1970s with broad coverage and detailed histories; there is a glossary, a bibliography listing many European publications, and selected annual discographies, as well as fuller record references distributed in the articles. Irwin Stambler's *Encyclopedia of Pop, Rock, and Soul* (1974) lists stars and some topics from 1965 to 1974; significant records are mentioned, but no lists are gathered of records not included in the narrative biographies. Norm N. Nite's *Rock On: The Illustrated Encyclopedia of Rock 'n' Roll—The Solid Gold Years* (1974, updated in 1982) gives one or a few paragraphs on each of about one thousand pop performers, not all belonging to rock 'n' roll or to rock, who had hits in the 1950s, with lists of those hit singles. It was succeeded by a larger *Rock On: The Illustrated Encyclopedia of Rock 'n' Roll—The Modern Years, 1964-Present* (1978) describing the artists who had top-100 records or hit albums in later rock. Phil Hardy and Dave Laing's economical *The Encyclopedia of Rock* (1976) was issued in three volumes: *The Age of Rock 'n' Roll; From Liverpool to San Francisco;* and *The Sounds of the Seventies;* the following year they were published in a single volume. Hardy and Laing have many hundred-word entries on British and American stars, perhaps stronger on the British, and also various record-company executives, producers, session musicians, and songwriters. There are no illustrations and no discographies. Nick Logan and Bob Woffinden's *The Illustrated Encyclopedia of Rock* (1977) has over six hundred entries, about half of them decorated with color pictures of record jackets and other photographs, and with album lists. Only marginally a member of this company is Lucy Emerson's *The Gold Record* (1978) which has pop notes and pictures but little else for fifty stars of the 1970s. The most recent of these encyclopedias at present is not the best: Michael Bane and Kenny Kertok's *Who's Who in Rock* (1981) gives very brief notations on rock and some blues performers; records are not listed.

Magazine-format collective presentations of rock stars have been a British fashion. *The Stars and Superstars of Rock* is a garish color-photograph album based on a series of magazine-article histories of British and American stars from Bill Haley to Gilbert O'Sullivan. *Pop Today,* edited by Gavin Petrie from *Disc* magazine, has an overlapping collection of twenty-five stars and groups. Petrie's *Rock Life* is collected from *Melody Maker* magazine features and includes prominent earlier acts such as the Beatles, the Rolling Stones, and the Jefferson Airplane. All three books are from 1974. *Superstars of the 70s* (1976) has nineteen more rock, soul, and pop stars. An American relative is John Tobler's *Guitar Heroes* with thirty-one profiles of rock guitarists and one of Les Paul, the electric guitar pioneer; another is Jay Saporita's *Pourin' It All Out* (1980), a medley of brief superficial interviews and vignettes. A special subgroup is displayed in Anthony Fawcett's *California Rock, California Sound: The Music of Los Angeles and Southern California;* pictures and relatively slight text introduce Crosby, Stills, Nash, Young, Joni Mitchell, Jackson Browne, America, Linda Ronstadt, the Eagles, J. D. Souther, Karla Bonoff, and Warren Zevon. There is some information on records.

The Rolling Stone Interviews collects the extended conversations that have been printed in that tabloid paper, the leading journal of the rock culture. A first volume has interviews made between 1969 and 1971 with Eric Clapton, Ravi Shankar (owing to rock's brief, Beatles-derived enthusiasm for Indian music), Mike Bloomfield, Frank Zappa, Peter Townshend, Booker T and the MGs, Mick Jagger, Chuck Berry, John Lennon, Jim Morrison, Phil Spector, Bob Dylan, Robbie Robertson, John Fogarty, Little Richard, David Crosby, and Grace Slick and Paul Kantner. A second volume, 1967 to 1972, has second interviews with Dylan and Townshend along with B. B. King, Van Morrison, Roger McGuinn, Ray Davies, Leon Russell, Rod Stewart, Stephen Stills, Joe McDonald, Keith Richard, Johnny Otis, Marvin Gaye, Paul Simon, and a recording executive. Less wide-ranging interviews, emphasizing instrumental technique, are printed regularly in *Guitar Player Magazine,* and there are two collections of them. *Rock Guitarists* collects seventy interview-articles from 1967 to 1974; *Rock Guitarists* (volume 2) presents sixty-two more players and groups (see also the *Jazz Guitarists* volume). Katherine Orloff's *Rock 'n' Roll Woman* presents interview portraits concerned with personal and career challenges to women in pop music including Nicoel Barclay, Toni Brown, Rita Coolidge, Terry Garthwaite, Claudia Lennear, Maria Muldauer, Bonnie Raitt, Linda Ronstadt, Carly Simon, Grace Slick, Alice Stuart, and Wendy Waldman. (See also Pavletich's *Rock-a-Bye, Baby* in section D, below.) Bruce Pollock's *In Their Own Words* is a book of interviews with twenty songwriters, with historical introductions to groups by five-year spans, from 1955 to 1974. The writers are Hal David, Doc Pomus, Gerry Goffin, Phil Ochs, Buffy Sainte-Marie, Peter Townshend, Keith Reid, Frank Zappa, Robert Hunter, John Sebastian, Felice and Boudleaux Bryant, Melvin Van Peebles, Randy Newman, Loudon Wainwright, John Prine, Melanie Safka, Tim Rice, Harry Chapin, and Linda Creed. (See also Sarlin's *Turn It Up!* in section D, below.) Robert Stephen Spitz' *The Making of Superstars: Artists and Executives of the Rock Music Business* has interviews with eight stars— Jim Messina, Barry Manilow, Janis Ian, Dion DiMucci, Neil Sedaka, Peter Frampton, Barry White, Grace Slick—and twice as many representatives of various business roles, including Don Kirshner, John Hammond, Sr., Arif Mardin, Ron Delsener, and Jerry Wexler.

INDIVIDUAL FIGURES AND GROUPS

ABBA: The Ultimate Pop Group by Marianne Lindvall is a large paperback of promotional text and photographs, with some song lyrics and an album list, for the bland Swedish pop-rock group that has amassed international (including American) record sales among the largest for any musicians.

Bachman-Turner Overdrive: Rock Is My Life, This Is My Song. The Authorized Biography by Martin Melhuish is a surprisingly long career journal of a heavy-sound Canadian rock band with a large impact in this country. Numerous candid photographs are kept subordinate to telling the story. There is a discography.

The Beach Boys were the champions of a style and cult of soft-rock surfing music from 1963, and the arrangements and production by their member Brian Wilson created some of the most complex and musically interesting records in rock. Bruce Golden's *The Beach Boys: Southern California Pastoral* is a short, serious essay on the group's music, with notes, a discography, an annotated bibliography, and no photographs at all. *The Beach*

Boys: A Biography in Words and Pictures by Ken Barnes has brief, song-by-song critical description of their records. David Leaf's *The Beach Boys and the California Myth* is an elaborate group biography and black-and-white photograph and souvenir album, not the critical or sociological study that the title might suggest. John Tobler's *The Beach Boys* is a British fan's history and photograph album, much of the photography in color. The U.S. discography included is much less full than than in a shorter book, the most recent, Byron Preiss' *Beach Boys,* a large format, souvenir book, heavy with promotional pictures and decorative paintings. The narrative text is interrupted by brief quotes from interviews and by many lyrics so that the effect is of a collage to browse over.

The Beatles have been written about at great length and with an intensity of interest fitting their enormous impact on world rock. Neither Elvis Presley, for whom a whole reference guide volume has been published, nor the Rolling Stones, for whom a university press has published two editions of a bibliography, have occasioned as much print as have the Beatles. The representative book list here can be extended by reference to separate entries below for Harrison, Lennon, and McCartney. *All Together Now: The First Complete Beatles Discography, 1961-1975,* by Harry Castleman and Walter J. Podrazik, is a huge collection of data on all records made by the Beatles or by others of songs written but not released by the Beatles or belonging to other Beatle-related categories. The authors' sequel volume *The Beatles Again* updates and supplements; it has a section of career chronicle with detailed attention to the years 1976-1977, various other facts on the Beatles and their associates, and a cumulative index to both volumes. *The Beatles A to Z* by Goldie Friede, Robin Titone, and Sue Weiner is an encyclopedia with three thousand entries of discographic fact, biographical detail on each Beatle and many associates, locations, institutions, and trivia. Each Beatle has a photograph section, all record jackets are pictured, and there are lists of tours, "special performances," and TV appearances. *The Beatles: An Illustrated Record,* by Roy Carr and Tony Tyler, is a large scrapbook, the frontal size of a record album, cataloging events and records year by year. *The Beatles,* with text by Geoffrey Stokes, is an album of unusual photographs printed in half-tone, color memorabilia, and *Rolling Stone* commentary. Beatles' lyrics have been printed in several forms in addition to their sporadic appearance in school and college literary anthologies. *The Beatles Illustrated Lyrics* edited by Alan Aldridge scatters song texts among florid illustrations by forty-four graphic artists; his *The Beatles Illustrated Lyrics 2* displays the works of another fifty-three. *The Beatles Lyrics Illustrated,* on the other hand, is a small "pocketbook" collection of about the same list of songs—189 of them—with a section of photographs. Perhaps the single most astonishing piece of rock scholarship is Colin Campbell and Allan Murphy's *Things We Said Today: The Complete Lyrics and a Concordance to the Beatles' Songs, 1962-1970.* Lyrics are transcribed from records rather than reprinted from print sources, and these transcriptions have been made the base of a computer-generated concordance of all words in those songs, significant and insignificant, printed in the full lines in which they occur. (There are three pages of *it*'s.) Facsimiles of fourteen Beatle lyric manuscripts are printed. *The Beatles,* a biography by Hunter Davies (1978), slightly extends the solid journalistic account Davies wrote in 1968 of the lives of the Beatles before and during stardom, not revelatory but reliable. Philip Norman's *Shout! The Beatles in Their Generation* (1981) is a long chronicle illustrated with a hundred previously unpublished photographs from 1957 to 1970. *The Beatles: A Day in the Life. The Day-by-Day Diary 1960-1970,* compiled by Tom Schultheiss, orders business, creative, performing, and personal data into calendar entries for most days of the decade. Particular phases of their saga appear in some more specialized books. *The Man Who Gave the Beatles Away* by Allan Williams and William Marshall gives the informal reminiscences of Williams, who was the group's manager in the Beatles' Liverpool and Hamburg days, with candid photographs and some reproductions of documents. Williams' successor was Brian Epstein, who wrote a short autobiography called *A Cellarful of Noise* (1964) about his own life and the Beatles' early days of glory up through their first American appearance. Epstein was the strategist of that early triumphal career until his early death in 1967. George Martin is the producer who came to be called the fifth Beatle for his role in shaping their more ambitious studio albums. He has written a book of recollections and technical briefings on his craft called *All You Need Is Ears.* Richard DiLello wrote *The Longest Cocktail Party: An Insider's Diary of the Beatles, Their Million-Dollar Apple Empire and Its Wild Rise and Fall* in 1972, history and gossip in 140 minichapters from 1968 to 1970, with many photographs. At the end he prints a collection of news items from the London *Times* on the group's legal dissolution. Peter McCabe and Robert D. Schonfeld's *Apple to the Core: The Unmaking of the Beatles* is half devoted to the group history and half an account of the business politics and legal tangles leading to their split. *The Beatles Apart* by Bob Woffinden is an illustrated narrative that follows the four ex-Beatles through the 1970s. John Blake's *All You Needed Was Love: The Beatles after the Beatles* also pursues each Beatle separately up to the time of Lennon's death, emphasizing the downs and disasters of their lives and careers. A book of musical commentary stands apart from the library of books about the Beatles themselves. *Twilight of the Gods: The Music of the Beatles,* by Wilfrid Mellers, a distinguished musicologist and composer, is a lively but serious study analyzing many specific musical examples, continuing through the Beatles' early separate recordings at the beginning of the 1970s.

The Bee Gees had success as a folkish pop group in the 1960s and achieved an improbable resurgence in the middle 1970s with a new disco style: their double album of soundtrack songs for the movie *Saturday Night Fever* became the biggest selling album in record history with 25 million sales. *The Bee Gees* by Kim Stevens is a short, illustrated paperback career story, through their *Sergeant Pepper* movie in which they and others acted characters and sang songs from the Beatles' album a decade before. *Bee Gees: The Authorized Biography* (1979) is credited to the brothers Gibb, the singers themselves, as told to David Leaf; the format is the common one of a large, illustrated fan book.

Blondie by Lester Bangs also has that format, profiling a punk-pop group at the end of the 1970s. The reportorial text is better than the average in such books.

The David Bowie Story by George Tremlett is a biography for fans of the English rock performer, through 1974. *David Robert Jones Bowie: The Discography of a Generalist, 1962-1979,* by David Jeffrey Fletcher, actually a third edition in 1979, is an illustrated, annotated discography and trove of other lore for even more serious fans.

Eric Clapton: A Biography by John Pidgeon is a British paperback, carefully researched and written, with some subordinated photographs, notes, a discography, and a "groupography" of the ensembles around Clapton, whose stardom rose in rock guitar virtuosity. (See also the study of a Clapton album cover by Waldinger in section B, above.)

Dick Clark hosted the record and dance television show, "American Bandstand," broadcast nationally from Philadelphia beginning in 1957. In *Rock, Roll & Remember* he tells his story of that show and other ventures and his version of his prominent role in the "payola" scandal and subsequent congressional hearings.

Alice Cooper, born Vincent Damon Furnier, generated a decadent-spectacular stage entertainment around his rock singing. Bob Greene, now a nationally syndicated newspaper columnist, was hired by Cooper's traveling show for a minor costumed part so he could write an account of the tour, *Billion Dollar Baby* (1974). His long book is balanced, unsensational, and generally sympathetic to members of the party. (It may be compared as a tour log with Shepherd's *Rolling Thunder Logbook* on Dylan and Greenfield's *S.T.P.* on the Rolling Stones, below.) *Me, Alice: The Autobiography of Alice Cooper,* by Cooper with Steven Gaines, is a first-person account of touring adventures in the early 1970s, with photographs on and off stage.

Elvis Costello by Krista Reese is a large, illustrated paperback history, unauthorized and reasonably objective, of the antiestablishment British rock star of the late 1970s who has had some impact in this country but less than he has had at home.

Bob Dylan is one of a handful of popular entertainers, and among them probably the chief, whose creative work as a songwriter has been given widespread critical study and respect. In folk-minstrel, rock, and country styles, but always in his own idiom, he has produced an evolving succession of challenging songs for twenty years during a charismatic and influential performing career. *Writings and Drawings by Bob Dylan* collected one decade of his songs (not music; as with many entertainers' work, there are also songbooks), from 1962 to 1972. *Bob Dylan: His Unreleased Recordings* by Paul Cable is a catalog of various tapings of Dylan between 1961 and 1976, including as an appendix a discography of his regulation releases and bootleg recordings updated to 1980. Anthony Scaduto's *Bob Dylan: An Intimate Biography* (1971) concentrates on Dylan's life and career up to 1965, covering another five years very quickly. In 1973 an updating afterword was added by Steven Gaines. Craig McGregor edited *Bob Dylan: A Retrospective* (1972), an anthology of articles and reviews from 1962 to 1971. *Bob Dylan: An Illustrated History* by Michael Gross is a fan's biographical scrapbook through 1976. Less informative is *Bob Dylan in His Own Words,* compiled by "Miles" (in a series of similar books), a paperback of pictures and Dylan's public remarks: the latter, a rather sparse collection, consists mainly of ironic misrepresentations. *Rolling Thunder Logbook* by Sam Shepherd is a photographic and lyrically celebratory narrative record of a tour by Dylan and friends through New England and New York in 1976; much attention is expended on the author himself. *Dylan: A Commemoration* (the reclusive Dylan has often been treated with the awe more often accorded the departed), edited by Stephen Pickering (second edition 1971), represents the cultic side of Dylan study; it is a tabloid scrapbook of reviews, interviews, and appreciation. Pickering's own writing in it insists on a Jewish-mystical version of the artist. Michael Gray's *Song and Dance Man: The Art of Bob Dylan* was an early full-scale critical analysis of Dylan's lyrics through the 1960s, pointedly invoking many established literary writers in an attempt to justify Dylan's place among them. Gray has an extensively annotated discography. Much more subtle and valuable is Betsy Bowden's *Performed Literature: Words and Music by Bob Dylan,* which analyzes and compares the artistry of particular recorded performances of the songs.

Fleetwood Mac: The Authorized History (1978) by Samuel Graham is an illustrated pocketbook story of that group. In the same year, Roy Carr and Steve Clarke published *Fleetwood Mac: Rumours n' Fax,* a fan's photograph-and-gossip album. Its yearly chronicle is organized by albums released by the various configurations of the group.

Peter Frampton is the title of two fan biographies, one by Marsha Daly and one by Irene Adler—both include pictures and record lists.

The Grateful Dead were leaders of San Francisco rock in the 1960s. Hank Harrison's *The Dead Book: A Social History of the Grateful Dead* (1973) is a psychedelic collage of prose, photographs, interviews, and Bay Area social context to portray the group members and their associates. More connected is Harrison's *The Dead* (1980), a continuation that includes a discography.

George Harrison: Yesterday & Today (1977), by Ross Michaels, has the standard fan-book form but is unusual in including a chapter that quotes many lyrics by the ex-Beatle with brief commentary. Harrison himself has published *I Me Mine* (1980), an anthology of his lyrics introduced by a long interview narrative and a photograph collection. There are many reproductions of Harrison's scratchpad song manuscripts.

Jimi Hendrix: Voodoo Child of the Aquarian Age by David Henderson is a very long, popular biography with evocative descriptions of Hendrix' playing and stream-of-consciousness recreations of his experiences. A condensed version of the book has been published under the title *'Scuse Me while I Kiss the Sky: The Life of Jimi Hendrix*.

Buddy Holly: His Life and Music by John Goldrosen (1975) is a full, serious critical biography delving into details of Holly's life and carefully appraising his 1950s rock 'n' roll songs. There is a technical and annotated discography. Goldrosen revised the book, with some new material, for an illustrated paperback *The Buddy Holly Story* (1979).

Elton John, a British rock pianist, singer, and showman, achieved his very large success with songs written for him by Bernie Taupin (see also below under Taupin's name) until the partnership ended in the late 1970s. Both are featured in Paul Gambaccini's *A Conversation with Elton John and Bernie Taupin* (1975), which includes a discographic chart. Dick Tatham and Tony Jasper's *Elton John* is a photomagazine book; it has an illustrated directory of John's sidemen. David Nutter's *Elton: It's a Little Bit Funny* is a photograph album with few captions.

Tom Jones by Peter Jones is a fan's unillustrated biography of the Welsh pop-rock singer and sex symbol whose following has tended to be an older and largely nonrock segment of the population.

Janis Joplin is the subject of *Buried Alive* by Myra Friedman, a best-selling biography from a friend's vantage point, with much dramatized conversation, published after the singer's death in 1970.

Murray Kaufman presents his career as a nationally prominent New York disc jockey in *Murray the K Tells It Like It Is, Baby,* a scrapbook of self-advertisements.

Carole King: A Biography in Words and Pictures by Mitchell S. Cohen is a large paperback presentation of King, whose first success as a songwriter was followed by greater success as a pianist-singer when her 1971 album, *Tapestry,* became the best-selling rock album up to that time.

Al Kooper recalls his studio and touring experiences as a rock and blues keyboard player, who collaborated with various stars, in *Backstage Passes: Rock 'n' Roll Life in the Sixties*.

Jerry Leiber and Mike Stoller were songwriters whose songs were among the most successful in the 1950s for such performers as the Drifters, the Coasters, and Elvis Presley. Robert Palmer's *Baby, That Was Rock & Roll: The Legendary Leiber and Stoller* tells the story of their writing and record-producing careers in a scrapbook of photographs, lyrics, printed music, a narrative, and tables.

John Lennon: One Day at a Time. A Personal Biography of the Seventies by Anthony Fawcett is a large, illustrated report on Lennon and his wife Yoko Ono in 1968-1969 and notes on their lives up to 1976; a chronology of Lennon's life and discography through 1975 are appended. Lennon's first wife Cynthia wrote her own story, bearing on Lennon's Beatle career, in 1978, with her own photographs, sketches, and poems: *A Twist of Lennon. John Lennon in His Own Words* (1981), compiled by "Miles," gathers photographs and excerpts from interviews year by year, extended to brief notice of Lennon's assassination just before the book went to press. The British Broadcasting Corporation interviewed the Lennons two days before John Lennon's death, and it has published a small book of the transcripts, *The Lennon Tapes: John Lennon and Yoko Ono in Conversation with Andy Peebles 6 December 1980.*

Jerry Lee Lewis was a piano-playing singing star of 1950s rockabilly, reappearing in the early 1980s in a softer country style. Robert Cain's *Whole Lotta Shakin' Goin' On: Jerry Lee Lewis* is a large-format, illustrated paperback biography. Robert Palmer's *Jerry Lee Lewis Rocks!* is a scrapbook essay on Lewis in the 1950s and after, perhaps overdramatic.

Paul McCartney in His Own Words, by Paul Gambaccini, is one of three similar photo-biographies of McCartney in his post-Beatle years, this one with interview text. John Mendelsohn's *Paul McCartney: A Biography in Words and Pictures* and Tony Jasper's *Paul McCartney and Wings* are the others. The last has the most photographs and the least text.

Barry Manilow by Ann Morse is of little interest as a thirty-page booklet aimed at juvenile readers, but it may be mentioned here to notice the series that it represents, which in 1978 ran to twenty-six such books on pop and rock stars published by Creative Education.

Joni Mitchell by Leonore Fleischer is a brief photo-biography of a troubadour, pop, and rock singer and songwriter (she has also produced a jazz album in tribute to Charles Mingus); the book includes a chapter on "Her Music" with commentary on her songs, which are indeed unusually interesting and have drawn some academic comment (see Charles Hartman, *Centennial Review,* fall 1977).

Jim Morrison was the lead singer of the group The Doors. His life and his death (in 1971) are reported in a best-selling biography *No One Here Gets Out Alive* by Jerry Hopkins and Danny Sugerman.

The Osmond Story by George Tremlett is a fan's biography of various members of the pop family group, with photographs, through early 1974.

Pink Floyd: A Visual Documentary by Miles, edited in Britain, printed in Japan, published in New York, is a diary scrapbook of that rock group with discography and color pictures of record jackets as well as of the group.

The Police Released is almost purely a photographic souvenir promoting that group at the turn of the 1980s.

Elvis Presley, from the early days of rock 'n' roll, was the greatest single star of that music. He had million-selling records with between forty and eighty different singles in addition to seventy best-selling albums—a sales success for one performer rivalled only by that of Bing Crosby. His performing style, partly his own and partly borrowed from black rhythm and blues, had great influence. A long string of starring movie roles extended and mellowed his mystique, and, despite reclusiveness in the years before his death in 1979, he retained the deep loyalty of a huge public. How much has been written about him is measured by John A. Whisler's *Elvis Presley: Reference Guide and Discography*. Drawing on *Readers' Guide* and other indexes, Whisler catalogs books, magazines, and articles—there are over a hundred Elvis books and magazines—and adds a discography and a song title index. His general index locates people and subjects not only in his own book but in the two books by Hopkins and the first by Lichter mentioned below. Ron Barry's *All American Elvis: The Elvis Presley American Discography* lists albums with contents and lists singles by title. Record numbers are given but not personnel credits or recording dates. The fullest of many display books is *Elvis Presley: An Illustrated Biography* by Rainer Wallraf and Heinz Plehn, a scrapbook with record-album-size pages, compiled in Germany, printed in Japan, and distributed from New York. Contents include some color photos and many other pictures, a chronology, a film catalog with long summaries, movie posters, album covers, and a discography. W. A. Harbinson's *The Illustrated Elvis,* which also exists in abridgements, is an annotated photographic history with many but not unusual pictures, most of them supplied by the Elvis Presley Appreciation Society or taken from his films. *Elvis* (1976) is a British scrapbook history. Paul Lichter's *The Boy Who Dared to Rock: The Definitive Elvis,* compiled by a self-described "world-renowned Elvisologist," presents a huge collection of publicity shots, some of them in color, around an admiring text. Appendixes tabulate live performances, recording sessions, and records. *Elvis* by Jerry Hopkins (1971) is a large, popular biography, the best during Presley's career. In 1980, Hopkins brought out *Elvis: The Final Years* chronicling Presley's life in the 1970s after the first book breaks off, based on interviews with many of Presley's associates. Albert Goldman's *Elvis* (1981) is a massive investigatory biography of Presley's personal life, revealing sordid details with great thoroughness. *Elvis, We Love You Tender* by Dee Presley and Billy, Rick, and David Stanley, is recollections by his stepmother-in-adulthood and her sons, with family and other photographs. Alfred Wertheimer's *Elvis '56: In the Beginning* is an album of informal photographs taken by the author on assignment in the first year of Presley's stardom. May Mann's *The Private Elvis* (first called *Elvis and the Colonel*) is an admiring narrative by a reporter, not as intimate as its cover suggests, written near the end of Presley's life and republished with brief additions after his death. It assembles materials from several interviews beginning in 1957. *Elvis in Hollywood,* by Paul Lichter, is a picture catalog of Presley's films with credits, long synopses, and fans' criticism, including a discography of the film music. *Elvis: The Films and Career of Elvis Presley* by Steven and Boris Zmijewsky is half a career photo-biography and half a film catalog similar to Lichter's. Neal and Janice Gregory's *When Elvis Died* is a detailed account of media and public response to Presley's death, including photographs of Presley, a section of sixty-eight reprinted editorials, and an extensive bibliography. No mundane information can be found in Ilona Panta's *Elvis Presley: King of Kings,* a book of psychic mystifications. Joe Kelly's *All the King's Men* is a brief, annotated photographic study of the phenomenon of Elvis impersonators.

The Rolling Stones have had the longest continuous run in the front ranks of rock. Beginning their career as rivals of the early Beatles, they have kept and raised their standing for a generation as recording and performing attractions and as symbols of general impudence. Mary Laverne Dimmick has compiled *The Rolling Stones: An Annotated Bibliography* of books and articles from 1962 to 1977. David Dalton edited *Rolling Stones* (1972), a collection of illustrated articles, interviews, and reviews, along with words and music for ninety-seven songs, and a discography through 1972. Tony Jasper's *The Rolling Stones* (1976) offers in large photomagazine format a history, chronology, set of biographies, directory of associates, and discography. David Dalton and Mick Farren compiled *Rolling Stones in Their Own Words,* a collage of interview texts and pictures. *S.T.P.: A Journey through America with the Rolling Stones* by Robert Greenfield is a journalistic account of their 1972 concert tour of the United States. *Up and Down with the Rolling Stones* by Tony Sanchez is an insider's gossip, with many of his photographs, emphasizing seamy revelations about the stars' personal lives.

Linda Ronstadt (1978) by Vivian Claire is a brief paperback biography with many promotional pictures and a track-by-track account of her records. Mary Ellen Moore's competing book *The Linda Ronstadt Scrapbook* (1978) has many pin-up-like photographs and a quick text.

Simon and Garfunkel: A Biography in Words and Pictures by Mitchell S. Cohen is another of the illustrated fan books, including commentary on records and discographies for the pair as well as for Paul Simon and Art Garfunkel in their separate careers after 1971.

Grace Slick: The Biography by Barbara Rowes is "authorized" fan journalism about the star singer of the Jefferson Airplane ensemble of San Francisco rock in the late 1960s and later of the Jefferson Starship and on her own.

Patti Smith: Rock & Roll Madonna by Dusty Roach is an illustrated survey of the career, records, and writings of a rock poetess of the later 1970s.

Phil Spector was one of the most successful and influential record producers of 1960s rock 'n' roll records. *Out of His Head: The Sound of Phil Spector,* by Richard Williams, is an illustrated career biography with a list of songs he wrote and a discography of the records made from them, including those that made his arranging and producing as famous as the performing of his star singers.

Bruce Springsteen by Peter Gambaccini is a relatively full photo-biography of the 1970s rocker whose discovery by the public was heralded in simultaneous cover stories in *Time* and *Newsweek*. An even more extensive one is Dave Marsh's *Born to Run: The Bruce Springsteen Story,* which also lists records and unrecorded songs and has a tour appearance chronology.

Rod Stewart (1977) by Tony Jasper is a standard photo-biography, with a discographic chapter and a career calendar. *Rod Stewart* (1981) by Paul Nelson and Lester Bangs joins a photograph album with competent critical discussion.

Bernie Taupin, mentioned above with Elton John, has his lyrics displayed with art graphics in *Bernie Taupin, the One Who Writes the Words for Elton John: Complete Lyrics from 1968 to Goodbye, Yellow Brick Road* (1976), patterned after Alan Aldridge's Beatles books, by Aldridge and Mike Dempsey.

Frank Zappa has been a puzzling rock and put-on artist since the mid-1960s. David Walley's *No Commercial Potential: The Saga of Frank Zappa Then and Now* is a fan's fairly serious biography, with interviews, photographs, discography, and mention of books on Zappa published in Holland and France.

D. ROCK HISTORY AND COMMENTARY

A good analytic history through the 1960s is Charlie Gillett's *The Sound of the City: The Rise of Rock & Roll* (1970 and 1972), which traces the musical and cultural forces that brought about rock 'n' roll in the early 1950s (most directly out of rhythm and blues) and that developed the soul and rock musics of the 1960s. Carl Belz' *The Story of Rock* (1969 and 1972) is another general history, 1954 through 1971, with good treatment of the technological elements in rock evolution; the book is dominated by the thesis that rock should be thought of as a folk music of its youth culture. *The Rolling Stone Illustrated History of Rock & Roll* (1976 and 1980), edited by Jim Miller, is the most comprehensive history now, though not a connected and synthesizing narrative: it collects 111 chapters by various writers on artists and movements, with selected discographies and many excellent large photographs. Nik Cohn's *Rock from the Beginning* (1969) is a popular chronicle of rock in England and America from the early 1950s to the mid-1960s, with lively critical commentary. Mike Jahn's *Rock: From Elvis Presley to the Rolling Stones* (1973) is a fairly quick yearly survey up to the beginning of the 1970s in one-to-two-page subchapters on performers and fashions, footnoted with record suggestions. Richie Yorke's *The History of Rock 'n' Roll* (1976) is a souvenir book, half text and half record company photographs, many in color, by year from 1955 to 1975; it developed from a forty-eight hour "History of Rock 'n' Roll" program for a Toronto radio station. Loyd Grossman's *A Social History of Rock Music: From the Greasers to Glitter Rock* (1976) is a serious but brief survey, critical as well as socioanalytic. David Dalton and Lenny Kaye's *Rock 100* (1977) is a history in about a hundred brief chapter profiles of stars, groups, and types of groups, most of them illustrated, from Elvis to David Bowie. Peter Lane's *What Rock Is All About* (1979) is a bland survey history through the early 1970s with some publicity photographs, perhaps aimed at a teenage reading public. A special angle on rock history is provided by Jenkinson and Warner's *Celluloid Rock,* noted in chapter 3.

Some histories limit themselves to particular periods, fashions, and phenomena. The roots of rock 'n' roll occupy Robert Palmer's *A Tale of Two Cities: Memphis Rock and New Orleans Roll,* two lectures on the contribution of these regional recording centers to the creation of rock 'n' roll from preexisting country and rhythm-and-blues styles. The early period, roughly the 1950s, has several retrospective studies. The fullest and most analytic is Arnold Shaw's *The Rockin' 50s,* written from Shaw's inside view as a music publishing executive. The book incorporates ten brief interviews with major figures. Gene Busnar's *It's Rock 'n' Roll,* called on its cover "a musical history of the fabulous fifties," gives short history, a few pages of profiles of half a dozen substyles and fifteen particular groups and artists, and annual chronicle and hit record lists from 1954 to 1963; Busnar concludes by interviewing Bobby Robinson, a black recording entrepreneur in the period. Bruce Pollock's *When Rock Was Young: A Nostalgic Review of the Top 40 Era* has short chapters of history by years from 1955 to 1964 and profiles of the Five Satins, Phil Everly, Jo-Ann Campbell, Hank Ballard, the Shirelles, the Kingston Trio, Neil Sedaka, Brenda Lee, and Little Anthony, tracing their careers to the time of the writing (1981).

The next decade is celebrated in David Pichaske's *A Generation in Motion: Popular Music and Culture in the Sixties,* an associative chronicle of the counterculture that strings together song lyrics, photographs, and other people's written and spoken statements with the author's commentary. *Trips: Rock Life in the Sixties,* by Ellen Sander, is inside-observer memoirs of various circles of rock stars, through the time of Woodstock (summer 1969). A ninety-page "Rock Taxonomy" by Sander and Tom Clark categorizes artists and groups of the time with brief admiring characterizations. Robert Somma edited a somber book called *No One Waved Good-bye: A Casualty Report on Rock and Roll,* a collection of articles on the deaths of four rock music figures: Beatles' manager Brian Epstein, Brian Jones of the Rolling Stones, guitar virtuoso Jimi Hendrix, and singer Janis Joplin. Jerome Kinkowitz' *The American 1960s: Imaginative Acts in a Decade of Change* is a more general study beyond the music, but has a chapter, "Bob Dylan and Neil Young: The Song of Self," with album-by-album commentary on their work as an index to American culture in the decade.

A phenomenon of great symbolic importance emerging in the 1960s was the massive outdoor concert. *Festival! The Book of American Music Cele- brations,* by Jerry Hopkins, is a history and photograph album of the folk, country, and rock festivals of the decade; some of the material is reprinted from *Rolling Stone.* Robert Santelli's *Aquarius Rising: The Rock Festival Years* carries the movement from the Human Be-In in San Francisco in 1967 to the Ontario Motor Speedway California Jam II in 1978, with crowd and stage photographs; the author's point of view is one of sympathy for the rock culture and the festival idea. There is a catalog of the festivals and a bibliography. The most important of the festivals as affirmation was Woodstock, and as disillusion, Altamont, four months later. Both were recorded in feature films, and the former in at least three books. *Woodstock Festival Remembered* by Jean Young and Michael Lang is a large album history, some of its pictures in color. Lang was one of the planners of the event. Robert Stephen Spitz' *Barefoot in Babylon: The Creation of the Woodstock Music Festival, 1969* is a 500-page reportorial account of the preparation and maneuverings leading up to the festival. *Young Men with Unlimited Capital,* by Joel Rosenman, John Roberts, and Robert Pilpel, is a jaundiced account from the perspective of the investors who sponsored the event but failed to profit from it.

A movement of rock in the late 1970s is the subject of Caroline Coon's *1988: The New Wave Punk Rock Explosion,* a British rock journalist's large paperback album of pictures and articles written in 1976 and 1977 with interviews and quoted lyrics. *"The Boy Looked at Johnny": The Obituary of Rock and Roll* by Julie Burchill and Tony Parsons is a booklet of flashy journalism by writers for the British rock magazine *The New Musical Express,* on the punk scene.

The social and economic implications of rock music have occupied a large proportion of writing about rock. The first extensive study of such implica- tions was Dave Laing's *The Sound of Our Time* (1970). Laing begins with a survey of the commercial history of popular music leading to the watershed of the 1950s when rock 'n' roll arrived, and he continues with specific atten- tion to the works in the 1960s of the Beatles, the Rolling Stones, the Who, and Bob Dylan. In a concluding note, he discusses method for sociological and semiological analysis of the music. Three British books from around the same time all attempt to survey the pop music business and culture for outsiders, beginning with Richard Mabey's *The Pop Process* (1969). Tony Jasper's *Understanding Pop* (1972) is a somewhat breathless but broad survey in nineteen topical chapters ("Pop Business," "Rock and Politics," "Pop and Religion"), quoting extensively from academic and journalistic commentators. Michael Wale's *Voxpop: Profiles of the Pop Process* (1972) collects interviews with representatives of various corners of the British industry. *Singers of an Empty Day: Last Sacraments for the Superstars* (1971), by Karl Dallas, is an essay on the careers of rock stars, considering them to be ritual figures for their audiences and for that reason vulnerable to destructive pressures. William J. Schafer's *Rock Music: Where It's Been, What It Means, Where It's Going* (1972) again addresses rock outsiders in a brief history and study that attempts to place rock musically, socially, and spiritually. David A. Noebel's *The Marxist Minstrels: A Handbook on Communist Subversion of Music,* a heavily footnoted polemic, lumps together folk-protest and rock music as a political conspiracy by Communists to destroy America. There are half a dozen similar books by Noebel and by Bob Larson. Chapple and Garofalo's *Rock 'n' Roll Is Here to Pay* (1977), a critique from the political left, has been cited in chapter 1. Aida Pavletich's *Rock-a-Bye, Baby* is a feminist chronicle of women in popular music from 1960 to 1980. H. Stith Bennett's *On Becoming a Rock Musician* is a sophisticated study, informed by contemporary sociological theory, of the role and career patterns of the many thousands of performers in local rock bands. Bennett offers much information as well on the technology of rock. He appends a thorough survey of previous sociological study of popular culture. Simon Frith's *Sound Effects: Youth, Leisure, and the Politics of Rock 'n' Roll* (1981) is an American and slightly less formal and scholarly reworking of the author's British book *The Sociology of Rock* (1978), combining professional sociology and rock criticism in studying the meaning of the music, the economics of its production, and the culture of its youth audience. Michael Bane's *White Boy Singin' the Blues* traces the racial borderline in pop music through various styles of white adaptation of black music in jazz and rock. The style of the book is that of rock journalism.

Rock criticism is still mainly a matter of critical journalism—that is, of reviews and articles published in newspapers and magazines about the performers and performances of the day. A few writers have attempted whole books of critical history or critical biography, already listed in this chapter, and a few others, notably Meltzer and Marcus, have written explanatory books about rock music as music at large. Most of a list of rock criticism in book form, however, consists of compilations of shorter pieces originally published in periodicals. An early and elementary collection is *The New Sound/Yes!* (1966) edited by Ira Peck; the sources are general-readership magazines, and the implied audience is young. Jonathan Eisen's *The Age of Rock* is a "reader" of thirty-eight pieces by many authors from the period 1966-1968 giving particular attention to the Beatles and to Dylan. *The Age of Rock 2,* a year later, compiles a similar set of articles for that year. Eisen's *Twenty-Minute Fandangos and Forever Changes: A Rock Bazaar* (1971) is spoof rock journalism, which may have literary merit but not informational value. *Rock and Roll Will Stand,* edited by Greil Marcus in 1969, reprints journalism on rock and society in the late 1960s by seven Berkeley and San Francisco writers; there are record suggestions after each article and an additional list at the end. In 1970 Richard Meltzer published *The Aesthetics of Rock,* not a collection but an odd whole book of free-associative reflections on rock with many cryptic references to the history of philosophy. Bob Sarlin's *Turn It Up! (I Can't Hear the Words)* (1973) is a series of essays commenting on songs written by Bob Dylan, Robert Hunter, Van Morrison, Joni Mitchell, Randy Newman, Laura Nyro, and Don McLean, with brief notes on the work of other songwriters and four background interviews with industry figures and other critics on the rise of such songs. (Compare with this book Bruce Pollock's *In Their Own Words,* above under collective biography.) Greil Marcus' *Mystery Train: Images of America in Rock 'n' Roll Music* (1975) is an essay on rock in American culture, less sociological than critical; Marcus dwells especially on the music and lyrics of The Band, Sly Stone, Randy Newman, and Elvis Presley. A long appendix annotates relevant records and books. Marcus later edited *Stranded: Rock and Roll for a Desert Island* (1979) for which he invited twenty critics to choose and defend a single favorite album. Choices range from Little Willie John's hits of the 1950s to Linda Ronstadt in 1978. In an epilogue, Marcus gives an annotated list of several hundred favorites of his own. Ben Fong-Torres has edited two books of selections from *Rolling Stone: The Rolling Stone Rock 'n Roll Reader* in 1974 and *What's That Sound?* in 1976.

Several individual critics have collected anthologies of their own periodical pieces. Paul Williams published *Outlaw Blues* in 1969 from his writings in the previous three years for his *Crawdaddy* magazine. Richard Goldstein's *Goldstein's Greatest Hits* (1970) is made up of articles from the same period, 1966 to 1968, that appeared in magazines and newspapers in Los Angeles and New York. Tony Palmer, a British critic, is inclined to impressionistic essays on the social implications of rock; his collection is *Born under a Bad Sign,* 1970. Albert Goldman's *Freakshow* (1971), mostly about rock, reprints his essays from general and intellectual magazines and from the *New York Times* from 1959 to 1970. John Landau's *It's Too Late to Stop Now* (1972) collects his pieces from *Rolling Stone* and elsewhere from 1966 to 1971. Robert Christgau's *Any Old Way You Choose It* (1973) has pieces from the *Village Voice, Newsday,* and the *New York Times,* 1967-1973; for a large directory of his briefer opinions see *Christgau's Record Guide* in section A, above. Peter Guralnick's *Lost Highway: Journeys and Arrivals of American Musicians* (1979) consists of pieces on rockabilly and country and blues singers that, for the most part, appeared in the rock press. Derek Jewell's *The Popular Voice* (1980), from the London *Sunday Times* in the previous two decades, covers jazz, pop, and rock. Gary Giddins in *Riding on a Blue Note* (1981) has some rock and pop along with jazz writing from the *Village Voice.*

The visual presentation of rock has made a succession of books. With some similarity to the photo-and-text encyclopedias and biographies, these differ in emphasizing the art of photography (or, in one case, painting) for its independent testimony about the rock scene. Perhaps the first such book, though a hybrid with editorial comments and quotations from the musicians, is *Rock and Other Four Letter Words* by J. Marks, with some of the photographs by Linda Eastman. *Rock: A World Bold as Love* by Douglas Kent Hall is a black-and-white album of Hall's pictures, again mixed with a collage of passages from interviews with performers. Abby Hirsch edited *The Photography of Rock* collecting full-page black-and-white candid and performing pictures of rock and blues artists from 1965 to 1971. Guy Peellaert and Nik Cohn's *Rock Dreams* is a portfolio of eerie, lurid paintings by Peellaert evoking images in rock 'n' roll music with similarly evocative captions by Cohn. *The Concerts* by Laurie Lewis has no text, only an unobtrusive key at the end, to its color photograph record of peak performance moments at rock concerts.

The dominant magazine of rock has been *Rolling Stone* since its origin in 1968 as a biweekly national tabloid of the counterculture, taking in social and political subjects as well as entertainment. *Crawdaddy,* a monthly founded in 1966, was the strongest competitor of *Rolling Stone;* it ceased publication in 1979 after a few experimental issues as *Feature* magazine. *Creem,* from 1969, and *Rock,* from 1976, have also provided rock features and reviews. The Charlton Company's *Hit Parader* magazine has rock industry coverage as well as song lyrics; their *Rock and Soul Songs* is mainly songs. *Circus* magazine aims its rock coverage at a younger readership. *Trouser Press* is an American magazine assertedly devoted to British rock, though American music does get some attention, especially the "New Wave" rock 'n' roll. A symmetrical phenomenon, *Zigzag,* covered American rock from Britain until it became more interested in the British punk scene. The principal British magazine of pop including rock is the weekly *Melody Maker.*

BIBLIOGRAPHY

Adler, Irene. *Peter Frampton.* New York: Quick Fox, 1979.

Aldridge, Alan, ed. *The Beatles Illustrated Lyrics.* New York: Delacorte Press, 1969.

———. *The Beatles Illustrated Lyrics 2.* New York: Delacorte Press, 1971.

———, and Dempsey, Mike, eds. *Bernie Taupin, the One Who Writes the Words for Elton John: Complete Lyrics from 1968 to Goodbye, Yellow Brick Road.* New York: Alfred A. Knopf, 1976.

Atkinson, Bob, ed. *Songs of the Open Road: The Poetry of Folk Rock and the Journey of the Hero.* New York: Signet/New American Library, 1974.

Bacon, Tony, ed. *Rock Hardware: The Instruments, Equipment and Technology of Rock.* New York: Harmony Books, 1981.

Bane, Michael. *White Boy Singin' the Blues.* New York: Penguin Books, 1982.

———. *Who's Who in Rock.* Researcher: Kenny Kertok. New York: Facts on File, 1981.

Bangs, Lester. *Blondie.* New York: Fireside Book/Simon and Schuster, 1980.

Barnes, Ken. *The Beach Boys: A Biography in Words and Pictures.* Ed. Greg Shaw. New York: Sire Books/Chappell Music Co., 1976.

———. *Twenty Years of Pop.* London: Kenneth Mason, 1973.

Barry, Ron. *All American Elvis: The Elvis Presley American Discography.* Phillipsburg, N.J.: Spectator Service, Maxigraphics, 1976.

The Beatles. Text by Geoffrey Stokes. New York: Times Books/Rolling Stone, 1980.

The Beatles Lyrics Illustrated. New York: Dell Publishing, 1975.

Belz, Carl. *The Story of Rock.* 2d ed. New York: Oxford University Press, 1972.

Bennett, H. Stith. *On Becoming a Rock Musician.* Amherst: University of Massachusetts Press, 1980.

Berry, Peter E. *"And the Hits Just Keep on Comin'."* Syracuse, N.Y.: Syracuse University Press, 1977.

Blair, John, comp. *The Illustrated Discography of Surf Music, 1959-1965.* Riverside, Calif.: J. Bee Productions, 1978.

Blake, John. *All You Needed Was Love: The Beatles after the Beatles.* New York: A Perigee Book, 1981.

Bob Dylan in His Own Words. Comp. "Miles." Ed. Pearce Marchbank. New York: Quick Fox, 1978.

Bowden, Betsy. *Performed Literature: Words and Music by Bob Dylan.* Bloomington: Indiana University Press, 1982.

Brown, Len, and Friedrich, Gary. *Encyclopedia of Rock & Roll.* New York: Tower Book, 1970.

Burchill, Julie, and Parsons, Tony. *"The Boy Looked at Johnny": The Obituary of Rock and Roll.* London: Pluto Press, 1978.

Busnar, Gene. *It's Rock 'n' Roll.* New York: Julian Messner, 1979.

Cable, Paul. *Bob Dylan: His Unreleased Recordings.* New York: Schirmer Books, 1980.

Cain, Robert. *Whole Lotta Shakin' Goin' On: Jerry Lee Lewis.* New York: Dial Press, 1981.

Campbell, Colin, and Murphy, Allan. *Things We Said Today: The Complete Lyrics and a Concordance to the Beatles' Songs, 1962-1970.* Ann Arbor, Mich.: Pierian Press, 1980.

Carr, Roy, and Clarke, Steve. *Fleetwood Mac: Rumours n' Fax.* New York: Harmony Books, 1978.

——, and Tyler, Tony. *The Beatles: An Illustrated Record.* New York: Harmony Books, 1975.

Castleman, Harry, and Podrazik, Walter J. *All Together Now: The First Complete Beatles Discography, 1961-1975.* Ann Arbor, Mich.: Pierian Press, 1976.

——. *The Beatles Again.* Ann Arbor, Mich.: Pierian Press, 1977.

Chipman, Bruce, ed. *Hardening Rock: An Organic Anthology of the Adolescence of Rock 'n' Roll.* Boston: Little, Brown, 1972.

Christgau, Robert. *Any Old Way You Choose It: Rock and Other Pop Music, 1967-1973.* Baltimore: Penguin Books, 1973.

——. *Christgau's Record Guide: Rock Albums of the Seventies.* New Haven, Conn.: Ticknor and Fields, 1981.

Circus. New York, 1966- .

Claire, Vivian. *Linda Ronstadt.* New York: Flash Books, 1978.

Clark, Dick, and Robinson, Richard. *Rock, Roll & Remember.* New York: Thomas Crowell, 1976.

Cohen, Mitchell S. *Carole King: A Biography in Words and Pictures.* Ed. Greg Shaw. New York: Sire Books/Chappell Music Co., 1976.

——. *Simon and Garfunkel: A Biography in Words and Pictures.* Ed. Greg Shaw. New York: Sire Books/Chappell Music Co., 1977.

Cohn, Nik. *Rock from the Beginning.* New York: Stein and Day, 1969.

Coon, Caroline. *1988: The New Wave Punk Rock Explosion.* New York: Hawthorn Books, 1978.

Cooper, Alice, with Steven Gaines. *Me, Alice: The Autobiography of Alice Cooper.* New York: G. P. Putnam's Sons, 1976.

Crawdaddy. New York, 1966-1979.

Creem. Birmingham, Mich., 1969- .

Dallas, Karl. *Singers of an Empty Day: Last Sacraments for the Superstars.* London: Kahn and Averill, 1971.

Dalton, David, ed. *Rolling Stones.* New York: Amsco Music Publishing Co., 1972.

————, and Farren, Mick, comps. *Rolling Stones in Their Own Words.* New York: Quick Fox, 1980.

————, and Kaye, Lenny. *Rock 100.* New York: Grosset and Dunlap, 1977.

Daly, Marsha. *Peter Frampton.* New York: Tempo Books/Grosset and Dunlap, 1978.

Damsker, Matt, ed. *Rock Voices: The Best Lyrics of an Era.* New York: St. Martin's Press, 1980.

Davies, Hunter. *The Beatles.* Rev. ed. New York: McGraw-Hill, 1978.

DiLello, Richard. *The Longest Cocktail Party: An Insider's Diary of the Beatles, Their Million-Dollar Apple Empire and Its Wild Rise and Fall.* Chicago: Playboy Press, 1972.

Dimmick, Mary Laverne. *The Rolling Stones: An Annotated Bibliography.* Rev. and enlarged ed. Pittsburgh: University of Pittsburgh Press, 1979.

Dylan, Bob. *Writings and Drawings by Bob Dylan.* New York: Borzoi/Alfred A. Knopf, 1973.

Edwards, Joseph. *Top 10's and Trivia of Rock & Roll and Rhythm & Blues 1950-1973.* St. Louis: Blueberry Hill Publishing, 1974.

Eisen, Jonathan, ed. *Age of Rock: Sounds of the American Cultural Revolution.* New York: Vintage/Random House, 1969.

————. *The Age of Rock 2: Sights and Sounds of the American Cultural Revolution.* New York: Random House, 1970.

————. *Twenty-Minute Fandangos and Forever Changes: A Rock Bazaar.* New York: Random House, 1971.

Elvis. Secaucus, N.J.: Chartwell Books/Phoebus, 1976.

Emerson, Lucy. *The Gold Record.* New York: Fountain Publishing Co., 1978.

Epstein, Brian. *A Cellarful of Noise.* Garden City, N.Y.: Doubleday, 1964.

Fawcett, Anthony. *California Rock, California Sound: The Music of Los Angeles and Southern California.* Los Angeles: Reed Books, 1978.

————. *John Lennon: One Day at a Time. A Personal Biography of the Seventies.* New York: Grove Press, 1976.

Fleischer, Leonore. *Joni Mitchell.* New York: Flash Books, 1976.

Fletcher, David Jeffrey. *David Robert Jones Bowie: The Discography of a Generalist, 1962-1979.* Ed. Rose Winters. 3d ed. Chicago: F. Fergeson Productions, 1979.

Fong-Torres, Ben, ed. *The Rolling Stone Rock 'n Roll Reader.* New York: Bantam Books, 1974.

————. *What's That Sound? The Contemporary Music Scene from the Pages of Rolling Stone.* New York: Rolling Stone Press/Anchor Books/Doubleday, 1976.

Frame, Pete. *Pete Frame's Rock Family Trees.* New York: Quick Fox, 1980.

Friede, Goldie; Titone, Robin; and Weiner, Sue. *The Beatles A to Z.* New York: Methuen, 1980.

Friedman, Myra. *Buried Alive: The Biography of Janis Joplin.* New York: William Morrow, 1973.

Frith, Simon. *The Sociology of Rock.* London: Constable, 1978.

_____. *Sound Effects: Youth, Leisure, and the Politics of Rock 'n' Roll.* New York: Pantheon Books, 1981.

Gambaccini, Paul. *A Conversation with Elton John and Bernie Taupin.* New York: Flash Books, 1975.

_____. *Paul McCartney in His Own Words.* New York: Flash Books, 1976.

_____, comp., with Susan Ready. *Rock Critics' Choice: The Top 200 Albums.* New York: Quick Fox, 1978.

Gambaccini, Peter. *Bruce Springsteen.* New York: Quick Fox, 1979.

Gibb, Barry; Gibb, Robin; and Gibb, Maurice; as told to David Leaf. *Bee Gees: The Authorized Biography.* New York: Delilah Communications/Delta/Dell, 1979.

Giddins, Gary. *Riding on a Blue Note: Jazz and American Pop.* New York: Oxford University Press, 1981.

Gillett, Charlie. *The Sound of the City: The Rise of Rock & Roll.* New York: Outerbridge and Dienstfrey, dist. Dutton, 1970.

Golden, Bruce. *The Beach Boys: Southern California Pastoral.* The Woodstock Series, Popular Music of Today, vol. 1. San Bernardino, Calif.: R. Reginald/Borgo Press, 1976.

Goldman, Albert. *Elvis.* New York: McGraw-Hill, 1981.

_____. *Freakshow: The Rocksoulbluesjazzsickjewblackhumorsexpoppsych Gig and Other Scenes from the Counter-Culture.* New York: Atheneum, 1971.

Goldrosen, John. *Buddy Holly: His Life and Music.* Bowling Green, Ohio: Popular Press, 1975.

_____. *The Buddy Holly Story.* New York: Quick Fox, 1979.

Goldstein, Richard. *Goldstein's Greatest Hits: A Book Mostly about Rock 'n' Roll.* Englewood Cliffs, N.J.: Prentice-Hall, 1970.

_____, ed. *The Poetry of Rock.* New York: Bantam Books, 1969.

Goldstein, Stewart, and Jacobson, Alan. *Oldies but Goodies: The Rock 'n' Roll Years.* New York: Mason/Charter, 1977.

Graham, Samuel. *Fleetwood Mac: The Authorized History.* New York: Warner Books/Sire Records, 1978.

Graves, Barbara Farris, and McBain, Donald J. *Lyric Voices: Approaches to the Poetry of Contemporary Song.* New York: John Wiley and Sons, 1972.

Gray, Michael. *Song and Dance Man: The Art of Bob Dylan.* New York: E. P. Dutton, 1972.

Greene, Bob. *Billion Dollar Baby.* New York: Atheneum, 1974.

Greenfield, Robert. *S.T.P.: A Journey through America with the Rolling Stones.* New York: Saturday Review Press/E. P. Dutton, 1974.

Gregory, Neal, and Gregory, Janice. *When Elvis Died.* Washington, D.C.: Communications Press, 1980.

Gross, Michael. *Bob Dylan: An Illustrated History.* New York: Grosset and Dunlap, 1978.

_____, and Jakubowski, Maxim. *The Rock Year Book 1981.* New York: Delilah/Grove Press, 1980.

Grossman, Loyd. *A Social History of Rock Music: From the Greasers to Glitter Rock.* New York: David McKay Co., 1976.

Guitar Player Magazine. Saratoga, Calif., 1967- .

Guralnick, Peter. *Lost Highway: Journeys and Arrivals of American Musicians.* Boston: David R. Godine, 1979.

Hall, Douglas Kent. *Rock: A World Bold as Love.* Ed. Douglas Kent Hall. New York: Cowles Book Co., 1970.

Harbinson, W. A. *The Illustrated Elvis.* New York: Grosset and Dunlap, 1976.

Hardy, Phil, and Laing, Dave, eds. *The Encyclopedia of Rock: The Age of Rock 'n' Roll,* vol. 1. Frogmore, St. Albans, Herts., England: Granada/Pantheon, 1976.

_____. *From Liverpool to San Francisco,* vol. 2.

_____. *The Sounds of the Seventies,* vol. 3.

_____. *The Encyclopedia of Rock.* London: Aquarius Books, 1977.

Harrison, George. *I Me Mine.* New York: Simon and Schuster, 1980.

Harrison, Hank. *The Dead.* Millbrae, Calif.: Celestial Arts, 1980.

_____. *The Dead Book: A Social History of the Grateful Dead.* New York: Links, 1973.

Helander, Brock. *Rock 'n' Roll to Rock: A Discography.* N. p.: Brock Helander, 1978.

Henderson, David. *Jimi Hendrix: Voodoo Child of the Aquarian Age.* Garden City, N.Y.: Doubleday, 1978.

_____. *'Scuse Me while I Kiss the Sky: The Life of Jimi Hendrix.* New York: Bantam, 1981.

Hill, Randal C. *The Official Price Guide to Collectible Rock Records.* Orlando, Fla.: House of Collectibles, 1979.

Hirsch, Abby, ed. *The Photography of Rock.* Indianapolis: Bobbs-Merrill, 1972.

Hit Parader. Derby, Conn., 1954- .

Hoffman, Frank. *The Literature of Rock, 1954-1978.* Metuchen, N.J.: Scarecrow Press, 1981.

Hopkins, Jerry. *Elvis.* New York: Simon and Schuster, 1971.

_____. *Elvis: The Final Years.* New York: St. Martin's Press, 1980.

_____. *Festival! The Book of American Music Celebrations.* New York: Macmillan, 1970.

_____, and Sugerman, Danny. *No One Here Gets Out Alive.* New York: Warner Books, 1980.

Jahn, Mike. *Rock: From Elvis Presley to the Rolling Stones.* New York: Quadrangle/ New York Times Book Co., 1973.

Jasper, Tony. *Paul McCartney and Wings.* Secaucus, N.J.: Chartwell Books, 1977.

_____. *Rod Stewart.* Secaucus, N.J.: Chartwell Books, 1977.

_____. *The Rolling Stones.* London: Octopus Books, 1976.

_____. *Understanding Pop.* London: SCM Press, 1972.

Jewell, Derek. *The Popular Voice: A Musical Record of the 60s and 70s.* London: Andre Deutsch, 1980.

John Lennon in His Own Words. Comp. "Miles." New York: Quick Fox, 1981.

Jones, Peter. *Tom Jones.* Chicago: Henry Regnery Co., 1970.

Kaufman, Murray. *Murray the K Tells It Like It Is, Baby.* New York: Holt, Rinehart and Winston, 1966.

Kelly, Joe. *All the King's Men*. New York: Ariel Books, 1979.

Kinkowitz, Jerome. *The American 1960s: Imaginative Acts in a Decade of Change.* Ames: Iowa State University Press, 1980.

Kooper, Al, with Ben Edwards. *Backstage Passes: Rock 'n' Roll Life in the Sixties.* New York: Stein and Day, 1977.

Laing, Dave. *The Sound of Our Time*. Chicago: Quadrangle Books, 1970.

Landau, Jon. *It's Too Late to Stop Now: A Rock and Roll Journal*. San Francisco: Straight Arrow Books, 1972.

Lane, Peter. *What Rock Is All About*. New York: Julian Messner, 1979.

Leaf, David. *The Beach Boys and the California Myth*. New York: Grosset and Dunlap, 1978.

Lennon, Cynthia. *A Twist of Lennon*. New York: Avon, 1978.

The Lennon Tapes: John Lennon and Yoko Ono in Conversation with Andy Peebles 6 December 1980. London: British Broadcasting Corporation, 1981.

Lewis, Laurie. *The Concerts*. New York: Paper Tiger/Dragon's World/A & W Visual Library, 1979.

Lichter, Paul, comp. *The Boy Who Dared to Rock: The Definitive Elvis*. Garden City, N.Y.: Doubleday/Dolphin, 1978.

_____. *Elvis in Hollywood*. New York: Simon and Schuster, 1975.

Lindvall, Marianne. *ABBA: The Ultimate Pop Group*. New York: A & W Visual Library, 1978.

Logan, Nick, and Woffinden, Bob, comps. *The Illustrated Encyclopedia of Rock*. New York: Harmony Books, 1977.

Mabey, Richard. *The Pop Process*. London: Hutchinson Educational, 1969.

McCabe, Peter, and Schonfeld, Robert D. *Apple to the Core: The Unmaking of the Beatles*. New York: Pocket Books, 1972.

McGregor, Craig, ed. *Bob Dylan: A Retrospective*. New York: William Morrow, 1972.

Macken, Bob; Fornatale, Peter; and Ayres, Bill. *The Rock Music Source Book*. Garden City, N.Y.: Doubleday/Anchor, 1980.

Mann, May. *The Private Elvis*. (*Original Title: Elvis and the Colonel*.) New York: Pocket Books, 1977.

Marcus, Greil. *Mystery Train: Images of America in Rock 'n' Roll Music*. New York: E. P. Dutton, 1975.

_____, ed. *Rock and Roll Will Stand*. Boston: Beacon Press, 1969.

_____, ed. *Stranded: Rock and Roll for a Desert Island*. New York: Alfred A. Knopf, 1979.

Marks, J. *Rock and Other Four Letter Words*. New York: Bantam Books, 1968.

Marsh, Dave. *Born to Run: The Bruce Springsteen Story*. New York: Dolphin Books/Doubleday, 1979.

_____, and Swenson, John. *The Rolling Stone Record Guide: Reviews and Ratings of Almost 10,000 Currently Available Rock, Pop, Soul, Country, Blues, Jazz, and Gospel Albums*. New York: Random House/Rolling Stone Press, 1979.

Martin, George, with Jeremy Hornsby. *All You Need Is Ears*. New York: St. Martin's Press, 1979.

Melhuish, Martin. *Bachman-Turner Overdrive: Rock Is My Life, This Is My Song. The Authorized Biography*. Toronto: Methuen/Two Continents, 1976.

Mellers, Wilfrid. *Twilight of the Gods: The Music of the Beatles.* New York: Richard Seaver/Viking Press, 1973.

Melody Maker. London, 1926- .

Meltzer, Richard. *The Aesthetics of Rock.* New York: Something Else Press, 1970.

Mendelsohn, John. *Paul McCartney: A Biography in Words and Pictures.* Ed. Greg Shaw. New York: Sire Books/Chappell Music Co., 1977.

Michaels, Ross. *George Harrison: Yesterday & Today.* New York: Flash Books, 1977.

Miles, Betty T., et al. *The Miles Chart Display: Top 100, 1955-1970,* vol. 1. Boulder, Colo.: Convex Industries, 1971.

Miles, Daniel J., and Miles, Martin J. *The Miles Chart Display of Popular Music. Top 100, 1971-1975,* vol. 2. New York: Arno Press, 1977.

Miller, Jim, ed. *The Rolling Stone Illustrated History of Rock & Roll.* 2d ed. rev. and updated. New York: Random House, 1980.

Miron, Charles. *Rock Gold: All the Hit Charts from 1955 to 1976.* New York: Drake Publishers, 1977.

Moore, Mary Ellen. *The Linda Ronstadt Scrapbook.* New York: Sunridge Press/ Grosset and Dunlap, 1978.

Morse, Ann. *Barry Manilow.* Mankato, Minn.: Creative Education/Childrens' Press, 1978.

Morse, David. *Grandfather Rock: The New Poetry and the Old.* New York: Delacorte Press, 1972.

Nelson, Paul, and Bangs, Lester. *Rod Stewart.* New York: Delilah Books, 1981.

Nite, Norm N. *Rock On: The Illustrated Encyclopedia of Rock 'n' Roll—The Solid Gold Years.* New York: Thomas Y. Crowell, 1974.

————, with Ralph M. Newman. *Rock On: The Illustrated Encyclopedia of Rock 'n' Roll—The Modern Years: 1964-Present,* vol. 2. New York: Thomas Y. Crowell, 1978.

Noebel, David A. *The Marxist Minstrels: A Handbook on Communist Subversion of Music.* Tulsa, Okla.: American Christian College Press, 1974.

Norman, Philip. *Shout! The Beatles in Their Generation.* New York: Fireside Book/Simon and Schuster, 1981.

Nugent, Stephen, and Gillett, Charlie, eds. *Rock Almanac: Top Twenty American and British Singles and Albums of the '50s, '60s, and '70s.* Garden City, N.Y.: Anchor/Doubleday, 1978.

Nutter, David. *Elton: It's a Little Bit Funny.* New York: Viking Press, 1977.

Orloff, Katherine. *Rock 'n' Roll Woman.* Los Angeles: Nash Publishing, 1974.

Osborne, Jerry. *Popular and Rock Records 1948-1978.* Ed. Bruce Hamilton. Phoenix, Ariz.: O'Sullivan Woodside & Co., 1978.

————. *Record Albums 1948-1978.* Ed. Bruce Hamilton. Phoenix, Ariz.: O'Sullivan Woodside & Co., 1978.

Palmer, Robert. *A Tale of Two Cities: Memphis Rock and New Orleans Roll.* New York: Institute for Studies in American Music, 1979.

————. *Baby, That Was Rock & Roll: The Legendary Leiber and Stoller.* New York: Harcourt Brace Jovanovich, 1978.

————. *Jerry Lee Lewis Rocks!* New York: Delilah Books/G. P. Putnam's Sons, 1981.

Palmer, Tony. *Born under a Bad Sign.* London: William Kimber, 1970.

Panta, Ilona. *Elvis Presley: King of Kings.* Hicksville, N.Y.: Exposition Press, 1979.

Pavletich, Aida. *Rock-a-Bye, Baby.* Garden City, N.Y.: Doubleday, 1980.

Peck, Ira, ed. *The New Sound/Yes!* New York: Four Winds Press, 1966.

Peellaert, Guy, and Cohn, Nik. *Rock Dreams.* London: Pan Books, 1974.

Petrie, Gavin, ed. *Pop Today.* London: Hamlyn, 1974.

_____. *Rock Life.* London: Hamlyn, 1974.

Pichaske, David. *A Generation in Motion: Popular Music and Culture in the Sixties.* New York: Schirmer Books/Macmillan, 1979.

Pickering, Stephen, ed. *Dylan: A Commemoration.* 2d ed. Menlo Park, Calif.: A No Limits Publication, 1971.

Pidgeon, John. *Eric Clapton: A Biography.* St. Albans, England: Panther/Granada, 1976.

Pink Floyd. A Visual Documentary by Miles. New York: Quick Fox, 1980.

The Police Released. London: Proteus Books, 1980.

Pollock, Bruce. *In Their Own Words.* New York: Macmillan, 1975.

_____. *When Rock Was Young: A Nostalgic Review of the Top 40 Era.* New York: Holt, Rinehart and Winston, 1981.

_____, and Wagman, John. *The Face of Rock & Roll: Images of a Generation.* New York: Holt, Rinehart and Winston, 1978.

Preiss, Byron. *Beach Boys.* New York: Ballantine Books, 1979.

Presley, Dee, et al. *Elvis, We Love You Tender.* New York: Delilah/Mike Franklin/Delacorte Press, 1980.

Propes, Steve. *Golden Goodies: A Guide to 50s & 60s Popular Rock & Roll Record Collecting.* Radnor, Pa.: Chilton Book, 1975.

_____. *Golden Oldies: A Guide to 60s Record Collecting.* Radnor, Pa.: Chilton Book, 1974.

_____. *Those Oldies but Goodies: A Guide to 50s Record Collecting.* New York: Macmillan, 1973.

Reese, Krista. *Elvis Costello.* London: Proteus Books, 1981.

Roach, Dusty. *Patti Smith: Rock & Roll Madonna.* South Bend, Ind.: And Books, 1979.

Rock. New York, 1976- .

Rock and Soul Songs. Derby, Conn., 1956- .

Rock Guitarists: From the Pages of Guitar Player Magazine, vol. 1. Saratoga, Calif.: Guitar Player Books, 1975.

_____. Vol. 2. Saratoga, Calif.: Guitar Player Books, 1977.

Rolling Stone. San Francisco, 1968- .

The Rolling Stone Interviews, vol. 1. Comp. by eds. of *Rolling Stone.* A Straight Arrow Book. New York: Warner Paperback Library, 1971.

_____. Vol. 2. Ed. Ben Fong-Torres. New York: Warner Paperback Library, 1973.

Rosenman, Joel; Roberts, John; and Pilpel, Robert, *Young Men with Unlimited Capital.* New York: Harcourt Brace Jovanovich, 1974.

Rowes, Barbara. *Grace Slick: The Biography.* Garden City, N.Y.: Doubleday and Co., 1980.

Roxon, Lillian. *Lillian Roxon's Rock Encyclopedia,* comp. Ed Naha. New York: Grosset and Dunlap, 1978.

_____. *Rock Encyclopedia.* New York: Grosset and Dunlap, 1969.

Sanchez, Tony. *Up and Down with the Rolling Stones.* New York: William Morrow, 1979.

Sander, Ellen. *Trips: Rock Life in the Sixties.* New York: Charles Scribner's Sons, 1973.

Santelli, Robert. *Aquarius Rising: The Rock Festival Years.* New York: Dell, 1980.

Saporita, Jay. *Pourin' It All Out.* Secaucus, N.J.: Citadel Press, 1980.

Sarlin, Bob. *Turn It Up! (I Can't Hear the Words.) The Best of the New Singer/ Songwriters.* New York: Simon and Schuster, 1973.

Scaduto, Anthony. *Bob Dylan: An Intimate Biography.* New York: Grosset and Dunlap, 1971.

Schafer, William J. *Rock Music: Where It's Been, What It Means, Where It's Going.* Minneapolis: Augsburg Publishing House, 1972.

Schmidt-Joos, Siegfried, and Graves, Barry. *Rock-Lexikon.* Mit Diskographien von Bernie Sigg. Reinbek bei Hamburg: Rowohlt Taschenbuch Verlag, 1973.

Schultheiss, Tom, comp. *The Beatles: A Day in the Life. The Day-by-Day Diary 1960-1970.* New York: Quick Fox, 1981.

Shaw, Arnold. *The Rockin' 50's: The Decade that Transformed the Pop Music Scene.* New York: Hawthorn Books, 1974.

Shepherd, Sam. *Rolling Thunder Logbook.* Richard Seaver Book/Viking Press, 1977.

Somma, Robert, ed. *No One Waved Good-bye: A Casualty Report on Rock and Roll.* New York: A Fusion Book/Outerbridge & Dienstfrey, 1971.

Spitz, Robert Stephen. *Barefoot in Babylon: The Creation of the Woodstock Music Festival, 1969.* New York: Viking Press, 1979.

_____. *The Making of Superstars: Artists and Executives of the Rock Music Business.* Garden City, N.Y.: Anchor Press/Doubleday, 1978.

Stambler, Irwin. *Encyclopedia of Pop, Rock, and Soul.* New York: St. Martin's Press, 1974.

The Stars and Superstars of Rock. London: Octopus Books, 1974.

Stevens, Kim. *The Bee Gees.* New York: Quick Fox, 1978.

Superstars of the 70s: including Helen Reddy, Stevie Wonder, Olivia Newton-John, David Bowie, Elton John and many more. London: Octopus Books, 1976.

Tatham, Dick, and Jasper, Tony. *Elton John.* London: Octopus Books/Phoebus, 1976.

Thorgerson, Storm, and Dean, Roger, eds. *Album Cover Album.* New York: A & W Visual Library, 1977.

Tobler, John. *The Beach Boys.* Secaucus, N.J.: Chartwell Books, 1978.

_____. *Guitar Heroes.* New York: St. Martin's Press, 1978.

Tremlett, George. *The David Bowie Story.* New York: Warner Paperback Library, 1975.

_____. *The Osmond Story.* New York: Warner Paperback Library, 1975.

Trouser Press. New York, 1974- .

Tudor, Dean, and Tudor, Nancy. *Contemporary Popular Music.* American Popular Music on Elpee. Littleton, Colo.: Libraries Unlimited, 1979.

Waldinger, Karl-Georg. *Semiotische Analyse eines Popmusik-Covers.* Möglichkeiten interdisziplinärer Projektarbeit in der Sekundarstufe I. Ratingen. Kastellaun: A Henn Verlag, 1975.

Wale, Michael. *Voxpop: Profiles of the Pop Process.* London: George G. Harrap & Co., 1972.

Walley, David. *No Commercial Potential: The Saga of Frank Zappa Then and Now.* New York: E. P. Dutton, 1980.

Wallraf, Rainer, and Plehn, Heinz. *Elvis Presley: An Illustrated Biography.* Trans. Judith Waldman. Dreieich, W. Germany: Abi Melzer Productions, dist. N.Y.: Quick Fox, 1978.

Wertheimer, Alfred. *Elvis '56: In the Beginning.* New York: Collier Books, 1979.

Whisler, John A. *Elvis Presley: Reference Guide and Discography.* Metuchen, N.J.: Scarecrow Press, 1981.

Whitburn, Joel. *Joel Whitburn's Pop Annual, 1955-1977.* Menomonee Falls, Wisc.: Record Research, 1978.

_____. *Joel Whitburn's Top LP's, 1945-1972.* Menomonee Falls, Wisc.: Record Research, 1973.

_____. *Top Pop Records, 1955-1970: Facts about 9,800 Recordings Listed in Billboard's "Hot 100" Charts, Grouped under the Names of the 2,500 Recording Artists.* Detroit: Gale Research Co., 1972.

Williams, Allan, and Marshall, William. *The Man Who Gave the Beatles Away.* New York: Macmillan, 1975.

Williams, Paul. *Outlaw Blues: A Book of Rock Music.* New York: E. P. Dutton, 1969.

Williams, Richard. *Out of His Head: The Sound of Phil Spector.* New York: Outerbridge & Lazard, 1972.

Woffinden, Bob. *The Beatles Apart.* London: Proteus Books, 1981.

Wood, Graham. *An A-Z of Rock and Roll.* London: Studio Vista, 1971.

Yorke, Richie. *The History of Rock 'n' Roll.* New York: Methuen/Two Continents, 1976.

Young, Jean, and Lang, Michael. *Woodstock Festival Remembered.* New York: Ballantine Books, 1979.

Zalkind, Ronald. *Contemporary Music Almanac 1980/81.* New York: Schirmer Books, 1980.

Zigzag. Reading, Berkshire, England, 1970- .

Zmijewsky, Steven, and Zmijewsky, Boris. *Elvis: The Films and Career of Elvis Presley.* Secaucus, N.J.: Citadel Press, 1976.

APPENDIX A

Some Significant Dates in the History of American Popular Music

1814	"The Star-Spangled Banner" by Francis Scott Key
1827	"The Coal Black Rose" popularized by George Washington Dixon
1837	Henry Russell composes and performs "Woodman! Spare That Tree"
1842	Beginning of the singing career of the Hutchinson family
1843	First performance by the Virginia Minstrels, including Dan Emmett
1848	"Oh, Susanna" by Stephen Foster, his first success
1855	"Listen to the Mocking Bird" by Septimus Winner
1862	"The Battle Hymn of the Republic" by Julia Ward Howe
1864	"Beautiful Dreamer" by Stephen Foster in the year of his death
1865	Tony Pastor's first opera house opens in New York
1866	*The Black Crook*—first major success in New York musical theater
1873	Ned Harrigan and Tony Hart become popular with their first Mulligan play
1877	Thomas A. Edison invents the phonograph
1878	*HMS Pinafore* by Gilbert and Sullivan begins American fashion for English comic opera
1886	Founding of M. Witmark & Sons, publishers
1892	"After the Ball" by Charles K. Harris, the first song hit of its magnitude, selling several million copies
1895	Buddy Bolden playing trumpet in New Orleans
1897	"The Stars and Stripes Forever" by John Philip Sousa
1899	"Maple Leaf Rag" by Scott Joplin
1903	Enrico Caruso records "Vesti la Giubba" from *Pagliacci*, the first million-selling record
	Twenty-eighth Street in Manhattan comes to be called Tin Pan Alley
1904	"Give My Regards to Broadway" by George M. Cohan, from his first hit show *Little Johnny Jones*
1907	The first Ziegfeld *Follies*, New York
1910	"Let Me Call You Sweetheart" by Beth Slater Whitson and Leo Freidman, one of two biggest sheet-music hits ever (see 1918)
1911	"Alexander's Ragtime Band" by Irving Berlin
1912	"The Memphis Blues" by W. C. Handy
1914	Formation of the American Society of Composers, Authors, and Publishers (ASCAP)
1916	Victor Herbert writes (live performance) score for *Birth of a Nation*
1918	"Till We Meet Again" by Raymond Egan and Richard Whiting, the other (see 1910) sheet music best seller

1920   Selvin's Novelty Orchestra records "Dardanella," the first million-selling popular dance record

KDKA in Pittsburgh begins first regular commercial broadcasting, including music

1922   WSB in Atlanta begins to broadcast local country music performers

Louis Armstrong comes to Chicago to join the King Oliver Orchestra

1923   Bessie Smith records "Down Hearted Blues"

Fletcher Henderson forms his first big jazz band

1924   George Gershwin's *Rhapsody in Blue* with symphonic use of jazz played by Paul Whiteman's Orchestra

Lady, Be Good! the first Broadway hit of George and Ira Gershwin

Vernon Dalhart records "The Wreck of the Old 97" and "The Prisoner's Song"

1925   WSM in Nashville, under George Hay, broadcasts "Barn Dance," later the "Grand Ole Opry"

Carbon microphones introduced for high-quality recording

1926   Jelly Roll Morton records with his Red Hot Peppers

National Broadcasting Company formed, the first radio network

1927   Ralph Peer records Jimmie Rodgers and the Carter Family

Duke Ellington plays the Cotton Club in Harlem

Al Jolson sings in *The Jazz Singer*, the first soundtrack film

Show Boat by Jerome Kern and Oscar Hammerstein II

Les Paul creates the first electric guitar

1928   Louis Armstrong records "West End Blues"

1929   "Star Dust" by Hoagy Carmichael and Mitchell Parish

Rudy Vallée mobbed by a youth audience at a New York theater

1930   Ethel Merman's Broadway debut, in *Girl Crazy*

1931   Bing Crosby begins his radio singing career

1933   *42nd Street* begins era of the modern film musical

Fred Astaire and Ginger Rogers co-star for the first time, in *Flying Down to Rio*

1934   First Oscar awarded for a film song, to "The Continental"

Anything Goes by Cole Porter

Founding of the Muzak company in New York

1935   Benny Goodman's big band inauguarates the Swing era

First broadcast of the "Lucky Strike Hit Parade"

Gene Autry's first starring role as singing cowboy, in *Tumbling Tumbleweeds*, introducing the song of that name

1937   *On Your Toes* by Richard Rodgers and Lorenz Hart

1938   Roy Acuff joins the Grand Ole Opry

Jelly Roll Morton tells his story at the Library of Congress

1939   Film *The Wizard of Oz*

Coleman Hawkins records "Body and Soul"

1940   Bob Wills records "San Antonio Rose"

Formation of Broadcast Music Incorporated (BMI)

(or 1941) Charlie Parker, Dizzy Gillespie, Thelonius Monk and others at Minton's in New York, the beginning of bop

1941   ASCAP radio performance ban

1942   Bing Crosby records "White Christmas," best selling record ever
       Acuff-Rose publishing founded in Nashville
       American Federation of Musicians strike against record companies, the
       Petrillo ban
       Frank Sinatra emerges as a teenagers' idol
1943   *Oklahoma!* by Rodgers and Hammerstein
       Mills Brothers release "Paper Doll," signalling end of the big-band era of
       hit records
1946   *Annie Get Your Gun* by Irving Berlin
       Jolson sings and Larry Parks acts in film *The Jolson Story*
1948   First long-playing records; first 45 rpm records
       Fats Domino records "The Fat Man," the first hit of his rhythm-and-blues
       career
1949   Hank Williams appears on the Grand Ole Opry; his "Lovesick Blues" sells
       a million copies
       South Pacific by Rodgers and Hammerstein
       Miles Davis records *The Birth of Cool*
       The Weavers record "Good Night, Irene"
       Gene Autry records "Rudolph the Red-Nosed Reindeer"
1950   "Your Hit Parade" goes to television
1951   Alan Freed begins to broadcast "Moondog's Rock 'n' Roll Party" on WJW
       in Cleveland, playing rhythm and blues records
       Patti Page records four million-selling songs
1952   Leroy Anderson records "Blue Tango"
       "Philadelphia Bandstand" goes on television, later to become "American
       Bandstand"
1953   "The Lawrence Welk Show" begins run on network television
1954   Bill Haley and His Comets record "Shake, Rattle and Roll" and "Rock
       around the Clock"
       Major shift to 45 rpm records; sheet music sales drop
1955   Chuck Berry records "Maybellene"; Little Richard records "Tutti-Frutti"
1956   *My Fair Lady* by Alan Jay Lerner and Frederick Loewe
       James Brown records "Please, Please, Please," his first hit
       Elvis Presley records "Heartbreak Hotel," his first hit; his various records
       sell 10 million copies
1957   *West Side Story* by Leonard Bernstein and Stephen Sondheim
1958   The Kingston Trio records "Tom Dooley"; their first album begins 195
       weeks on the sales charts
       Johnny's Greatest Hits by Johnny Mathis begins 490 weeks, the longest run,
       on sales charts
       First stereo long-playing records marketed in the United States
1959   Ornette Coleman records *The Shape of Jazz to Come*
       The disc-jockey "payola" scandal breaks
1960   Chubby Checker records "The Twist"
       Camelot by Lerner and Loewe
1961   Bob Dylan comes to Greenwich Village
1963   The Beatles record "She Loves You," their first hit in the United States
       The Beach Boys record "Surfin' USA," their first hit
1964   The Beatles visit America

The Rolling Stones record *The Rolling Stones*, their first album

The Supremes record "Where Did Our Love Go?" their first hit

1965   At the Newport Folk Festival, Bob Dylan joins rock

John Coltrane records *Ascension*

The Sound of Music film, from the Rodgers and Hammerstein show of 1959; soundtrack record becomes the best-selling album to that date

1967   The Jefferson Airplane records *Surrealistic Pillow*

Aretha Franklin records "I Never Loved a Man the Way I Love You," her first major hit

The Beatles record *Sgt. Pepper's Lonely Hearts Club Band*

1968   Johnny Cash records *Johnny Cash at Folsom Prison*

Hair by Galt MacDermot, Gerome Ragni, and James Rado

1969   Merle Haggard records "Okie from Muskogee"

Woodstock festival, August

Altamont festival, December

Miles Davis records *Bitches Brew*

Led Zeppelin plays in the United States and their first two albums sell a million each

1970   *Woodstock* and *Gimme Shelter* (Altamont) films

Death of Jimi Hendrix

Death of Janis Joplin

1971   Carole King records *Tapestry*, biggest selling rock album to date

1972   *Grease* by Jim Jacobs and Warren Casey begins longest Broadway run to date

1973   Elton John records *Goodbye Yellow Brick Road*

A Little Night Music by Stephen Sondheim

1975   Bruce Springsteen records *The Wild, the Innocent, and the E Street Shuffle*

1976   Stevie Wonder records *Songs in the Key of Life*

1977   Fleetwood Mac records *Rumours*

Instrumental soundtrack of *Star Wars* (music by John Williams) sells a million albums

1978   The Bee Gees release *Saturday Night Fever*, four sides, the biggest selling album to date

1979   Kenny Rogers records "The Gambler"

1980   Death of John Lennon

1981   Paul Simon and Art Garfunkel perform for half a million people at a free reunion concert in New York

The Rolling Stones U.S. tour sells over $25 million in tickets

1982   Economic difficulties and home taping cut record sales in half in a single year, after several years of smaller declines

Addresses of Selected Reference Collections

American Antiquarian Society, Library
  185 Salisbury Street
  Worcester, Mass. 01609
  (617) 755-5221

Sheet music, songsters, broadside ballads.

Arkansas Arts Center, Elizabeth Prewitt Taylor Memorial Library
  Box 2137, MacArthur Park
  Little Rock, Ark. 72203
  (501) 372-4000

New Orleans jazz, 1930-1950.

Barnard A. and Morris N. Young Library of Early American Popular Music
  270 Riverside Drive
  New York, N.Y. 10025

Twenty thousand items, mostly 1790-1910, including a black American collection.

Berklee College of Music, Library
  1140 Boylston Street
  Boston, Mass. 02215
  (617) 266-1400

Jazz books, records, tapes, and scores.

Bowling Green State University, Popular Culture Library and Audio Center
  Bowling Green, Ohio 43402
  (419) 372-2450

Popular recordings, including twenty thousand 78 rpm records.

Brown University
  John Hay Library, Special Collections
  20 Prospect Street
  Providence, R.I. 02912
  (401) 863-2146

Sheet music, songsters, songbooks.

Country Music Foundation, Library and Media Center
  4 Music Square E.
  Nashville, Tenn. 37203
  (615) 256-7008

Sheet music, songbooks, records, radio transcription discs, and other materials.

Fitz Hugh Ludlow Memorial Library
  P.O. Box 99346
  San Francisco, Calif. 94109

Musicians' use of psychoactive drugs—two hundred books and six hundred records.

Free Library of Philadelphia, Music Department
  Logan Square
  Philadelphia, Pa. 19103
  (215) 686-5316

One hundred ninety thousand items of sheet music and many other materials.

Indiana University, Archives of Traditional Music
  Maxwell Hall 057
  Bloomington, Ind. 47405
  (812) 337-8632

Some popular materials among more from various folk musics.

Indiana University, Music Library
  School of Music Library
  Bloomington, Ind. 47405
  (812) 337-8541

Black music collection of materials by and about black American composers.

Institute of the American Musical, Inc., Library
  121 N. Detroit Street
  Los Angeles, Calif. 90036
  (213) 934-1221

The musical theater from about 1880: records, sheet music, and many other materials.

John Edwards Memorial Foundation
  Center for the Comparative Study of Folklore and Mythology
  University of California, Los Angeles
  Los Angeles, Calif. 90024

American folk music, hillbilly, country and western, blues, gospel, and so forth on commercial recordings: twenty-seven thousand records and other materials.

Library of Congress, American Folklife Center, Archive of Folk Song
  Thomas Jefferson Building G 136
  Washington, D.C. 20540
  (202) 287-5505

  Collection includes some jazz, blues, and folk-troubadour materials.

Library of Congress, Music Division
  Thomas Jefferson Building G 144
  Washington, D.C. 20540
  (202) 287-5507

  Sheet music of 150,000 songs; many other materials. (Consult also the Motion
  Picture, Broadcasting, and Recorded Sound Division.)

Louisiana State Museum: Louisiana Historical Center; New Orleans Jazz Club
Collection
  751 Chartres Street
  New Orleans, La. 70116
  (504) 568-6979

  Photographs, sheet music, and records.

New York Public Library, Performing Arts Research Center:
  Billy Rose Theatre Collection
  111 Amsterdam Avenue
  New York, N.Y. 10023
  (212) 870-1639

  Clippings, books, and other materials, some on musical theater.

  Music Division
  (same address)
  (212) 870-1650
  Forty thousand items of sheet music; books and other materials.

  Rodgers and Hammerstein Archives of Recorded Sound
  (same address)
  (212) 799-2200
  Four hundred thousand recordings; discographic reference books.

North Texas State University
  Music Library
  Denton, Tex. 76203

  Sheet music 1920-1960; Duke Ellington materials; 78 rpm jazz records; Stan
  Kenton charts.

Rutgers University, The State University of New Jersey, Institute of Jazz Studies
  Bradley Hall
  Warren and High Streets

Newark, N.J. 07102
(201) 648-5595

Fifty thousand recordings, three thousand books, many other materials. See also
the separate John Dale Owen collection of jazz records here.

Trinity College, Watkinson Library
300 Summit Street
Hartford, Conn. 06106
(203) 527-3151

Songbooks and sheet music.

Tulane University of Louisiana, Hogan Jazz Archive
Howard-Tilton Memorial Library
New Orleans, La. 70118
(504) 865-5688

New Orleans jazz: twenty-three thousand recordings, thirteen thousand items of
sheet music, and many other materials.

University of California, Los Angeles, Archive of Popular American Music
267 Kinsey Hall
University of California, Los Angeles
Los Angeles, Calif. 90024
(213) 825-1665

Meredith Wilson Library of Popular American Sheet Music, 430,000 items; many
records. (See also above, John Edwards Memorial Foundation.)

University of Florida, Belknap Collection for the Performing Arts
512 Library W
Gainesville, Fla. 32611
(904) 392-0322

Sheet music, 1830-1950.

University of Miami, School of Music
Albert Pick Music Library
Coral Gables, Fla. 33124
(305) 284-2429

Thirty-three thousand recordings.

University of Oregon
University Library
Eugene, Ore. 97403

Two hundred thousand items of sheet music, some popular.

University of Pittsburgh, Stephen Foster Memorial, Foster Hall Collection
Pittsburgh, Pa. 15260
(412) 624-4100

Ten thousand items of various kinds relevant to Foster.

University of Rochester, Eastman School of Music, Sibley Music Library
44 Swan Street
Rochester, N.Y. 14604
(716) 275-3018

Seventy-five thousand sheet music items, 1790-1940.

Women's Music Archives
208 Wildflower Lane
Fairfield, Conn. 06430

Recordings and materials pertaining to feminist music.

Yale University Collection of the Literature of the American Musical Theatre
Sterling Memorial Library, Room 226
New Haven, Conn. 06520
(203) 436-1822

(Collection housed in the Beinecke rare book library.) Thirty thousand items of sheet music, Harburg and Porter materials, and others.

Index

ABOUT THE AUTHOR

MARK W. BOOTH is Associate Professor of English at Virginia Common-wealth University. He has written *The Experience of Songs* and articles for *SEL*, *SAB*, *Chaucer Review*, *Quarterly Journal of Speech*, *Georgia Review*, and *Spenser Encyclopedia*.